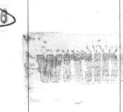

EZRA POUND:
Tactics for Reading

EZRA POUND:
Tactics for Reading

edited by
Ian F. A. Bell

VISION
and
BARNES & NOBLE

Vision Press Limited
11–14 Stanhope Mews West
London SW7 5RD

and

Barnes & Noble Books
81 Adams Drive
Totowa, NJ 07512

ISBN (UK) 0 85478 045 9
ISBN (US) 0 389 20283 5

Printed and bound in Great Britain by
Unwin Brothers Ltd.,
Old Woking, Surrey.
Phototypeset by Galleon Photosetting,
Ipswich, Suffolk.
MCMLXXXII

b 000667396

Contents

Preface

The present collection offers no 'school' of thought about Pound, no united body of opinion or perspective. Indeed, I suspect that it contains views which would occasion vigorous debate amongst its contributors, visible, perhaps, in the typographical clashes of the essays themselves. The editorial position should be made clear. Since the 1950s, when one or two more daring academic critics began to confer upon Pound the respectability of book-length studies, many of the commentaries have had the double effect of sealing their subject off not only from the reader of his poetry but also from any analysable history. This is not to deny that much valuable, and necessary, work of exegesis has been accomplished, nor that Pound's enterprise has attracted some of the best critical attention during the past thirty years. What is increasingly apparent, however, is the need to re-evaluate the terms whereby Pound is examined in order to reconstruct our means of talking about him in a more historical, less privileged manner than that which has informed so many earlier discussions. The ambition of the present book is to widen the contexts which usually determine readings of Pound's poetry and his poetics; to move beyond the curriculum itemized by those poetics, in order to suggest a fuller picture of the ambiguities and contradictions constituting Pound's historical place for modernist writing.

Such is the rubric within which the present essays have sited themselves, choosing to move widely through the full range of Pound's *oeuvre* to cover the bases of his aesthetics formed during the London years and the determinant issues of the *Cantos*, principally the essential questions of politics and economics. The diversity of material is shared by the modes of reading offered: yet a further means of appropriating Pound is a strategy this collection strongly disavows. Hence it emphasizes a free-play necessary to resist the authoritarianism inevitably implicit in those commentaries designed to confine Pound within his own curriculum, or to salvage the lyrical moments of the *Cantos*, or to deny the urgent issues of his history by condoning the liberal dualism of poetry and the fractures of its enabling conditions. Pound, to a greater extent than almost any other major writer, has had his work falsified and devalued by the elusive, defensive claim that it is a sensitive appreciation of the poem on the page which matters, an appreciation sinuously articulated by the anaesthetizing discourse and narrow scholarship of the academies. Each of the following essays, in its different way, thus refuses the official voice of literary criticism to seek methods of fragmenting the sacred text so assiduously constructed on behalf of Pound's writing by that debased voice. Each attempts to demystify the metaphysical bubble which usurps occasions for proper evaluation.

I.F.A.B.

7

Acknowledgements

Extracts are reprinted by permission of Faber and Faber Ltd. and New Directions Publishing Corp., from the following: *The Cantos of Ezra Pound*, copyright 1934, 1937, 1940, 1948, © 1956, 1959, 1962, 1963, 1968, 1972 by Ezra Pound; *The Collected Shorter Poems, Personae*, copyright 1926 by Ezra Pound; *The Translations of Ezra Pound*, copyright 1953 by Ezra Pound. *The Literary Essays of Ezra Pound* (edited by T. S. Eliot), copyright 1918, 1920, 1935 by Ezra Pound; *Selected Letters of Ezra Pound 1907–1941* (edited by D. D. Paige), copyright 1950 by Ezra Pound; *Selected Prose of Ezra Pound* (edited by William Cookson), © 1973 by The Trustees of the Ezra Pound Literary Property Trust; *ABC of Reading* by Ezra Pound, copyright 1934, 1951.

Extracts are reprinted by permission of New Directions Publishing Corp., and Faber & Faber Ltd. on behalf of The Trustees of the Ezra Pound Literary Property Trust, from the following: *Gaudier-Brzeska* by Ezra Pound © 1970 by Ezra Pound; *Pavannes and Divigations* by Ezra Pound © 1958 by Ezra Pound; *The Classic Noh Theatre of Japan* by Ezra Pound and Ernest Fenollosa © 1959 by New Directions Publishing Corporation; *The Chinese Written Character as a Medium for Poetry* by Ezra Pound, copyright 1936 by Ezra Pound.

Extracts from the Paris Review Interview and other radio broadcasts are reprinted by permission of The Trustees of the Ezra Pound Literary Property Trust © The Trustees of the Ezra Pound Literary Property Trust.

Extracts from *The Classic Anthology Defined by Confucius* are reprinted by permission of Faber & Faber Ltd. and Harvard University Press, copyright 1954, 1955 by Ezra Pound. Extracts are reprinted by permission of New Directions Publishing Corp., from the following: *Patria Mia* by Ezra Pound, copyright 1950 by Ezra Pound; *Guide to Kulchur* by Ezra Pound, copyright 1938 by Ezra Pound; *Spirit of Romance* by Ezra Pound © 1968 by Ezra Pound.

1

The Lesson of Ezra Pound: An Essay in Poetry, Literary Ideology and Politics

by PETER BROOKER

1

In 1945 Ezra Pound was arrested on a charge of treason following his wartime broadcasts over Rome Radio, and incarcerated in a military stockade in Pisa. He was returned to America, but found unfit to stand trial and confined to St. Elizabeth's Hospital in Washington, to be released in 1958 through the efforts of a sympathetic literary intelligentsia. In 1949 his *Pisan Cantos* had been awarded the Bollingen Prize for poetry. The main effect of the award and of Pound's release was to authorize a distinction between his politics and his poetry, obscuring the one in the high claims made for the other. Pound mattered, it could be felt, because he was a 'great poet'. His politics could be seen as eccentric or tragic or even obnoxious, but as unrelated still to judgement upon his 'art'. The extensive academic criticism of Pound has perpetuated this distinction and its accompanying criteria: until recently, that is to say, it has been literary and/or biographical, and has concerned itself conventionally with Pound's progress through an avant-gardist apprenticeship in London to the writing of the *Cantos*. Critical interest in the *Cantos* themselves, where it

9

has not been narrowly textual, has gravitated towards the question of the *Cantos'* form, judging the poem's success or failure in terms of its final or underlying and potential order, or its ultimately disabling formal incoherence. Pound's economic and political ideas have been presented biographically, or have been discussed separately from his poetry and treated most often with reasoned apologia or regret.[1]

The one competent account of Pound's politics has been made by a political scientist,[2] and the one recent occasion where his poetry has been considered in terms of its politics has resulted in a trenchant, but straightforward, mapping of fascist attitudes in the *Cantos*, regardless of questions of poetic form.[3]

In this way bourgeois criticism has shown itself as primitively incompetent in face of the uneasy relations between poetic form and political ideology, while it has at the same time, and with considerable sophistication, reinforced distinctions between the literary text and politics and history which are necessary to its own self-definition as a specialist discipline. Pound emerges as a canonized poet of major talent, worthy of practically endless study, but politically as a deluded crank or misguided liberal humanist, who can be on these grounds either dismissed or accommodated. The same process, I would suggest, has been followed in the erratic publication of Pound's prose works, notably of *Jefferson and/or Mussolini*, the Rome Radio talks, a series of 'Money Pamphlets', and many articles from Italian, American and English journals[4] (most conspicuously his writings for the *Morning Post*, the *Fascist Quarterly*, the *British-Italian Bulletin*, and *Action*, none of which have been reprinted). Criticism and publishing have in this way colluded in the tacit suppression of material which would to say the least complicate and embarrass the presentation of Pound as he is publicly marketed and consequently largely studied.

There is more at stake here however than the unavailability of certain texts or even the singular relation between poetry and politics, crucial and exacting though this is. The presentation and criticism of Pound offers one instance of the dispersed but unitary promulgations of bourgeois literary ideology, which in reproducing literature with a partiality which renders it assimilable, also, by the same token, assists in maintaining

10

an innocuous political place for the arts under capitalism. In addressing and attempting to explain the internal relations between Pound's literary texts and authorial ideology, the following argument is offered as a corrective to dominant critical priorities, as a critique also of their informing ideology, and is concerned in its latter stages, though it is a primary aim, with the lessons a radically oppositional poetry might learn from Pound's example.

2

Like other literary intellectuals in the 1920s and '30s, Pound became politically conscious and indeed active in response to the crisis of World War I, post-war economic depression and the attendant demise of liberal values. Like Henry James and Whistler earlier, and like Eliot in his own generation, Pound came to Europe in search of a traditional culture, and to England especially because it offered a cultural capital absent in America.[5] His complaint in *Patria Mia* against the philistinism of America had been accompanied by a hope for a native renaissance which would pay due credit to its artists, and this he sought to effect, at a distance, through a belligerent literary bohemianism with its source in the English nineties. Under the influence of Ford Madox Ford, the example of the French novel and French poets, Pound accelerated through the 1910s so as to outpace and affront a literary orthodoxy he had lagged behind on his arrival, rigorously reshaping its concept of tradition, its critical and poetic idiom as he proceeded. But Pound's polemics during this period, within imagism and vorticism, remained those of an artistic avant-garde, as busy with questions of craft and technique as with lambasting the bureaucratic, provincial mind, and whose suppositions were deep in Romantic theory. 'Artists are the antennae of the race', wrote Pound in 1918,[6] and later in 'How to Read'—

> Has literature a function in the state, in the aggregation of humans, in the republic . . .? It has . . . the individual cannot think and communicate his thought, the governor and legislator cannot act effectively or frame his laws, without words, and the solidity and validity of these words is in the care of the damned and despised *litterati*.[7]

11

Pound's characteristic attention to language is important, but his general position here is familiar and persistent with its most prominent antecedents in Shelley, Carlyle, Ruskin and principally Matthew Arnold. A nation's language and mental health, in such a view, are in the care of its *litterateurs*. If the world, Pound insists, had listened to Flaubert there would have been no war of 1870.[8] Art then is not only an index of social conditions, it is set in advance of them and if attended to, a proper guide to future conduct. These are early statements by Pound but his emphasis is an essential and continuing one through the *ABC of Reading* and *Guide to Kulchur* in the thirties, to the Rome Radio Broadcasts, where Pound explains,

> I thought in 1908 and before then, that a nation's literature is important/state of a nation's literature. The most condensed form of communication, communication of the most basic and essential facts/ideas necessary for the good life registered in the best books. And man's duty . . . is to keep those books and that tradition available.[9]

Pound began and continued to think in terms of this claim for art's social relevance. In itself, this is an aspect of a consistent position which informs both his aesthetic and his attachment to fascism, but it presents too, in Pound's own person, the extreme logic of an argument which assumes that an élite artistic consciousness does or ought to condition general social being: an argument which is deeply imbued in English literary ideology. Pound's poetry in the period of the First War is in its way a defence of this same thinking. Though claims have been made for *Cathay* (1915) as an example of 'war poetry'[10] and for *Homage to Sextus Propertius* (1917) as, true to Pound's stated motives, an attack on imperialism,[11] the argument of these poems resides in their very distance from contemporary events. The oblique strategies they employ of 'creative translation' and of an adopted persona, in Propertius, who eschews imperial verse for the irony of self-deflating love lyric in fact minimize their actual historical occasion in an implicit claim for the autonomy and transcendence of their originals, whose germ waits only to be resuscitated for its timely relevance to be felt. In 1919–20 the effects of the war had become too

12

immediate and too profound for it to be held off with quite such condescension. In *Hugh Selwyn Mauberley* Pound reviewed in retrospect the preceding literary generations from Ruskin to Arnold Bennett and Ford in an eclectic idiom and fluctuating persona which express the particular form of the social dilemma they had experienced and he had inherited. Faced with victims of vilification, neglect and entropy, or with examples of compromise, Pound had swung not to the deliquescent aestheticism the figure Mauberley suggests but to an aggressive evangelical bohemianism, only to find with the dilution of Imagism and the deaths of Vorticist *confrères* in the war that its social base, narrowly located as it was in an artistic movement and stance, had been cut from under him. He is pressed therefore into a defiant and direct identification of the cause of decline, directing his animus against, '. . . usury age-old and age-thick/ and liars in public places.'[12]

England that had offered the proxy culture absent in America stands in *Mauberley* as an 'old bitch gone in the teeth', indicted for neglect of her own past traditions which only an American in exile can properly respect. London, Pound wrote, was as 'dead as mutton'[13]; it had cheated him of the culture it promised and of a literary orthodoxy and sustaining liberal ideology which, though it was Pound's looked-for support, had proved hostile, and was now as defunct for him as for the petty bourgeoisie it had more directly served. Pound now shared the position of the class he had reviled. Caught between a lying plutocracy and working-class militancy, it too was without bearings; its class identity threatened into abeyance. For the petty bourgeoisie the post-war period offered the possibilities of realignment on either side of a stark class struggle, or of renewed self-assertion.[14] For Pound the first possibility barely presented itself: the ruling class stood exposed through its own machinations as the enemy, and Pound remained significantly ignorant of working class militancy and of the nature of socialism, seeing it only as misguided idealism, and latterly in the example of Russia, as part of a world conspiracy.[15] Thrown back but off balance onto his role as cultural emissary, Pound elected instead to relaunch himself and his cultural crusade in Europe. The following years, before Pound settled in 1924 in Italy, were for him, as for the

13

European petty bourgeoisie, a period of gestation and re-orientation. In these years he gathered in Homer, Ovid and Dante the components of a literary ideology which enabled him to revise the shambling Ur-Cantos into their present form, thus giving his projected poem an impetus and structural base-line, and found also in Confucius, Leo Frobenius and the social credit theory of Major C. H. Douglas a combined ethical and political standard, a 'kulturmorphologie' and an economics which would sanction his own synchronic cultural sweep and arm him against the ubiquitous crime of usury.

Pound's effort appears grotesque, but it was in proportion to the ideological deflation and redefinition consequent upon the war, and in itself indeed, consistent. Rather than depart from aestheticism, Pound broadened and strengthened its base, evading an embattled and narrow aestheticism which would exclude history, and which history itself had already proved futile, to embark with comparable arrogance upon an epic poem which in his description would 'include history and therefore economics'.[16] History presented itself, in common with the literary tradition, as material to be raided, moulded, revivified, transformed and, in short, rewritten as art. Rather also than abandon liberal ideology, Pound, in tandem with the petty bourgeoisie, awakened its potential extremism to realize an affinity with British and Italian Fascism, through, in his case, a renewed acquaintance with the ambiguities of the liberal tradition in America.

3

In 1942, Pound wrote of discovering in 1928 a tradition of family interest in questions of monetary reform.[17] His grand-father Thaddeus Coleman Pound had been Congressman for Wisconsin under President Hayes and close apparently to a cabinet seat under Garfield. He had issued his own paper scrip backed by lumber, tabled an amendment to a bill on silver coinage to ensure the circulation of non-interest bearing debt and had, Pound learned, already in 1878, at the height of the Greenback Party, 'been writing about or urging among his fellow congressman [sic], the same essentials of monetary and statal economics that I am writing about today.'[18] Pound's father, Homer Pound, was in his turn, register of the Hailey Land Office, Idaho, in the period of general land boom in the North Western States, and at its close had moved the family East to take up an appointment as assistant assayer at the U.S. Mint in Philadelphia in 1889.[19] The late 1880s and 1890s were years of populist agitation and the campaign for the remonetization of silver. In 1890, two years before the formation of the Populist Party, the Sherman Silver Purchase Act had put the Government under the obligation to buy 4,500,000 m. ounces of silver annually so as to maintain gold and silver at parity, but by 1893 the prosperity which had made this compromise possible was reversed.[20] The fall of the gold reserve led to a financial panic, to Grover Cleveland's repeal of the Silver Purchase Act and a recount of silver coinage, an event Pound witnessed as a boy at the Philadelphia mint. In these years, as Noel Stock writes, 'politics was in the air' and it was no doubt family discussion which moved Pound, as he reports, to his violent indignation at Cleveland's election in 1892, and alerted him later to the Free Silver campaign and William Jennings Bryan's 'Cross of Gold' speech in 1896.[21]

W. J. Bryan had opposed Cleveland's repeal of the Sherman Act in 1893, and was in 1896 nominated as the Democratic and later the Populist Presidential candidate.[22] Already, however, he had narrowed the Populist offensive to the single issue of free silver, shelving its original broader demands for the Government reclamation of land, the nationalization of railroads and communication systems, and its argument for the united interests of rural and urban labour.[23] For Bryan the restoration of silver was paramount. Once this was ensured he said 'all other necessary reforms will be possible; but . . . until this is done there is no other reform that can be accomplished.'[24] Bryan also accentuated, while he deradicalized, the Populist distinction between a nation of producers and a self-seeking business élite. While the Populist platform of 1892 had harangued both Republican and Democratic parties for proposing 'to drown the outcries of a plundered people with the uproar of a sham battle over the tariff, so that capitalists, corporations, national banks, rings, trusts, watered stock, the demonetization of silver and the oppressions of the usurers may be lost sight of',[25] Bryan initiated a compromise with the

15

Democratic Party which was to assist in the failure of Populism as a third party force. He spoke for American individualism, for the cause, he said in the 'Cross of Gold' speech, of 'humanity' in the interests of a new definition of the business-man: the wage earner, the country attorney, the small merchant, the farmer, the miner were all, Bryan argued, as much businessmen as the employer, the corporation council, the big city merchant, the speculator and financial magnate. 'We come to speak', he said, 'for this broader class of business men',[26] confirming in his autobiographical *The First Battle* that, 'the most important business men of the country [are] the real creators of wealth.'[27] Bryan's calling in the same speech upon the authority of Jefferson, Jackson and Thomas Benton also set parameters which effectively claimed a descent for populism from an orthodox liberalism which had traditionally defended the interests of the small property owner against big city financiers and monopoly holdings. The contradiction in American liberal ideology which made this possible, between a revolutionary mission which served only to reinforce capitalist enterprise and a notion of liberty which depended on property rights and slave holding, had been latent of course since the 1770s.[28] Once exploited, however, the ideological ground was prepared for Pound, as for the American fascist movements of the 1930s, to look back for legitimacy, through the already conservative prism of Bryan's populism, to the heroes of American liberalism.

Bryan himself was not an important explicit reference for Pound, although again in 1942, speaking over Rome Radio, he remembered both Bryan's 'Cross of Gold' and his grandfather as antecedents in his own by this time paranoidal mission.[29] The personal significance, in their different ways, of both figures was that they gave apparently clear expression to an American tradition which Pound could rediscover and re-enter in 1928, so gaining an assurance for his own developing ideas of monetary reform and of economic history, founded, true to populist credentials, upon the principal clash of usurious and non-usurious interests. The idiom and polemics of Pound's prose writing and poetry on these subjects between the late '20s and mid '40s consequently belong with those of a compromised and monomaniacal populism. His explicit adop-

tion over these years also of fascism, including the combined
anti-semitism and anti-communism more characteristic of
Nazism, can be recognized as a parallel instance to the culti-
vation of a reactionary germ in American populism which was
to produce the fascism of Father Coughlin and Huey Long,
both of whom could claim a descent from Bryan with ease.[30]

Pound's prose writings during this period were especially
extensive and show a mounting concern with questions of
American politics, economics and fascism, containing amongst
other items his (never republished) estimate of Huey Long
and Father Coughlin, and a letter to the Nazi-style Silver Shirt
Legion of America.[31] During the '30s also Pound produced a
block of 40 cantos, bracketed by the Jefferson Nuevo Mundo
Cantos (31–41) and the Chinese and Adams Cantos (52–71),
drawing here emphatically upon primary historical documen-
tation of the early American presidencies.[32] These he contrived
to splice, by way of intermittent references to Mussolini's
Italy, with the ratifying histories of Imperial China (Cantos
52–61) and of exemplary economic reform in Tuscany under
the Grand Duke Leopold from 1765–90 (Cantos 42–51).
Pound's evidence and sources provide a particular historical
reference and standard, and as such draw in a base-line to
which he can add social credit and canonized examples of a
selective literary tradition (Chaucer, Cavalcanti, Homer, early
Chinese) in a conglomerate and would-be totalizing authentic
culture whose corrective force can then be brought, if Pound's
vorticist method is to work, upon the suffocating 'hebrew
affections ... of Mitteleuropa' (Canto 35), the crimes of
munitions magnates (Canto 38), and everywhere the encroach-
ing infection of usury.

Pound's recourse to history in these Cantos has been judged
invariably in terms of its artistic failure or success. The
American and Chinese Cantos are seen in this way to fail in so
far as they depend unjustifiably on external and sometimes
tedious sources, and in so far as Pound's arbitrary selections
fail to bring them to independent life. Or, conversely, they are
thought to succeed because of the vicarious experience they
offer, when consulted with their sources, of the process of
Pound's artistic composition.[33] The important point, however,
lies not in questions of artistic worth, but in Pound's method

17

and object, in his choice of sources and in his selection from these in the making of a poem which seeks to master and control history for its own purposes. The problem lies then in the priority accorded to art and synonymously, for Pound, to 'civilization'. It is this dimension of zealous Arnoldian extremism which Pound's poetry brings to the populist undertow of these Cantos, and which he finds ratified in social credit theories and in Italian fascism.[34] His emphasis is clear in the summary complaint against usury in Cantos 45 and 51 which are central not only to the Cantos completed in the 1930s, but arguably to the whole of the *Cantos* as a prospective unity. Canto 45 draws into itself the accumulating evidence not only of immediately preceding Cantos, but the earlier indictment in *Mauberley* and specifically also the picture of London as a usurious hell in Cantos 14 and 15. The complaint itself is familiar from populism (indeed from Jefferson, Jackson and Van Buren), from Bryan and the American fascist movements of the '30s.[35] In its Old Testament cadence Pound's Canto throbs with the nervous religious venom of Bryan's speeches, and shares too Coughlin's sense of an anti-usurious Catholic middle-ages, invoking typically a threatened, predominantly agrarian order:

> with usura, sin against nature,
> is thy bread ever more of stale rags
> is thy bread dry as paper,
> with no mountain wheat, no strong flour
> with usura the line grows thick
> with usura is no clear demarcation
> and no man can find site for his dwelling.
> Stone cutter is kept from his stone
> weaver is kept from his loom
> WITH USURA
> wool comes not to market
> sheep bringeth no gain with usura
> Usura is a murrain, usura
> blunteth the needle in the maid's hand
> and stoppeth the spinner's cunning.[36]

To this, however, Pound brings the implicit resonance from Cantos 14 and 15 of Dante's hell, the authority of François Villon ('the first voice of a man broken by bad economics'),[37] the classical reference of the agrarian rites of purity and renewal at Eleusis, and most pointedly a series of citations of medieval painters and architecture whose fineness was uncorrupted by usury.

> Duccio came not by usura
> nor Pier della Francesca; Zuan Bellin' not by usura
> nor was 'La Calunnia' painted.
> Came not by usura Angelico; came not Ambrogio Praedis,
> Came no church of cut stone signed: *Adamo me fecit*.
> Not by usura St. Trophime
> Not by usura Saint Hilaire,
> Usura rusteth the chisel
> It rusteth the craft and the craftsman
> It gnaweth the thread in the loom
> None learneth to weave gold in her pattern;
> Azure hath a canker by usura; cramoisi is unbroidered
> Emerald findeth no Memling
> Usura slayeth the child in the womb
> It stayeth the young man's courting
> It hath brought palsey to bed, lyeth
> between the young bride and her bridegroom
>   CONTRA NATURA
> They have brought whores for Eleusis
> Corpses are set to banquet
> at behest of usura.

The focus of Pound's concern then is ethical and artistic and it is revealing, but consistent, that he should in the earlier Canto 41 predicate his praise of the Fascist public works programme upon Mussolini's response in 1933 to his own *A Draft of XXX Cantos*:

> 'Ma questo,'
> said the Boss, 'è divertente.'
> catching the point before the aesthetes had got there;
> Having drained off the muck by Vada
> From the marshes, by Circeo, where no one else wd. have
>   drained it.
> Waited 2000 years, ate grain from the marshes;
> Water supply for ten million, another one million '*vani*'
> that is rooms for people to live in.
>   XI of our era.[38]

19

Pound's idealism and gullibility, however transparent here, proved tenacious ingredients in his admiration of fascism. By the end of the month following his sole interview with Mussolini, Pound had produced his most provocative rationale in *Jefferson and/or Mussolini*, a work as selective in its principal juxtaposition as any of Pound's reconstructions of the literary tradition. Ostensibly *Jefferson and/or Mussolini* offers an apologia for Mussolini in terms of an American democratic heritage, now regained in Europe, but it does this in an ideological reading of political history which not only overlooks the compromise, coercion and censorship of Mussolini's dictatorship, but also reveals while it intends to conceal the single argument it can depend upon: the *real* continuity between the latent conservatism of American liberalism and fascist totalitarianism. Pound's populist analysis is again evident: 'the main line' of American history in the first half of the nineteenth century, 'was the fight between public interest and the interests'[39]; Jefferson stands against national debt and for keeping money 'in the pockets of the people' (pp. 79, 80), while Italy, as the saviour of Europe, represents the only possible opposition 'to the infinite evil of the profiteers and the sellers of men's blood for money' (p. 61). Jefferson and Mussolini are presented as similarly opposed to mechanization (p. 63); as both activated by a ' "concern" for the good of the people' (p. 34); and as sharing, Pound concludes,

> three common denominators or possibly four: agriculture, sense of the 'root and the branch', readiness to scrap the lesser thing for the thing of major importance, indifference to mechanism as weighed against the main purpose, fitting of the means to that purpose without regard to abstract ideas, even if the idea was proclaimed the week before last. (p. 64)

Both men are praised therefore for their opportunism, their freedom from *idées fixes* and their ability to convert ideas unobstructed into action. Their affinity is affirmed in a total political vocabulary which accepts a concept of liberty as 'the right to do anything that . . . does not harm others' (p. 43), which subordinates means to ends ('Who wills the end wills the means', p. 34), and which justifies a 'STRONG ITALY' as an expedient measure towards Jefferson's ideal of government as 'that which governs least' (pp. 15, 35, 45).

Jefferson and/or Mussolini then is an eccentric contribution to fascist propaganda, different in temper, but not in kind, from Pound's later radio broadcasts. Its arguments, by which Pound sought to supply Italian fascism with a legitimizing American precedent, were necessary in an immediate sense to himself, but were also quite compatible with the combination in fascist ideology of nationalist with socialist or republican motifs.[40] Mussolini himself of course had entered political journalism as a socialist and later again in the period of the Salo Republic proposed to return fascism to its socialist origins.[41] Earlier in 1923, he had claimed there was an 'historical and ideal continuity' between Garibaldi and the Blackshirts,[42] a view assisted by the interpretation of his education minister Giovanni Gentile that fascism 'in harmony with the teachings of Mazzini is the most perfect form of liberalism and democracy'.[43] As Poulantzas and others have argued, however, the actual continuity between the Risorgimento and Italian fascism resided in their common class base in the petty bourgeoisie,[44] and if descriptions of the liberal character of the fascist movement accorded with its earliest phase, this was overtaken soon after 1922, and decidedly in the 1930s, by Mussolini's personal assumption of power in the name of the Party and the State.[45] The petty bourgeoisie on whose shoulders Mussolini acquired power in fact suffered most from his regime as the fascist alliance with big business and the interests of European capitalism became more apparent.[46] The inevitability of this Pound did not or could not accept,[47] although its historical logic lay first in the development of American capitalism which Jefferson and Jackson had helped confirm despite their resistance to private banking,[48] and then in the crisis of the Post World War I economic depression which had produced, in America as in Europe, the so-called fascist alternative which was only a reinforcement of capitalism.

Pound was duped, one might suppose, by fascist ideology, and certainly his admiration of Jefferson and Mussolini as 'entire men', as exemplars of Confucian discipline and social responsibility closely follows Mussolini's own canonical and mystificatory description:

The fascist state . . . is form, inner law and discipline of the whole

21

person. It permeates will and intellect. Its principal, the central inspiration of the human personality dwelling in the civic community, permeates to the depths and settles in the heart of the man of action as well as of the thinker, of the artist as well as of the scientist: as the spirit of the spirit.[49]

But the singular affinity Pound could draw from such thinking was not only between the American and Fascist revolutions, or between Jefferson and Mussolini as men of like Confucian political genius, but between politics and art. Brought in *Jefferson and/or Mussolini* to a distinction between types of opportunism, Pound adds,

> There is also the opportunism of the artist who has a definite aim and creates art of the materials present. The greater the artist the more permanent his creation. And this is a matter of WILL.

> It is also a matter of the DIRECTION OF THE WILL. And if the reader will blow the fog off his brain and think for a few minutes or a few stray half-hours he will find this phrase brings us ultimately both to Confucius and Dante. (pp. 15–16)

'To cut the cackle', Pound insists, 'you can have an OPPORTUNIST who is RIGHT, that is who has certain convictions and who drives them through circumstance, or batters and forms circumstance with them' (pp. 17–18). Mussolini and Pound's Jefferson are of course then not far behind, since there is also a more exceptional opportunist who can act out of a full but intuitive knowledge, or intelligence, and deal with 'NEW circumstances'. When this occurs 'we call it genius' and 'Jefferson was one genius and Mussolini is another' (p. 19). Pound's premise when it surfaces again is unmistakable.

> I don't believe any estimate of Mussolini will be valid unless it *starts* from his passion for construction. Treat him as *artifex* and all the details fall into place. Take him as anything save the artist and you will get muddled in contradictions. (pp. 33–4)

The adoption of a persona which had served Pound in dealing with literary circumstance serves him here also. Mussolini, like Pound, can strike to the root in any tangle; like the true critic he can 'pick out the element of immediate and major importance' (p. 66). Finding himself 'in the cluttered rubbish and cluttered splendour of the dozen or more strata of human

THE LESSON OF EZRA POUND

effort', Mussolini took to it the shaping passion of creative genius to wrench and dynamite 'that junkshop into a nation, a live nation on its toes like a young bull in the Cordova ring' (pp. 66–7). One is reminded by this of Pound's defence of Sigismondo Malatesta's Tempio at Rimini ('. . . If you consider the Malatesta and Sigismundo in particular, a failure, he was at all events a failure worth all the successes of his age. . . . If the Tempio is a jumble and a junk shop, it nevertheless registers a concept. There is no other single man's effort equally registered'[50]), and reminded too of his comparison of the *Cantos* with a performance of Bartok's Fifth Quartet as having alike 'the defects inherent in a record of struggle'.[51] A profound affinity between art and politics percolates in this way back and forth through Pound's thinking; their common motivation resides in a passionate drive for construction, their common means in a self-justifying opportunism and their common test in the creation of a permanent order freed from struggle.

4

Pound, one can see then, consistently aestheticizes history and politics, or more precisely reads back into art a conception of both as a contest between individual men and the disarray of life's materials. This is a tendency we might consider, following Walter Benjamin, as itself inherently fascistic.[52] But not every and any aesthetic will have such designs. A shorthand indication of the ramifications of Pound's particularly amoebic aestheticism is to be read in the sliding designations given to the term 'tò Kalón', glossed first as 'Beauty' but subsequently as a principle of 'Order' exemplified by Mussolini. This is a symptomatic transition,[53] but the elision of art, ethics and politics is proof of needs still to be unravelled particularly in the expansive realm of Pound's poetry in the *Cantos*.

Pound began the original Cantos in earnest in 1917 with a conception of chaos and the need for an epic poem as correspondingly loose and baggy:

> Hang it all, there can be but one *Sordello*!
> But say I want to, say I take your whole bag of tricks,

23

> Let in your quirks and tweeks, and say the thing's an art-
> form,
> Your *Sordello*, and that the modern world
> Needs such a rag-bag to stuff all its thought in . . .[54]

The revision of the *Cantos'* beginning which set Odysseus, the theme of metamorphosis, Dante's *Divine Comedy* and Malatesta's Italy as primary pigments in Pound's artist's palette gave the poem a prospective but still flexible scheme and direction. Here already a general analogy with Malatesta's construction of the Tempio and Mussolini's of Italy suggests itself. Again, Pound's epic rhymes with fascist ambitions in that it depends on the belief in an assumed end though the passage towards it is unplanned. As Pound wrote in *Jefferson and/or Mussolini*,

> Any thorough judgment of Mussolini will be in a measure an act of faith, it will depend on what you *believe* the man means, what you believe that he wants to accomplish. (p. 33)

The same might be said of Pound's *Cantos*. The first sixteen especially evolved out of false starts and substantial revisions in which Pound was moved more by an insistence and compulsion than a preconceived design. As he wrote in 1922 to Felix Schelling,

> Perhaps as the poem goes on I shall be able to make various things clearer. . . . I *have* to get down all the colours or elements I want for the poem. Some perhaps too enigmatically and abbreviatedly. I hope, heaven help me, to bring them into some sort of design or architecture later.[55]

His message to Hubert Greekmore later, in 1939, was the same:

> As to the *form* of *The Cantos*: All I can say or pray is: *wait* till it's there. I mean wait till I get 'em written and then if it don't show, I will start exegesis.[56]

The completion of both Pound's poem and Italian fascism manifestly require a similarly unqualified faith in the driving will towards order of the constructive single personalities at their centres. It is hence the nature of this desired order which defines the *Cantos* presiding aesthetic and as we shall see helps explain the relation of its poetic form to political ideology.

Pound criticism has of course recognized the problem of the *Cantos'* formal organization; indeed it has been preoccupied with it, the situation standing now much as it was presented by Daniel Pearlman in 1969, with critics divided on what he takes to be 'the crux of *Cantos* criticism, the question as to whether this physically enormous, sprawling poem has *major form*—an overall design in which the parts are significantly related to the whole.'[57] Clearly criticism which sets itself this sole objective, will not only patently ignore the questions posed here, but also, regardless of its conclusions, reinforce the primacy of formal unity within an organicist aesthetic. The persistence of this problematic, as Terry Eagleton has shown, is deeply entrenched in bourgeois criticism and literature.[58] It is true also that Pound evidently subscribed to organicist criteria, not only in the formal, literary and musical analogies he positively invoked for the *Cantos*, but also in the terms by which he judged it a failure (it was a 'mess', he 'botched it', he said in late interviews, confessing in Canto 116 'I cannot make it cohere', only to reaffirm in the same Canto 'it coheres all right').[59]

The *Cantos* do aspire emphatically towards a formal unity, and Pound's *conscious* effort is, as criticism has largely presented it, to shape water into stone, to convert flux into permanence and so pull the disarray of the poem's materials into order. The result in the poem is moments of would-be transcendence and stillness from which 'integrative' critics are prone to extrapolate its entire character. The *Cantos* are in this way for Hugh Kenner 'a timeless frieze',[60] and for Pearlman a conflict of time systems in which Pound's own 'ahistorical cyclical time-consciousness' is triumphant over the linear and mechanical clock-time of history.[61] Both Kenner and Pearlman understandably make much in this reckoning of the 'dimension of stillness' in Canto 49, for Kenner 'one of the pivots of the poem: the emotional stillpoint of the *Cantos*',[62] and for Pearlman a paean to 'Confucian order', which he relates to the definition of the essential or ideal form of love in Canto 36 as that which 'moveth not, drawing all to its stillness'. For Pearlman, Pound's translation of Cavalcanti's 'Donna me pregha' in Canto 36 represents 'a touchstone of aesthetic and intellectual order' and the idea of 'stillness' he sees as 'the metaphoric and conceptual center of the only sustained vision Pound has yet offered us of a paradise.'[63] Here in Canto 36, in revitalizing a 'luminous moment' in the literary tradition, Pound purportedly sets art in defiance of time, aligning its truth with the Confucian scheme of order in Canto 49 as a rebuff to an Einsteinian theory of relativity which would define 'time' itself and not 'stillness' as the 'fourth dimension'. The cost, however, is plainly very high. Not only is the informing concept of order in these Cantos cryptically closed to the least challenge, Pound's translation in 36 is also one of the most inaccessible sections of the poem, presenting an abstruse and privileged definition of 'love' by whose authority Pound, as much as Cavalcanti, can at its end arrogantly jettison those who neither understand nor sympathize:

> Go, song, surely thou mayest
> Whither it please thee
> For so art thou ornate that thy reasons
> Shall be praised from thy understanders,
> With others hast thou no will to make company.[64]

The connections over these Cantos between ideals of artistic and also social and political order become plain. The 'transcendence' which is claimed for the two 'literary' Cantos 36 and 49 is supported by the informing notion of the Confucian axis or 'unwobbling pivot', the 'calm principle' in man and in Nature, which permits an 'escape' from history while it offers a judgement upon it. Against the crime of usury, or increasingly of named Jewish usurers, Pound levels the supposed stability, clarity and uncorrupted natural abundance of former times, whose essence is preserved and renewed through a selective literature (as of these examples) and the recorded words and deeds of selective leading personalities. Not only Jefferson and Mussolini, but the several other 'factive' historical individuals upon whom the *Cantos* are threaded (Malatesta, Frederick II, Leopold, Hanno, Napoleon, the legendary Chinese Emperors, the Adamses), are seen variously to share beneath and above the accidents of history, the profound affinities of Odyssean 'polumetis' (many-mindedness), Confucian inner discipline, an ability to commit ideas unswervingly to action, and a 'will towards order'. In power, they are latter-day examples of the Confucian prince in whose will the well-being of the State and people are simultaneously entrusted and guaranteed.

Both these features of a radicalizing cultural nostalgia and a theory of personality are endemic in populism, and exacerbated and exploited in fascist ideology. The first, as Donald Macrae has argued, appears in populism's 'modified primitivism', its idealizing view of a simple spontaneous past order, a 'golden age' free of plutocratic villainy, whose quality is linked with the 'sacred, life-renewing soil', and by which it invokes,

> a holy, ritual cyclical time, immune in its revolutions from the corruptions of real historical time, change and decay.[65]

The resemblance of these terms to Pearlman's argument for the overriding unity of the *Cantos* could not be closer. The 'theory of personality', secondly, Macrae summarizes in part as 'in simple societies there is a paucity and a uniformity of institutions. Individuals in such societies are competent to fill many roles: they are "many-faceted", and therefore various, realized and integral personalities'.[66] In fascism these ideas reappear and are synthesized in the cult of the leader who embodies at once the State and the interests of its citizens, and is himself an example of the 'new man' who heralds a 'new world'.[67] The praise of Mussolini and the supportive ingredients of fascist, not to say Nazi ideology, in Pound's *Cantos* have been vigorously demonstrated by John Lauber. As he concludes,

> The *Cantos* are totalitarian and fascistic not only in such aspects as their praise of Mussolini or their anti-Semitism but in their basic ideology: in their paranoid interpretation of history, seeing in every event the signs of a 'usurocratic' conspiracy and the agency of the 'enemy'; in their concern for the unmasking of culprits; in their intense authoritarianism and élitism (inseparable from their paranoia—the truth is known to a privileged few, whose assertions are not to be challenged); in their 'aesthetic' view of politics, judging a leader by his vision, and viewing humanity as 'malleable mud' to be cast into a mould by its leaders and its artists; in their admiration for the inseparably associated virtues of the Will, of action, and of hardness (needed to carry out the vision of the leader).[68]

The populist antecedents I have suggested would, I think, qualify Lauber's categorical description of the *Cantos* as a

27

'fascist epic', but there is more at issue here than Pound's overt political attitudes. It is a question also of the ideological burden of the poem's formal organization. The types of evidence the *Cantos* assemble towards a promised terrestrial paradise, by way of past literatures and charismatic heroes who culminate in a Confucian Mussolini, converge also in the example of Pound's own 'factive' personality and literary enterprise, to be reworked there in patterned motifs of internal transcendence in a many-sided, but profoundly egocentric and totalitarian design. Pound's own Odyssean voyage towards a prospective centripedal whole which is prefigured only, like Odysseus' home-coming, by blind prophecy, proceeds in a formal synchrony with fascism's anticipated, but obscure destiny.[69] Both depend on the integrative will of their central personalities towards a created harmony, and crucially on their power and mastery over the malleable materials of art and people. Pound's artistic method we see is far from innocent: the moments of transcendent stillness which are so valued in the *Cantos'* putative formal unity collaborate in fact with a political ideology of mixed origin but of a decidedly fascist tendency, in a logic also which bourgeois criticism has failed to pursue, just as it has failed, inevitably, to inspect the ideological bearing of its own aesthetic priorities.

5

In a sense the warning note here had already been sounded by Wyndham Lewis's attack in *Time and Western Man* (1927) on the 'time cult' which treated reality as an unending 'process' rather than a 'system' to be properly understood by analogy with the static principles of a geometrical art. As Dimitri Mirsky recognized by the middle thirties, Lewis's transcendent 'statics' were as fascistic as the more rationalized fascist philosophy of 'pure action'.

> Lewis's anti-temporal 'statics' are no less glaring an expression of what fascism is about—that is to say of the attempt being made to arrest the course of history and put capitalist civilization, already putrescent, in a cold chamber, in the hope of keeping it fresh.[70]

28

More crucially, Lewis had accused Pound in *Time and Western Man* of too much 'process', a response in its way to the fundamental inner contradiction in the *Cantos* and a reminder *not* of its order but of its often, even ultimately, provisional and centrifugal character. Pound himself of course was registering the disruptive and wayward force of this aspect of the poem in announcing it a failure ('I picked out this and that thing that interested me, and then jumbled them into a bag. But that's not the way to make ... a *work of art*'[71]), but had also described the antagonistic aesthetics which divide the poem against itself and so confound its egoism and totalitarian ambition. There are, Pound had said, *à propos* William Carlos Williams, 'very important chunks of world-literature in which form, major form, is remarkable mainly for absence', and later in the same essay,

> Art very possibly *ought* to be the supreme achievement, the 'accomplished'; but there is the other satisfactory effect, that of a man hurling himself at an indomitable chaos, and yanking and hauling as much of it as possible into some sort of order (or beauty), aware of it both as chaos and potential.[72]

In art Pound was aware of both chaos and potential order, of change and permanence, of 'process' and 'statics'. And what the *Cantos* accustom us to *in spite* of Pound's express predilection for order over chaos, is the intermediary, fluctuating realm which is neither, but both. In this sense the *Cantos* are at their extremes both intermittently transcendent *and* incoherent, and the passage between such states is uncertain, exploratory and testing, requiring of us as readers, as of Pound, something akin to Keats's idea of 'negative capability'—'when man is capable of being in uncertainties, Mysteries, doubts, without any irritable reaching after fact & reason.'[73] It would seem to be in this spirit, amongst other instances, that Pound spoke in 1963 of realizing 'the consciousness of doubt' and 'the uncertainty of knowing nothing'.[74] Its effect in his poetry relates chiefly to the mode he identified as 'logopoeia':

> 'The dance of the intellect among words', that is to say, it employs words not only for their direct meaning, but it takes count in a special way of habits of usage, of the context we *expect* to find with the word, its usual concomitants of its known

acceptances, and of ironical play. . . . it is the latest come, and perhaps most tricky and undependable mode.[75]

'Logopoeia' is usually confined to irony but I suggest it extends to the vocabulary and syntax, the ellipses, the suspensions, the lapsed and accretional reference and literal foreignness of the *Cantos*. It is here as Pound checks and replenishes and surpasses habits of usage and known associations that his poem and his relation to its readers is at its most potentially enriching and most at risk. This would bear once again on the example of Canto 36. Pound's Cavalcanti translation of 1928 was, he suggested, a means to establishing a viable English,[76] and Canto 36, which is for Pearlman, 'a touchstone of artistic and intellectual order' is presumably a further stage in this process. But Pound's translation of Cavalcanti here is remarkable precisely to the extent that its broken and curiously unfamiliar locutions and syntax render it virtually unintelligible as English. Terms such as 'affect', 'diafan', 'intention', 'emanation', even *'virtu'* and 'quality', rise from the page as if detached from their common syntactic and semantic bearings. What they convey is their own aura, a sense of possible depth, or hollowness, above which they have surfaced. Here 'logopoeia' proves decidedly tricky and undependable, just in so far as Pound eschews common habits of usage and with it the possibilities of ironical play. (Most obviously in the preference for the term 'affect' over the more literal 'accident' because the second term was subject to extraneous associations.[77]) The suppression of contingency in this way is the linguistic equivalent of the timeless 'dimension of stillness' the Canto otherwise seeks to define. The ideological implications of organicist criteria here therefore carry through questions of form to questions of language, Pound seeking in this instance to exercise an authoritarian control which will confine and atomize discourse. But this is again only one aspect of the *Cantos'* self-contradictory whole. Just as the poem is in general terms structurally precarious, both rigidly sculpted and unshaped, so its language, if it is on occasion imprisoned, as in Canto 36, is elsewhere released, and allowed to run fluently through native and borrowed tongues. At these moments Pound's egotistical grasp is relaxed.

30

The corollary of 'negative capability', one remembers from Keats, is a preparedness to go out of the individual ego in a non-possessive empathy with others. The section titled *Thrones* in the *Cantos* was an attempt Pound said 'to move out from egoism and to establish some definition of an order possible or at any rate conceivable on earth',[78] and one notes both the idea still of such an order and the qualifications which hedge it. But Pound had arguably sought an alternative to open egoism prior to this through the adopted rhythms and idioms of his earliest translations, imitations and personae poems.[79] And in the *Cantos* too an alternative is most apparent, before *Thrones*, in the *Pisan Cantos*, written after the fall of fascism during Pound's confinement by the U.S. Army, and appears here again, most noticeably, in a series of tessellated voices and rhythms, especially as they recede and advance through Cantos 80 and 81. Pound, I would suggest, occupies but does not appropriate these voices, releasing them as freely back into their sources as into his own discourse. The *Cantos*, he had said in 1920 'come out of the middle of me and are not a mask',[80] but his poetry at a point such as this speaks more than anywhere through remembered authors, with the effect of at once dissolving and extending personal identity and 'self-expression' into a more impersonal and faceted idiom. If Pound does not inhabit a recognizable English in Canto 36, he here inhabits several received literary idioms (those, for example of Aubrey Beardsley, Arthur Symons, Yeats, Browning, William Stevenson, Fitzgerald's *Rubaiyat*, Tennyson, Richard Lovelace, Ben Jonson, Chaucer and the King James Bible), so that we witness something like the 'synthetic construction of speech' referred to by Eliot.[81] Nor does Pound organize his poem on these echoes, or through the associative memories which drift back and forth in Canto 80 over Edwardian London as though they are palpably recoverable in the present, or in a pretence to coherence. We are in the double realm here of chaos and potential order. His questions to England at the close of the same Canto, for example, are speculative if not cynical, and a hope such as that 'the bank may be the nation's' or that 'money be free again' is roundly answered, as soon as raised, by Pound's pessimism.[82] His general purpose here, as he put it elsewhere, was to discover 'his own ADDRESS (in time)' to know 'where his time and milieu stand in relation to other times and conditions'.[83] Pound's address, as this passage reminds us, was the Detention Training Centre, Pisa, and the enormous gulf between this reality and a remembered past is not one the poem fudges. The predominant tone of the passage indeed is one of loss, of 'Tudor indeed is gone' and of surviving remnants (the Serpentine, the gulls, the sunken garden) in the midst of a significantly shared sense of post-war uncertainty and dispossession, 'and God knows what else is left of our London/My London, your London.' In seeking his 'address', Pound finds in drastic circumstances that he has none, that he is 'linguistically un-housed' and culturally exiled, connected positively with none of the aspects of English or American, or Italian or Chinese culture he admired and would have willed into being. This 'negative awareness' is evident finally in the climactic moment of visitation in Canto 81 by Aphrodite, otherwise the leading symbol of all Pound's effort to extract permanence from flux. In the event, the experience is not one of vision but of partial fulfillment, 'careless or unaware it had not the/ whole tent's room/ nor was place for the full *eidos*'.[84] The strength of this moment lies not in its transcendence but in its demarcation of the known from the unknown, its awareness of the disparity between consummate form and a falling short of it.

Where then in the Cantos discussed earlier Pound had ordered history to his poem's convenience, here a real history, of the second war and of the fall of fascism, overtakes and itself shapes the poem, constructing in the *Pisan Cantos* a second personal hell which significantly throws the projected Dantesque scheme of the poem out of line. The *Pisan Cantos*, in effect, mis-shape and wreck the *Cantos'* totalitarian project in the aftermath of the wreck of Italian fascism. By their example they offer the poem's alternative sense of history, as one 'when the historians left blanks in their writings/ I mean for things they didn't know'.[85] The *Cantos* as a whole in this respect we can read as not only exploiting history, but as participating in a historical consciousness specific to a class and ideology whose rise and defeat is mapped in the twists and cancellations of the poem. In a sense the *Cantos* do then 'include' history, by very virtue of their ambitious bravura and its deflation, which produces the poem's ellipses and blanks, its record of loss, its *unfulfilled* paradise and its *uncompleted* journey home. It is the fact that Pound writes, especially from the *Pisan Cantos* onwards, not unwittingly, but in an awareness of this radical uncertainty which enables us to think of him as an example of 'negative capability'. Its force is to lay bare the poem's internally contradictory closures and fissures, its egoism and self-abnegation, its condition as stone and as water, so as to dramatically subvert the *Cantos* putative organicism by its aesthetic negation. It is this form of erosive self-critique too which distinguishes the *Cantos* from Pound's prose writings, and from which his poem emerges as of interest not simply as a 'fascist epic', or as an 'American fascist epic' but also as a 'failure' since where it 'fails' it also succeeds in undermining Pound's totalitarian ambition.

An obvious question remains however. If we are to learn from Pound's example, and pass beyond the adjudications of an organicist aesthetic and bourgeois criticism, we should look not only to the negative force of the *Cantos* auto-critique, but to the prospect, beyond Pound, of poetry's positively exercised critical potency in relation to ideology. What, we should ask, might be the ideological burden of a type of poetry which is, unlike Pound's own, purposively open and decentralized and which deliberately eschews the bourgeois criterion of 'major form'? The remainder of this discussion attempts to pursue this question in examining the implications of Pound's 'negative capability' and the 'failed' aspect of the *Cantos* where this is converted into a positively informing influence in the tenets of 'open-field poetry'.

6

Fascism has existed and exists still in several forms which require each in their turn the most thorough historical and ideological analysis. In Europe and in America, however, where it is at least clear that fascism has arisen in periods of economic crisis particularly affecting the petty bourgeoisie, one can argue that it has gained full or partial consensus to the degree that it has successfully operated within, and so built upon, the disabling contradictions in liberal ideology as these too have risen to the surface. Pound's own radical extremism, while a specific instance of a general tendency or disposition

33

towards the right amongst a European-based literary intelli-
gentsia, finds its particular explanation and context I suggest
in the ideological machinations of American fascism, especially
as, in one of its aspects, it twisted the course of the populist
tributary of American liberalism further to the right. The
populism of the 1890s was of course an already ambiguously
progressive and conservative movement, which it is well to
remember never campaigned, even at its most radical, for more
than an adjustment of capitalism.[86] The same ambiguity, in
different terms, might be detected a century earlier in the
seminal conceptions of liberty and the rights of man informing
both American and French Revolutions. As Marx coolly per-
ceived, a notion of liberty which is tied to property ownership
and a conception of rights which sanctioned the right to get
rich, in effect laid the foundations for modern capitalism.[87] The
main source in political philosophy which guided Jefferson in
framing the American Declaration of Independence is to be
found, Bernard Bailyn tells us, in John Locke.[88] But claims have
been made prior to, and in answer to Bailyn, for at least the
indirect influence also of Rousseau upon American democratic
ideals.[89] The debate is itself revealing since if Locke is the
theorist of the doctrine of 'checks and balances' which informed
the U.S. Constitution, Rousseau's conflation of the 'general
will' with the State is a harbinger, in its turn, of modern
so-called 'totalitarian democracies'. To put it at its bluntest, as
Bertrand Russell does, 'Hitler is an outcome of Rousseau;
Roosevelt and Churchill of Locke.'[90] Pound's *Jefferson and/or
Mussolini* is in a sense then, in the terms of intellectual history, a
recast 'Locke and/or Rousseau', and its confusion a late result
of the ambiguous applications of eighteenth-century political
philosophy. What makes Pound's argument possible, however,
and what Locke and Rousseau share, is not so much points of
theory as a common response to historical crises, the first
marking the advent of the bourgeoisie and the second its
remobilization and acquisition of political muscle in the period
of economic depression following World War I. Both develop-
ments, that is to say, and the responses they encourage, belong
to extreme points in the history of bourgeois capitalism.

It is not particularly surprising then that many of Pound's
crucial sources should converge, as they do, upon the late

eighteenth and early nineteenth centuries, not least his knowledge of Chinese history which he derived principally from a French translation made in 1777–83. (Pound's knowledge of the canonical Confucian texts was derived from a later source, but it is worth noting still that Confucius was introduced to the West by the French *philosophes*.[91]) What is significant, however, is not only that the locus of Pound's political and historical thinking is sited in this early period, but that the divided aesthetic which composes while it disrupts his *Cantos* has also its inception here. Of several possible instances, the most pronounced as it concerns the composition of the long, 'epic' poem, is the antagonism between Keats and Wordsworth. Keats's idea of 'negative capability' and of 'the poetical character' as having 'no self . . . no character . . . no identity' was conceived, under the immediate influence of Hazlitt, in direct opposition to the 'proper self' of the 'man of power' which Keats came to identify with the 'Wordsworthian or egotistical sublime'.[92] Both Keats's *Hyperion* poems can be understood in this light as much as attempted replies to Wordsworth as to Milton. Both poems, however, significantly 'fail', not simply because in the conventional sense they are 'unfinished', but because Keats's critique of romantic individualism is vitiated by the very self-consciousness on which it depends, rendering the poet and poetic composition as much his subject as it is Wordsworth's. What distinguishes Keats is the recognition of this failure, his consequently scuttling the poems, and his projection of a career outside of and superior to poetry, where 'negative capability' might take practical effect. Such an ambition appears in his 'idea of doing some good in the world' and in the type of model humanitarian in the *Fall of Hyperion*, those

> who love their fellows even to the death,
> who feel the giant agony of the world,
> And more, like slaves to poor humanity,
> labour for mortal good.[93]

But while Keats in this way checked and exposed romantic egoism, leaving poems which are fragments rather than organic wholes, he could offer no full reply to the insistence of either egoism or organicism. And neither could he offer a real alternative outside poetry, since the Victorian ethic of practical benevolence he prefigures here, while it might modify naked self-interest, could only 'humanize' but not radically undermine bourgeois individualism.

The distinction between Keats and Wordsworth has been raised, with reference to Pound, by Donald Davie.[94] Davie's double-edged point is that the modernist tendencies initiated by certain of the Romantic poets, and the argument by way of Pound for an alternative to 'the lyric-syntactic closures of first person experience'[95] can, when pursued through an erudite academic discourse, eschew the Wordsworthian virtue of a 'man speaking to men' and by the same token pay scant respect to the 'common reader'. Davie sets Wordsworth in this against Blake and Shelley 'and perhaps Keats'. But Keats has been particularly relevant to the American 'modernist' proponents of 'open field poetry' who have also wanted to acknowledge a debt to Pound's sense of a heterogeneous musical form, while warning of the contrary defects in his method and thinking. Both Charles Olson and Robert Duncan, the major theorists of 'composition by field', were disturbed in this way, to the point of disgust, by Pound's fascism, Olson reeling under 'the full shock of what a fascist s.o.b. Pound is'[96] in meetings with him at St. Elizabeth's hospital, and Duncan commenting perceptively but dismissively,

> It is the simplistic BLAST of Mussolini's Boss m and the simplistic rigor of the structure of total control that Fascism proposes in its authoritarian model for all social behaviour that excites Pound's fanatical defense against the need for 'order' that he felt in his own work.[97]

For Olson, the double lesson of Pound's *Cantos* was that 'the EGO AS BEAK is bent and busted' while they had shown also how historical materials might be freed, so as to 'bring any time abreast of us', turning 'time into . . . space and its live air'.[98] For Duncan, similarly, while Pound sought to introduce through Confucius a moral 'foundation of simplicity',

> he acts to make our European 'western' mind more heterogeneous and complex . . . Pound's inspiration in his Cantos, ultimately distressing to him, is in such an increase in the internal surface of the poem. It does not homogenize; for its operations are not archetypal or simple. Its organization is not totalitarian but co-operative.[99]

36

The general terms in which the *Cantos* have been rescued for these and other writers, and some critics, are expounded by Eric Mottram:

> The *Cantos* already required a dynamic freedom of form which assimilated image, vortex, ideogram (an adaptation of the Chinese sign into an English verbal cluster) and sentence into a field action, so that complex materials could be handled without losing speed of thinking and feeling, and without losing the precompositional form of the materials themselves. This method itself is part of that synchronicity taking place in all the arts of the period, the artist's desire to be inclusive, to respect the objectivity or thingness of his given materials, and to acknowledge the place of other logic than the linear, other speeds than the single or continuous. The poem could now use whatever material in whatever form that came into the process of composition, and to employ what Pound calls 'pleasure in counterpoint' (Canto 79), the continuous juxtaposition of melodic informational elements.[100]

Keats, I suggest, has been an important ingredient in this rehabilitation of Pound. Both Duncan and Olson again directly invoke the proposition of 'negative capability' as a seminal reference for a non-egotistical address to the world and as a guide to an authentic view of history and a true poetics. In *The Truth and Life of Myth*, myth is for Duncan, 'the true history hidden in history . . . the story of what is happening in history that we know in part', and Keats is cited as belonging with others, including Socrates, Milton and Darwin, in a tradition bearing a 'gnosis of not-knowing':

> Socrates knew he did not know. And with the Romantic movement, the intellectual adventure of not knowing, of 'Negative Capability', Keats called it in poetry, returns. The truth we know is not of What Is, but of What is Happening.[101]

Pound earns his place in this thinking via his lesson of accuracy and humility, for disclosing a recognized flaw in a 'hoped-for success'. The key ideograms of 'sincerity' ('the precise definition of the word . . . to perfect, bring to focus') and 'Fidelity' ('Fidelity to the given word. The man here standing by his word') as glossed by Pound, Duncan interprets respectively as 'Focusing in on the process itself as the field of the poem, the jarring discord must enter the poem' and 'that [the writer] face

the possibility of error and seek the truth of his statement'.[102]
Where, as Duncan writes,

> In the aftermath of the War, Pound stands in the full conse-
> quences of his Confucian myth of the State compounded with his
> Renaissance myth of the Prince brought over into his idealiza-
> tion of the Tyrant Mussolini. . . . Now in the Pisan Cantos we
> find among the properties of the poet's mind . . . the admission
> of a serious flaw, 'the six seeds of an error'; and in the great
> Cantos of his old age, the theme grows
> > 'Tho my errors and wrecks lie about me
> > And I am not a demigod
> > the damn stuff will not cohere?'[103]

In Duncan's reading therefore the grounds of Pound's sense of
the *Cantos'* artistic failure are reversed to become terms of an
achievement and acknowledged influence.

In Olson's *Special View of History*, Keats's original definition
of 'negative capability' forms the 'methodological' epigraph
and provides, in collation with Heraclitus, Einstein, A. N.
Whitehead and Heisenberg's 'uncertainty principle', the book's
presiding authority. Olson extrapolates from Keats' definition
in his first section as follows—

> So: as far as man goes, the attempt here is to establish in what
> sense man need not any longer be estranged from that with
> which he is most familiar. That would be the content, and is the
> reality in whose face anyone of us has to take a stance. And that
> the stance which yields the possibility of acts which are allow-
> ably historic, in other words produce, have to be negatively
> capable in Keats' sense that they have to be, they have to be
> uncertain.
> > Or what we would call today relative.[104]

'History itself', Olson says, drawing as he often does through
the text on Keats's distinction between a 'man of power' and a
'man of achievement',

> can be shown to be of two kinds, and that of these two kinds,
> one is negatively capable and the other is power. Men can and
> wilfully set in motion egotistical, sublime events. They have
> effect which looks like use. But in the scheme here presented,
> these are power, and history as primordial and prospective is
> seen to demand the recognition that the other history, what I
> would call anti-history, is not good enough.[105]

History, he further insists 'is the *function* of any one of us' and function is how a thing acts.

> Action, in its turn, is a determinant of will and there are 'two sorts of will: a will to power or a will of achievement. The first one is the one in which the will collapses back to the subjective understanding—tries to make it by asserting the self as character. The second makes it by non-asserting the self as self. In other words the riddle is that the true self is not the asserting function but an obeying one. . . . One is the self as ego and sublime. The other is the self as center and circumference.'[106]

'Negative capability' then presents itself as a way of 'staying in process', of attending to the manifold relativity of a 'prospective' reality in which 'events are absolute only because they have a future, not from any past.'[107] Such a conception requires an attitude of surrender and attention of a kind the poet undertakes in writing 'projective verse':

> From the moment he ventures into FIELD COMPOSITION—puts himself in the open—he can go by no track other than the one the poem underhand declares, for itself.[108]

If we can assume this thinking informs open-field poetry, particularly Olson's *Maximus Poems* and Duncan's *Passages* and *Structure of Rime*, we can see the nature of its debt in the writing of the long poem to a recuperated Keatsian aspect of Pound, and see by the same token its limitations. While Keats's *Hyperion* poems were frustratedly opposed to Wordsworth and Milton, and Pound's *Cantos* unwillingly subversive of themselves, 'projective verse' or 'composition by field' is here in comprehensive and unrepentant open rebellion against traditional organicist criteria, particularly in its attendant prescriptions for regular metrical and stanzaic forms. But this poetry is also notoriously cavalier in its regard of the 'common reader', and, one might add of a collective history as it is made by men in society rather than in myth or in poems. The practically neurotic aversion within open-field poetry to conventional punctuation and spacing, in the interests of following the warp and woof of speech, becomes in fact a rationale for a principle of measure ordered by individual patterns of breathing, with its source as much as anywhere in Pound's notion of an 'absolute rhythm'

39

which 'will be, therefore, in the end, (a man's) own, uncounter-feiting, uncounterfeitable.' In Olson this becomes,

> I measure my song,
> measure the sources of my song,
> measure me, measure
> my forces.[109]

The assault within open-field poetry on literary orthodoxy is then primarily individualist and aesthetic. As far as its broader corollaries are advanced through the authority of Darwin, Einstein, Whitehead, Gestalt psychology and modern physics it smacks of a quasi-scientific, but, in effect, religious optimism. Where Pound had perceived a primordial chaos of materials in need of the ordering ego of the 'man of power', open-field poetry assumes a deep order and unity within a world of variegated process to which man's life ('history') and poetic creation stand in the relation of allegory. As Denise Levertov has most categorically stated:

> Back in the idea of organic form is the concept that there is a form in all things (and in our experience) which the poet can discover and reveal . . . [he] seeks out inherent, though not immediately apparent form.[110]

The poet's method is one of 'aperception, i.e. of recognizing what we perceive, and it is based on an intuition of order, a form beyond forms, in which forms partake, and of which man's creative works are analogies, resemblances, natural allegories.' 'Such poetry', she adds, 'is exploratory.' But exploration, on these terms, can only proceed within a given circumference whose line is already drawn, if not by mortal hand. In its fundamental complacency this is a recipe for political quietism, an implication which indeed overtook Olson's early political involvement, and surfaces also in Duncan's adumbrated social vision.

Olson's revulsion from Pound's fascism and anti-semitism had been that of a confirmed democrat, who 'revered' Roosevelt, and who had risen by 1944 to become Foreign Nationalities Director of the Democratic National Committee.[111] In the same year, before meeting Pound, Olson had written in 'People v The Fascist U.S.'—'Attack is the first and final weapon of the fascist. Attack a leader, attack a class, attack a race—attack a peace. . . . the fascists strike at "Reds", "democrats", "Jews", "Liberals", "Negroes", "Catholics" ',[112] and in *Call Me Ishmael*, 'But the captains of industry ain't worth the powder etc. Take the revolution so long as we're on the subject: whose revolution was it but the "moneyed groups"; Breed's Hill two weeks after Lexington and it was all over for the "smaller people" until Jefferson gave them another chance.'[113] The significantly populist spirit of this is obvious, but it is equally obvious that its animus was blunted for Olson by the 'gutter politics of Truman' and by the fascist challenge, which 'captured criticism of democracy, & puts any critic in the camp of the enemy'.[114] The period of Olson's meetings with Pound, between 1946–48, marked the transition in his own career from an active involvement in practical politics to the occupation of 'writer', for whom the political phase of his life 'was over—just that and no more',[115] and for whom consequently the painful discrepancy between Pound's detestable politics and his personal charm and 'greatness' as a poet was unnegotiable. The grounds on which politics could reappear as a dimension of a developed poetics were proffered much later by Duncan. Drawing, in 1973, upon Charles Sherrington's biology of autonomous cell structure for an analogy with the 'life-form' of the poem, Duncan expatiates:

> Poetics, like politics, is an art of the intensification of what we take to be the principle of individuality in the realization of its identity and unity (or fulfillment) as essential part of a society. It is not in whatever social attitudes we protest that the politics of our poetries is to be read, but in the actual society of events that that given poetry presents and in the character of the life of the members of that society. The political counterpart of the body-image I read from Charles Sherrington's work I see in Vanzetti's proposition of a voluntary State, a social order utterly arising from just that social action that each autonomous cell-member volunteers. This is not an ideal State yet to be realized; any more than the present state of any physical body is an ideal state yet to be realized. Each existing state of every thing has no more order than its elements so volunteer. Every resource of a state (a physical body, a work of art in the working, a language, a human society) immediate to our need (free) and immediate to our wanting it (voluntary).[116]

41

The classic prescription of 'to each according to his needs' in such a formula is guaranteed plainly not by active struggle, but through a naïve trust in the evolutionist and relativistic scheme of things to take their natural, ordered course (by force, not accidentally, of analogy). At most this could issue in a species of libertarianism, or in Olson's 'pro-humanistic possibility.'[117]

7

It is tempting, given these conclusions, to reach for a clear and positive alternative to both Pound and open-field poetry. Modernism has been a protean and dispersed development with by no means an inexorable inner aesthetic or political logic. Wallace Stevens, Carlos Williams, Allen Ginsberg, and the insecurely post-modernist Robert Lowell, amongst American poets, illustrate some of its instructively divergent routes, one from the other, and from Pound and Black Mountain. More clearly, and outside America, Mayakovsky, Brecht and Enzensberger come immediately to mind as pursuing a left modernism to offset the present examples; in Brecht's case, given his imagistic practice, his interest in Villon and in Chinese literature, there is indeed a distinct if partial affinity, and at one point, his 'E.P. L'Election de son sepulcre', a conscious engagement with Pound.[118] The baffling weave of aesthetic, political and historical threads which swim into view here are sufficient warning against any brutal scissoring into stark alternatives. But if it has served any purpose the present essay indicates the need for precisely such comparisons in the more than academic interests of both contemporary poetry and criticism. The examples of Pound and open-field poetry should permit us at least then to draw some guiding conditions for future work.

Donald Davie's concern, referred to earlier, is with the fortunes of the 'common reader' and 'common discourse'. In itself this is right and admirable, but it does not follow that we must concede with him that 'it is only the Wordsworthians amongst us who can continue to ask for a non-specialized language, common discourse, the language that men *do* use.'[119] Nor does it mean that the 'us' of his statement need occupy the position of conservative dissent Davie himself speaks for, and which the history of modern criticism, in America as in England, has shown as invariably prone to encorporation.[120] A challenge to organicist criteria and the accompanying 'closures of first-person experience' would have to recognize how both they, and the criticism which confirms them, participate in maintaining bourgeois notions of 'literature', and in reply deliberately direct its ideological dissent, in one crucial respect, towards regaining the language men (and women) do use, in an awareness too that language is itself a field of class domination, subordination and resistance over which blanket terms such as 'men' and 'people' seek to draw the blind of apparent consensus. Always there is the question to whom discourse is 'common' and why. Clearly the aesthetic critique developed within open-field poetry does not take this lesson from Pound any more than he gives it. To an ideal of organic unity forced into shape through Pound's self-seeking thrust of will and power, it proffers a latent, intuited order, aperceived in the process of composition and in individual action. As such it is the obverse of traditional organicism, not a radically constructive alternative to it—no more an alternative we come to recognize than Keats is to Wordsworth, or Pound the restored pioneer of 'composition by field' is to Pound the poet of Fascism. Its true effect, as in Pound's *Cantos*, is the negative, cancelling effect of stalemate. The central and common weakness in both tendencies, in their aesthetic and political aspects, lies in an undialectical conception of 'the self' as either absorbing and dominant, or non-assertive and effacing. Self-abnegation in the face of the movement of history, as the left literature of England in the 1930s showed,[121] is only the complement to a self-inflation in Pound's *Cantos* which in its turn sought to usurp and reorchestrate history and politics. Both tendencies belong, over and above their antagonism and resistance, within the boundaries of bourgeois hegemony: in Pound's case most clearly within the informing problematic of a precariously situated petty bourgeoisie. One can project, if not point to, an ideal alternative on the basis of these limitations: an active and unsullied opposition to the bourgeois appropriation and ideological reproduction of art, language and the human subject in a class society. One can see too the tremendous demands

43

that would lie upon criticism and poetry in maintaining it. As a first step and a further lesson the aesthetic and political colours in the modernist umbrella are surely worth further hard (self) scrutiny.

NOTES

1. Cf. Charles Norman, *Ezra Pound, A Biography* (1960, revised 1969), Noel Stock, *The Life of Ezra Pound* (1970) also his *Poet in Exile* (1964), G. S. Fraser, *Ezra Pound* (1960). On Pound's economics, see Earle Davis, *Vision Fugitive: Ezra Pound and Economics* (Kansas, 1969), and on his politics, William M. Chace, *The Political Identities of Ezra Pound and T. S. Eliot* (Calif., 1973), C. David Heymann, *Ezra Pound: The Last Rower, A Political Profile* (1976), and the discussions in John Harrison, *The Reactionaries* (1966), and Alistair Hamilton, *The Appeal of Fascism* (1971).
2. Victor C. Ferkiss, 'Ezra Pound and American Fascism', *The Journal of Politics*, Vol. 17 (1955), 173–97.
3. John Lauber, 'Pound's *Cantos*: A Fascist Epic', *The Journal of American Studies*, Vol. 12, 1 (1978), 3–21.
4. Pound recorded how *Jefferson and/or Mussolini* was completed in 1933 but that forty publishers refused it before its publication in 1935 by Stanley Nott Ltd. The book was reissued in 1936, and in Italian in 1944, but then not again until 1970 by Liveright, New York. Apart from the scattered appearance of certain speeches in whole or in part, Pound's Rome radio talks have been published selectively in *If This Be Treason*, printed for Olga Rudge by Tip Nuova (1948), *Certain Radio Speeches of Ezra Pound*, ed. William Levy (Rotterdam, 1975), and finally in full in *'Ezra Pound Speaking'/Radio Speeches of World War II*, ed. Leonard Doob (Greenwood Press, 1978). Pound's 'Money Pamphlets' appeared with revisions in *Impact: Essays on Ignorance and the Decline of American Civilization*, ed. Noel Stock (Chicago, 1960), and again, with exclusions, in *Selected Prose*, ed. William Cookson (1973).
5. Cf. Pound's *Patria Mia*, written in 1912, but not published until 1950.
6. *Literary Essays* (1954), p. 297.
7. Ibid., p. 21. Cf. also Pound's remarks in the essay 'The State' in *Selected Prose*, p. 185.
8. Op. cit., p. 297.
9. In the broadcast titled, 'Question of Motive', Levy, op. cit., n.p.
10. Hugh Kenner, *The Pound Era* (1972), pp. 201–2.
11. Cf. *Selected Letters* (1971), p. 231.
12. *Hugh Selwyn Mauberley*, IV, in *Collected Shorter Poems* (1952), p. 208.
13. *Selected Letters*, p. 24.
14. Cf. Nicos Poulantzas, *Fascism and Dictatorship* (1974), pp. 240, 244–45, 252, and Renzo de Felice, *Fascism. An Informal Introduction to its Theory and Practice* (New Jersey, 1976), pp. 45–50.

15. For Pound's early remarks on socialism see *Selected Prose*, pp. 164, 166. The weakness of Marx's thought, Pound insisted, was that it ignored the problem of money. For Pound's attitude to Russian communism, see the Rome broadcast titled 'The Fallen Gent', in Levy, op. cit., n.p. 'Bolshevism', Pound writes, 'was created by the New York Jew millionaires.'

16. Pound wrote, 'An epic is a poem including history. I don't see that anyone save a sap-head can now think he knows any history until he understands economics', *Literary Essays*, p. 86.

17. Cf. Noel Stock, *Poet in Exile*, p. 212.

18. Quoted, ibid., p. 212.

19. For the biographical details referred to in this paragraph, see Stock, *The Life of Ezra Pound*, pp. 4–9.

20. For some discussion of the 'Sherman Silver Purchase Act' see J. D. Hicks, *The Populist Revolt* (University of Nebraska Press, 1961), pp. 306, 312, and R. Hofstadter, *The Paranoid Style in American Politics* (1961), pp. 261–63.

21. Cf. Stock, *The Life of Ezra Pound*, pp. 9–10, and Pound's 'Indiscretions' in *Pavannes and Divagations* (New York, 1974), p. 32.

22. For an account of Bryan's career, see R. Hofstadter, *The American Political Tradition* (1962), Ch. VIII. Bryan's 'Cross of Gold' speech is contained in his *The First Battle* (Chicago, 1896), pp. 199–206.

23. See Hicks, op. cit., especially pp. 406–7 for a description of the full populist demands. Hicks describes the silver issue as 'somewhat irrelevant' to populist thinking.

24. Bryan, *The First Battle*, p. 204.

25. From the People's Party Platform, 4 July 1892, included in *We Hold These Truths . . .*, ed. H. E. Hammond (New York, 1964), p. 250.

26. Bryan, op. cit., p. 200.

27. Ibid., p. 206.

28. For this basic ambiguity in American liberalism, see Karl Marx, 'On the Jewish Question', *Collected Works*, Vol. 3 (1975), pp. 146–74, R. Hofstadter, *The American Political Tradition*, pp. 3–17, and Louis Hartz, *The Liberal Tradition in America* (New York, 1955), pp. 110–13. For a response to Marx see Staughton Lynd, *Intellectual Origins of American Radicalism* (1969), pp. 10–13.

29. In the speeches titled, 'Pattern' and 'Universality', Levy, op. cit., n.p.

30. Cf. Victor Ferkiss, 'Populist Influences on American Fascism', *Western Political Quarterly* (June 1957), 350–73, and for a reply to Ferkiss, Michael Paul Rogin, *The Intellectuals and McCarthy: The Radical Specter* (Cambridge, Mass., 1967), especially p. 212. On American fascism, including studies of Long and Coughlin, see Raymond 'Gram' Swing, *Forerunners of American Fascism* (New York, 1935), especially pp. 34–107; Arthur M. Schlesinger Jr., *The Politics of Upheaval*, Vol. 3 of *The Age of Roosevelt* (Boston, 1960), pp. 15–28, 42–95; Seymour Martin Lipset, 'Three Decades of The Radical Right' in *The Radical Right*, ed. D. Bell (New York, 1963), especially pp. 317–26, and Seymour Martin Lipset and Earl Raab, *The Politics of Unreason* (1971), pp. 150–208. Long took the

slogan 'every Man a King' from Bryan, and Coughlin urged, 'Long enough have we been the pawns and chattels of the modern pagans who have crucified us upon a cross of gold' (quoted in Schlesinger, op. cit., p. 19).

31. Cf. Pound's 'Senator Long and Father Coughlin: Mr. Ezra Pound's Estimate', *Morning Post* (17 April 1935), p. 14; 'As for Huey . . .', *New English Weekly*, VII.18 (12 September 1935), p. 345; 'Again the Rev. Coughlin', *New English Weekly*, VIII.2 (24 October 1935), p. 26.

32. Pound's main sources were, *The Writings of Thomas Jefferson*, ed. A. A. Lipscomb and A. E. Bergh (Washington, D.C., 1907); *The Works of John Adams*, ed. Charles Francis Adams, 10 Vols. (Boston, 1850–57); *The Autobiography of Martin Van Buren* (Washington, D.C., 1920); *The Diary of John Quincy Adams*, ed. A. Nevins (New York, 1928); George Bancroft, *Martin Van Buren to the End of his Public Career* (New York, 1889); E. M. Shepard, *Martin Van Buren* (Boston and New York, 1890). See Stephen Fender, *The American Long Poem: an Annotated Selection* (1977), for the use of these sources in Cantos 31 and 37.

33. For these opposite arguments, see Donald Davie, *Ezra Pound: Poet as Sculptor* (1965), pp. 136, 160–64, and Fender, op. cit., p. 92.

34. Cf. 'Murder by Capital' in *Selected Prose*, p. 202, and *Jefferson and/or Mussolini* (1935), pp. 68, 127. The Arnoldian tones of Pound's 'A good government is one that operates according to the best that is known and thought' are unmistakable. Ibid., p. 91.

35. Cf. Schlesinger, op. cit., p. 18.

36. *Cantos* (Faber and Faber, 1975), pp. 229–30. This edition is referred to throughout and cited as *Cantos*. See my notes on Canto 45 in *A Student's Guide to the Selected Poems of Ezra Pound* (1979), pp. 285–89.

37. *ABC of Reading* (1934), p. 104.

38. *Cantos*, p. 202.

39. *Jefferson and/or Mussolini*, pp. 79, 80. Further page references to this volume are given in the text.

40. Cf. Ernst Nolte, *The Three Faces of Fascism* (1965), p. 574, and Poulantzas, op. cit., p. 265. Cf. also Gramsci, *Prison Notebooks* (1971), p. 119, De Felice, op. cit., pp. 67, 102–7, and the discussion of the roots of left wing totalitarianism in J. L. Talmon, *The Origins of Totalitarianism* (1970), to which Dr. De Felice refers.

41. Nolte, op. cit., pp. 303–11.

42. Ibid., p. 320.

43. Ibid., p. 322, and cf. the discussion of Gentile in Hamilton, op. cit., pp. 41–2, 56–9.

44. Poulantzas, op. cit., pp. 127–30, 265–67. Poulantzas quotes Trotsky's view that fascism was ' "basically [the] program of petty bourgeois currents" ' and Gramsci's that fascism was ' "the ultimate political incarnation of the petty bourgeoisie" ' (p. 245). He stresses, however, as both Trotsky and Gramsci do, that in fascism the ideological offensive of medium capital and the theme of national unification were exploited as camouflage by big capital: 'the specific characteristic of "fascist ideology" ', he writes, was, 'the indirect domination of imperialist

ideology, via the direct dominance of "petty bourgeois ideology"'
(p. 252).

45. Cf. Nolte, op. cit., pp. 334–36. Nolte writes, 'to all intents and purposes
Italian fascism's separation from its liberal foster parents was complete
by 1924' (p. 334). For the distinction between the Fascist movement and
the party or regime, cf. De Felice, op. cit., pp. 44–55.

46. Poulantzas, op. cit., p. 256, writes, 'The petty bourgeoisie traditional
and new, was the main economic victim of fascism together with the
middle and lower-middle peasantry. Petty commerce and small-scale
production were very badly hit by the fascist policy of support for big
capital.'

47. Cf. *Jefferson and/or Mussolini*, pp. 93, 128.

48. Cf. R. Hofstadter, *The American Political Tradition*, pp. 36–41, on
Jefferson's policy of 'laissez-faire' as being 'not anti-capitalist but anti-
mercantilist' and on the erosion of distinctions on manufacture and
banking between Republicans and Federalists by 1816. The Jacksonian
movement, similarly, Hofstadter argues, while 'commonly recognized'
as 'a phase in the expansion of democracy . . . was also a phase in the
expansion of liberated capitalism' (p. 55). Jackson's famous veto
message on the recharter of the Bank of the United States, also spoke
against monopoly and the unconstitutionality of the Bank in favour of
'the classic bourgeois ideal, equality before the law, the restriction of
government to equal protection of its citizens. This is the philosophy of a
rising middle class; its aim is not to throttle but to liberate business'
(p. 61).

49. Quoted in Nolte, op. cit., p. 314. Hamilton, op. cit., p. 57, suggests that
Gentile was the author, though the article carried Mussolini's signature
on its appearance in the *Enciclopedia Italiana*.

50. Frontispiece to *Guide to Kulchur* (1938).

51. Ibid., p. 135.

52. 'The Work of Art in the Age of Mechanical Reproduction' in
Illuminations, ed. Hannah Arendt (1973), pp. 243–44.

53. Cf. John Espey, 'The Inheritance of Tò Kalón' in *New Approaches to Ezra
Pound*, ed. Eva Hesse (1969), pp. 319–30.

54. 'Three Cantos I', *Poetry*, Vol. X, 3 (June 1917), 113.

55. *Selected Letters*, p. 180.

56. Ibid., p. 323.

57. D. Pearlman, *The Barb of Time: On the Unity of Ezra Pound's Cantos* (New
York, 1969), p. 3. Parts of the following argument represent a reworking
of the discussion in my *A Student's Guide to the Selected Poems of Ezra Pound*,
pp. 228–36.

58. In *Criticism and Ideology* (1977), especially Ch. 4.

59. *Ezra Pound. A Critical Anthology*, ed. J. P. Sullivan (1970), pp. 354, 375,
and the *Cantos*, p. 796.

60. 'New Subtlety of Eyes' in *Ezra Pound: A Collection of Essays to be Presented to
Ezra Pound on his 65th Birthday*, ed. P. Russell (1950), p. 91.

61. Pearlman, op. cit., especially pp. 21–7.

62. *The Poetry of Ezra Pound* (1951), p. 326.

63. Op. cit., pp. 154, 158.
64. *Cantos*, p. 178.
65. 'Populism as an Ideology' in *Populism. Its National Characteristics*, ed. G. Ionescu and E. Gellner (1969), p. 155. Cf. also R. Hofstadter, *The Age of Reform* (1962), pp. 62–3.
66. Ibid., p. 159.
67. Cf. especially De Felice, op. cit., pp. 54, 67–9, 75; also Nolte, op. cit., pp. 344, 570, and Poulantzas, op. cit., p. 254.
68. Lauber, op. cit., p. 21.
69. Cf. De Felice, op. cit., p. 96.
70. D. Mirsky, *The Intelligenzia of Great Britain* (1935), p. 126.
71. Sullivan, op. cit., p. 375.
72. *Literary Essays*, pp. 394, 396.
73. *Letters of John Keats*, ed. R. Gittings (1970), p. 43.
74. *Delta* (Montreal, 22 October 1963), pp. 3–4.
75. *Literary Essays*, p. 25.
76. Ibid., pp. 193–94.
77. Ibid., p. 159.
78. *Writers at Work. The Paris Review Interviews*, Second Series (1963), p. 52.
79. Cf. Andrew Crozier, *Poetry Nation Review*, 5 no. 2 (1977), 27–9.
80. Quoted in Pearlman, op. cit., p. 301.
81. T. S. Eliot, Introduction to *Ezra Pound. Selected Poems* (1928), p. 12.
82. *Cantos*, p. 514.
83. *Guide to Kulchur*, p. 83.
84. *Cantos*, p. 516.
85. Canto 13, ibid., p. 60.
86. The notable account of populism as a progressive social force is N. Pollack's, *The Populist Response to Industrial America* (Cambridge, Mass., 1962). For a reply to Pollack, see K. Minogue, 'Populism as a Political Movement' in Ionescu and Gellner, op. cit., pp. 198–99, 201, 203. Cf. also Hofstadter, *The Age of Reform*, pp. 41–2, 58–9, 61, 92–3.
87. Marx, op. cit., pp. 146–74.
88. Bernard Bailyn, *The Ideological Origins of the American Revolution* (Cambridge, Mass., 1967).
89. Staughton Lynd, op. cit., especially pp. 31–4.
90. *History of Western Philosophy* (1946), p. 660.
91. Cf. Ernst Cassirer, *The Philosophy of the Enlightenment* (Boston, 1951), p. 166.
92. Gittings, op. cit., pp. 36, 157, 88.
93. *Keats Poetical Works*, ed. H. W. Garrod (1970), p. 407.
94. *Poetry Nation Review*, 5 no. 4 (1978), p. 1.
95. The phrase is Andrew Crozier's, op cit., p. 28.
96. Quoted in Catherine Seelye, ed., *Charles Olson and Ezra Pound* (New York, 1975), p. xxii.
97. R. Duncan, 'Notes on the Structure of Rime' in *Maps* 6 (Pennsylvania, 1974), p. 49.
98. C. Olson, *Mayan Letters* (1968), pp. 27, 28.
99. Duncan, op. cit., p. 51.

100. Eric Mottram, 'Open Field Poetry', *Poetry International*, 17 (Summer, 1977), p. 6.
101. Duncan, *The Truth and Life of Myth* (Michigan, 1968), p. 60.
102. Ibid., pp. 62, 76. Pound's definitions are contained in his *Confucius* (New York, 1969), pp. 20, 22.
103. Ibid., pp. 64, 65.
104. Olson, *The Special View of History* (Berkeley, 1970), p. 16.
105. Ibid., pp. 17–18.
106. Ibid., p. 45.
107. Ibid., p. 16.
108. From the essay 'Projective Verse' in *Modern Poets on Modern Poetry*, ed. J. Scully (1966), p. 272.
109. *Maximum Poems* (New York, 1960), p. 44.
110. Quoted in Mottram, op. cit., pp. 16–17.
111. Seelye, op. cit., p. xviii.
112. Ibid., p. xx.
113. *Call me Ishmael* (New York, 1947), p. 21.
114. Seelye, op. cit., p. 20.
115. Ibid., p. xix.
116. Duncan, in *Maps*, ed. cit., p. 48.
117. Olson, *The Special View of History*, p. 35.
118. Bertolt Brecht, *Poems*, Pt. III (1976), p. 384. The translation is by Michael Hamburger. Cf. also Hamburger's comments on Brecht and this poem in *The Truth of Poetry* (1969), pp. 209–11.
119. Davie, op. cit., p. 1.
120. Cf. in particular John Fekete's study of American criticism in *The Critical Twilight* (1978).
121. Stan Smith argues that 'self-revulsion is everywhere present in the literature of the period' ('Scars and Emblems! 1936 and the Crisis of the Subject', a paper given at Essex University, 1978).

2

Pound-signs: Money and Representation in Ezra Pound

by DAVID MURRAY

'What can drive a man interested almost exclusively in the arts into social theory or into a study of the "gross material aspects" videlicet economic aspects of the present?'[1] Pound's own answer to his question helps to explain the nature and limitations of the economic and political views he came to espouse.

> I have blood lust because of what I have seen done to, and attempted against the arts in my time. . . . The unemployment problem that I have been faced with, for a quarter of a century, is not or has not been the unemployment of nine million or five million, or whatever I might be supposed to contemplate as a problem for those in authority or those responsible, etc., it has been the problem of the unemployment of Gaudier-Brzeska, T. S. Eliot, Wyndham Lewis the painter, E.P. the present writer, and of twenty or thirty musicians. . . .[2]

Pound's commitment to cultural morphology, the interrelation of social and cultural forms, leads him to emphasize the importance of the relation of the arts to society: 'Artists are the race's antennae. The effects of evil show first in the arts.' Clearly, though, artists are more important in Pound's scheme than an advance warning system, a dispensable miner's canary, and in fact Pound's emphasis on individual artists rather than the unemployed millions, is an accurate reflection of his élitism. These people *are* more important to society than the masses, and it is important to locate Pound specifically as an artist threatened by a lack of role in a democratic society. Neither traditional patronage nor the market system offered him the upholding of standards necessary for the recognition of creativity, and his attacks on British and American society are in terms not of the social injustice of disparities of wealth as such, but of the *cultural* failure of the rich.

> Those that govern, govern *on condition* of being a *beau-monde* of one sort or another. Their role cannot indefinitely survive their abrogation of 'culture' in the decent sense of that word.[3]

If artists need patronage, the leisure and security to work freely, then that society which best recognizes them and allows them this is to be advocated, not just selfishly but because élites matter to the whole society.

Pound's economic concerns must therefore be placed within a nostalgia for an ordered and hierarchical society, with corresponding concepts of 'high' culture, and a rejection of democracy and its apparent threat of 'low' culture. This position is not unusual amongst Pound's contemporaries, but Pound's particular combination of general precepts and specific remedies is, and needs clarification. In particular, Pound's long-standing concern with money, which operates almost to the exclusion of other economic issues, needs examination. It has usually been regarded by critics as an eccentric obsession which ruined a lot of his poetry. Some even blame it for his commitment to Fascism.[4] This paper argues, though, that Pound's concern for money relates directly to his major concerns, through money's dual and contradictory role as sign and transforming agent. The particular *terms* in which he chose to express these ideas, though, and his interpretation of historical events to support his theories, are not original to Pound, and are best understood by looking at Pound in a historical context, situated between American Populism and the Depression. The second part of the paper provides this context, with the intention of showing how Pound took over many of the terms and assumptions current among money reformers in America in the late nineteenth century and applied them to the '20s and '30s, but also how he related these ideas to his most fundamental moral and artistic concerns.

For Pound, economics is almost a branch of ethics. His economic thinking tends to presuppose an ordered and largely static society, with a centralized authority which holds a set of ethical assumptions about money, determining the direction of its economic control. For Pound, any economic system or cycle is purely a means to a primarily non-economic end, namely freedom from the physical hardship which would limit the individual's full spiritual and ethical development. A good economic system provides enough for material wants, and leisure (i.e. spare time free from anxiety) for an individual to enrich himself by his own actions as he wishes. This attitude is in direct contrast to the common abstraction of the capitalist tradition of economic thought, that of 'economic man'. Instead of seeing man as primarily motivated by selfish and *acquisitive* instincts, seen in economic terms as the 'profit-motive', Pound goes back to the economic thought of periods prior to the rise of capitalist thought, and especially to the Confucian/Mencian system and the economic doctrine of the medieval Catholic Church. Both of these systems subjugate the economic interests of man to his ultimate spiritual salvation.

The Mencian economic doctrine is an integral part of the whole Confucian conception of man in society and his relation to Process, and is basically concerned with setting up rules for justice in individual commercial dealings, with an equitable tax system designed for an agrarian society. With his stress on an ordered and static society, Mencius sees greed for excessive profit as completely immoral, as Pound points out:

> The profit-motive is specifically denounced. I mean that you will get no more accurate translation of the ideograms in Mencius' talk with King Hwey than 'profit-motive'. Mercantilism is incompatible with Mencius. Cheap evasion and evasiveness are impossible anywhere near him.[5]

The reference here is to Mencius Chapter IA where Mencius warns King Hui of Liang against thinking in terms of 'profit-and-advantage' (Pound prefers to translate it as 'Profit-motive'):

With this mutual exaction of profit-and-advantage pervading it from top to bottom, your very realm itself is threatened. In a state possessing 10,000 war chariots, the household with 1,000 will become the slayer of its prince. Now possession of ten per cent of power must be considered a large amount, but where propriety is placed second while the considerations of profit-and-advantage are foremost, there will be no satisfaction until one possesses all one hundred per cent. On the other hand, there has never been a case where manhood-at-its-best has neglected its relations. There has never been a case where the follower of propriety considered the interests of his prince secondary. Let your Majesty too use only the terms manhood-at-its-best and propriety! Why must you use that word profit-and-advantage?[6]

The same mistrust of personal greed for profit, and belief in a community of interest which should rule such things as the tax-system underlies Chapter 3 of Mencius called 'T'ang Wan Kung', where he outlines the ideal policy of a ruler towards maintaining justice in agriculture. The main recommendation is for a flexible tax based on proportion rather than a fixed charge:

> If you would bring order into land-holding nothing is better than the render-help method; nothing is worse than the tribute method.[7]

Both of these passages are brought together by Pound in the *Cantos*:

> 'Nowt better than share (Mencius)
>   nor worse than a fixed charge.'
> That is the great chapter, Mencius III, 1,111,6
> T'ang Wan Kung
>
> pu erh. 'Why must say profit
>
>   (the grain cut).
> No dichotomy.'[8]

For the medieval Canonists, too, economics was a moral issue, taking its place in a much larger context of moral action and organization:

> Man's path in life was a spiritual progress. No one aspect of his existence could properly or safely be separated from the

53

remainder. Economic activity was far from an exception, for if anything a Christian encountered more danger to his soul in buying and selling, in the temptations of avarice, than in most other of life's occupations. To organise life around the quest for unlimited profit was as inconceivable to St. Thomas as the organisation of life around the gratification of sexual passion.[9]

Pound is in agreement with this basic scale of economic values, and, seeing economics in moral terms, he therefore sees the basic issues as unchanging.

He is able, then, to present economic history not as a world of changing and developing resources, and of institutions and practices developing in response to these, but as a series of moral tableaux where one can see acted out repeatedly the struggle between good and evil. The *Cantos* may be an epic, a poem that contains history, as Pound insists, but they 'contain' it in several senses. By insisting on an unchanging schema beneath the changing accidentals Pound is denying the importance of historical change and with it the possibility that value-systems might be within history, determined by historical and material changes, contained by it rather than containing it. This is crucial because Pound's insistence on relating the economic to the ethical and religious means that he presents as unchanging ideals, outside history, precepts that are clearly culture-specific. When this is combined with his long-standing concern for rectification of language and clear definition it produces Pound's insistence that clear and simple definitions have been made in the past and need only be rescued. Their relevance has not changed because the basic issues are unchanging. These definitions can be technical and specific, and used by Pound as talismanic reminders (e.g., fragments from Aristotle) or more general, as in the repetition of ideograms for equity, justice, law, etc., from Confucius and Mencius. In both cases, the assumption is that, having been once fixed, these definitions are outside of ideology and change, and can act as bulwarks against slippage of language.

It is this insistence on clear and simple definitions which motivates a great deal of his economic writings, but it is also, when it is combined with Pound's particular style, one of the reasons why these texts are so unsatisfactory. It is worth examining a fairly typical text in some detail to show the characteristic movement of Pound's thought. *ABC of Economics* was published in 1933 but it does not differ substantially in this respect from a later work like *Gold and Work* of 1944. It is a confusing text, partly because of Pound's 'ideogrammic' method which he defines here as 'first heaping together the necessary components of thought'.[10] This relates directly to his concern for precision, and his defence, following Fenollosa, of the ideogram as 'scientific' since it works with concrete particulars from which it makes inductions. This method, rigorously used, would of itself, make for discontinuities, and jumps, from one set of data to another, but what really causes the confusion here, and they are important clues to what happens in Pound's thinking, are the gaps in the assembled data itself. There is a rapid shift from very general moral and political statements to a very limited and specific economic issue, namely distribution. For example, we have on the second page a progression from an assertion of the need for men to have responsibility, 'No social order can exist very long unless a few, at least a few, men have such sense',[11] to the limitations of democracy, and then, with no preparation, 'Probably the only economic problem needing emergency solution in our time is the problem of distribution.' A few pages later we have an assertion that

> The science of economics will not get very far until it grants the existence of will as a component; i.e. will toward order, will toward 'justice' or fairness, desire for civilisation,[12]

followed in the next paragraph by a discussion of money specifically as certificate. This I take to be a very characteristic leap, from ethics to money, involving all sorts of omissions and short circuits, and it is worth examining this leap more closely.

'The problem of production is solved',[13] Pound asserts. Only distribution needs to be reformed. But reform of distribution does not mean *re*-distribution of wealth (i.e. a political matter and related directly back to production) but to the mechanisms of distribution via *money*. He calls for 'ADEQUATE (and more or less just) distribution of credit slips' and adds 'I have put "ADEQUATE" in capitals and "just" in lower case because that is the order of their importance.'[14] This is a particularly explicit example of Pound's curious leap over the political to the limitingly technical, but elsewhere he equates 'the orders of an omniscient despot and of an intelligent democracy' in their effect on 'the main body of the country's economics'.[15] By ignoring production Pound also ignores the larger political issue of who is producing and who is owning. This relates importantly to Pound's tendency to ignore the real changes in the modes of production in different periods of history, itself related to his concern with the recurrent and unchanging.

To insist that Pound's concern is with the *un*changing may seem perverse, given both the mass of historical material from different periods and the theme of metamorphosis in the *Cantos*, but metamorphosis implies both something that changes and something that doesn't, the wave holding its form in the water, the avatar of Aphrodite. As such it posits a world of change, but one informed by unchanging generative sources:

> . . . the deathless,
> Form, forms and renewal, gods held in the air.[16]

To 'make it new' is to change something ('it') that is already there, but this tension between seeing the world as infinitely transformable—a world of energy, and exchange of energy—and only being able to confront this by holding to an unchanging centre, an unwobbling pivot, is relevant to Pound's economics as well as his use of literature and mythology. The unchanging centre, the key to equity, stability, and justice in economic terms is, for Pound, money and the correct use of it. He even describes it in the same terms as the Confucian ideas which were so important to him: 'Money is the pivot. It is the middle term',[17] and elsewhere he talks of this pivot wobbling: 'A money ticket under a corrupt system wobbles.'[18] What he wants money to be in his system of values, is the fixed element in a series of transformations of value. Otherwise the pivot wobbles, the fixed point of certainty disappears. The trouble is, that money has been more usually treated as in itself a repository of value, and an agent of transformation rather than a sign, and Pound's historical materials involve many different types of money.

Money, for Pound, is potentially a threat to values and categories which should *not* be transformable, which should be clearly separated out from each other, and also a potential block, if misused, of the natural exchange of energies. Pound's childhood memories of the Mint at Philadelphia, and the processes of refining and assaying gold and silver have been recognized as influential on his concern for coinage as such ('the spectacle of coin being shovelled around like it was litter—these fellows naked to the waist shovelling it around in gas flares—things like that strike your imagination'),[19] but I want to stress the image of *transformation* involved in smelting and coining. Values are being transmuted and then fixed before one's eyes—particularly if one believes that either the metals or the coins have an *intrinsic* value—and it is against this idea that Pound endlessly campaigns. He refers to the coinage of money as alchemy,[20] whereby precious metal is created from base metal, in other words, where value is fraudulently created, and sees the creation of money by banks without anything to correspond to it, as being equivalent. Coining as alchemy, though, also relates to the more general transformation involved when gold, silver or paper take on value in *themselves*, that is, when they are substituted for the real sources of value, rather than representing them.

This role of money as *representative* is crucial in Pound. He refers in the Chinese Cantos to Hien Tsong, who dabbled in alchemy, as

> another Lord seeking elixir
> seeking the transmutation of metals
> seeking a word to make change

21

Money can only be a *representation* of value, not valuable in itself, just as any sign is not the thing it signifies. Money actually represents a unit of value, but the source of that value resides elsewhere. Signs cannot have value, words cannot make change. They refer to the real, and should do so clearly. Here, in fact, is the deepest level of connection between

57

Pound's ideas, and it helps also to account for Pound's sweeping generalizations about usury and its effect on the arts, as I show later. Money, then, as the representation of the *relation* between things of value is an abstraction which should remain fixed. As Georg Simmel expressed it,

> As a visible object, money is the substance that embodies abstract economic value, in a similar fashion to the sound of words which is an acoustic-physiological occurrence but has significance for us only through the representation that it bears or symbolises. If the economic value of objects is constituted by their mutual relationship of exchangeability, then money is the autonomous expression of this relationship. . . . Thus it becomes comprehensible that money as abstract value expresses nothing but the relativity of things that constitute value; and at the same time, that money, as the stable pole, contrasts with the eternal movements, fluctuations and equations of the objects.[22]

Only when that pole is stable, or in Pound's terms, the pivot is unwobbling, can the relations of value between things be clarified. If not, the transformations and exchanges of economic life can be deceptive and dangerous, and in Canto 74 he relates this to the transformation of Odysseus' men to swine:

> every bank of discount is downright iniquity
> >   robbing the public for private individual's gain
> >   nec benecomata Kirke, mah! . . .
> neither with lions nor leopards attended
> >   but poison, veleno
> in all the veins of the commonweal.[23]

This degrading transformation is in contrast to the inter-related images of illumination connected with the recurring and metamorphosing female deities, and the battle between the positive and negative transformations is well illustrated by a passage which combines these mythological materials with Pound's concern for definition—in this case, the single word, taken from Aristotle, Xpeia. His primary concern with it is as an example of the obscuring of accurate definition:

> The mistranslation or rather the insertion of the word 'value' where Aristotle said Xpeia, demand. Money is not a measure of value. The price is caused by demand.[24]

The explanation is necessary to the reader's understanding of the isolated word as it appears in Canto 106, where he uses the word to contrast with the description of the coinage of money in China, but in a context of spiritual illumination:

> coin'd Artemis
> all goods light against coin-skill
> if there be 400 mountains for copper—
> under cinnabar you will find copper—
> river gold is from Ko Lu;
> pricc from XREIA;
> Yao and Shun ruled by jade
> That the goddess turns crystal within her
> This is grain rite
> Luigi in the hill path
> this is grain rite
> near Enna, at Nyssa:
> Circe, Persephone[25]

Pound exploits the connection of Artemis with coinage (as patroness of silversmiths, Diana often figured on coins) to make the connection with the various female deities he uses as images of fertility and natural process, and there is a contrast here between 'coin-skill' and images of light and fertility. The basic inorganic commodities, extracted from rivers or out of the ground take on, by being coined, and being treated as having inherent value, the organic qualities of grain, and this contrast between inorganic money and the organic self-reproducing world controls the opposition throughout the *Cantos* and much of Pound's prose, between Usury and Eleusis. Eleusis I am using as an image of energies which are sexual and reproductive, and the seminal energies of artists come into this category. Energy exchanges in this area are productive and life-enhancing, and related to Mencian/Confucian 'process' by the images linking the metamorphosing Aphrodite to both fertility and light. Usury is linked to gold, money and to hoarding, described in terms reminiscent of Freud's connection between money and faeces. 'Filthy lucre', N. O. Brown calls it, and Pound's scatological language firmly associates money that is hoarded or artificially abstracted from the natural exchanges of energy, with excrement. The 'usurer's dunghill', the 'putrid gold standard' are standard terms in Pound, and his well-known association of usury with sodomy, as being equally unnatural, 'contra naturam', in Canon law corresponds to this division of anal and genital. Usury, then, blocks and corrupts natural energies, substituting for clarity and distinction (visual imagery) the soft and the slimy (tactile imagery), and the passage on 'neschek', written about 1941 but not published until *Drafts and Fragments* exemplifies these themes. Having described it as 'Syphilis of the State' he continues

> *'neschek'*, the crawling evil
>   slime, the corrupter of all things,
> Poisoner of the fount
>   of all fountains, *neschek*
> The serpent, evil against Nature's increase.[26]

The fountain as image of clarity and purity, but also a perpetual and unchanging source of change is related to Nature's increase, poisoned by syphilis, sodomy, excrement.

This broad opposition between natural energies and the stopping of them by the hoarding of purchasing-power has often been recognized in Pound, but the role of labour in this scheme has not been so fully discussed. Grain, which Pound opposes to gold, is not simply 'natural', in that it is the product of human labour as well as 'nature's increase', and while Pound acknowledges this ('All value comes from labour and nature. Wheat from ploughing, chestnuts from being picked up')[27] he is at pains finally to subsume labour under nature: 'Work does not create wealth, it *contributes to the formation of* it. Nature's productivity is the root.'[28] This appears in the *Cantos* as

> the true base of credit, that is
>   the abundance of nature
> with the whole folk behind it[29]

The logical landscape which follows this is the 'naturalizing' of workers in the fields, the harmony of peasants with nature presented in the Chinese landscapes in the *Cantos*, and the only legitimate source of increase on which money can be advanced is natural increase, like the sheep on which the bank of Monte dei Paschi is founded.[30]

Some distinctions have to be made here, the first being

between wealth and value. While it may be true that the wealth (i.e. total goods and services available) is created by nature and labour in interaction (the role of technology will be dealt with later), the determination of *value* is quite different, and it is useful here to return to Pound's use of Aristotle's Xpeia. Pound is at pains to point out that Aristotle meant 'demand' and not value by it, but he does not pursue Aristotle's thinking any further. Marx did, though, and his remarks are very relevant to Pound's subsuming of labour under nature. Aristotle, Marx tells us, recognizes that exchange cannot take place without some grounds of equality and commensurability, i.e. a standard of value, but is at a loss to locate 'that equal something, that common substance' which gives one object a value relative to another object. For Marx the missing element is human labour, and he explains why Aristotle could not see this:

> There was, however, an important fact which prevented Aristotle from seeing that, to attribute value to commodities, is merely a mode of expressing all labour as equal human labour, and consequently as labour of equal quality. Greek society was founded upon slavery, and had, therefore, for its natural basis, the inequality of men and of their labour-powers. The secret of the expression of value, namely, that all kinds of labour are equal and equivalent, because, and so far as they are human labour in general, cannot be deciphered, until the notion of human equality has already acquired the fixity in a society in which the great mass of the produce of labour takes the form of commodities, in which consequently, the dominant relation between man and man, is that of owners of commodities.[31]

Pound's strategy in the *Cantos* of ignoring the changes in social organization and in the ways of thinking generated by these changes indicates partly that his ideal society may not be unlike Aristotle's, but also that labour is a term not fully examined by him, and it is worth defining more clearly the differences between the role of labour in different economic views.

Marx's stress on labour and production reflects in a very distinctive form a more widespread conception of value and money which develops with capitalism. Previously wealth had been regarded as a fixed entity which was accurately represented by (because embodied in) coin. Money, then, was a commodity, and the main economic issues were seen as distribution and the just price. Later developments in industry and commerce, though, entailed an emphasis on wealth-creating capabilities, which meant that value was created by labour and technology. As Michel Foucault sees it,

> Value can no longer [after Smith and Ricardo] be defined, as in the Classical age, on the basis of a total system of equivalences, and of the capacity that commodities have of representing one another. Value has ceased to be a sign, it has become a product.[32]

Foucault locates the shift with Ricardo:

> Ricardo, by dissociating the creation of value from its representativity, made possible the articulation of economics upon history. 'Wealth', instead of being distributed over a table and thereby constituting a system of equivalences, is organised and accumulated in a temporal sequence: all value is determined, not according to the instruments that permit its analysis, but according to the conditions of production that have brought it into being.[33]

This has effects directly relevant to Pound's monetarism:

> after Ricardo, the possibility of exchange is based upon labour: and henceforth the theory of production must always precede that of circulation.[34]

Pound's attitude to these crucial changes is complicated and ultimately contradictory. On the one hand the changes allow the shift away from a view of wealth reliant on commodity money, the fetishization of metals, and therefore allow a consequent realization of the real meaning of money, as sign. Money then, as Foucault describes it 'receives its value from its true function as sign'.[35] Pound should clearly approve of this, but he is appalled by the accompanying shift in attitudes to credit. The very change and expansion which made possible the realization that money was a sign also allowed, in Pound's view, an erosion or obliteration of the real relationship between money and things. Money created 'ex nihilo', as in the founding of the Bank of England, took on value *in itself*, rather than being a sign representing something actually extant (goods, labour). As a result Pound dismisses developments since the fifteenth century in Europe and since Hamilton in the U.S., as the victory of usury. As a result he praises societies and periods of history which were free of this, but inevitably these are mostly societies based on money as commodity. Pound needs, then, somehow, in combating the slippage involved in capitalism, to fix sign back on to thing, but not, as in his examples from earlier societies, by means of 'hard' money, based on metals. As a result he talks of money as certificate of work done, or certificate of goods available, but the real problem— and it is at the heart of Pound's ambivalence about money—is that money as he wants it to operate is an abstraction, a sign referring to a *relation* between things of value, not to something concrete. By dismissing the importance of production in the creation of value, and the role of credit within it, and returning to the concerns of pre-capitalist economists Pound chooses to ignore crucial historical changes. In particular, his subsuming of labour under nature, as producer of wealth needs to be examined further. For Pound, labour is part of a harmony *with* nature, rather than being for most men the means of their alienation from their full humanity. Although he does acknowledge the role of culture in its fullest terms as opposed to nature, i.e. the co-operation of men in groups, the 'increment of association' and the role of transmitted knowledge and skills, 'the increment of tradition', his absolute lack of interest in technology means that these ideas and their relation to labour are never really developed. The fact that labour in an unequal society is an alienation of men's energies rather than a free exchange of them, and that money as wealth is an embodiment of that alienation in *itself*, rather than just when accumulated by usurers, is where Pound fails to follow or understand Marx, and he therefore attacks Marx on false grounds:

> Fascinated by the lustre of a metal, man made it into chains. Then he invented something against nature, a false representation in the mineral world of laws which apply only to animals and vegetables. The nineteenth century, the infamous century of usury, went even further, creating a species of monetary Black Mass. Marx and Mill, in spite of their superficial differences, agreed in endowing money with properties of a quasi-religious nature. There was even the concept of energy being 'concen-

trated in money' as if one were speaking of the divine quality of consecrated bread.[36]

In fact, far from holding these views, Marx makes the same basic criticism of capitalism as Pound. In 'The Power of Money in Bourgeois Society' Marx refers to the presentation of money in *Timon of Athens*, as 'the visible divinity—the transformation of all human and natural properties into their contraries, the universal confounding and overturning of things; it makes brothers of impossibilities.' The reason for money's ability to do this, though, is clearly defined by Marx, and his definition surely demystifies the magical element. Its power 'lies in its *character* as man's estranged alienating and self-disposing *species-nature*. Money is the alienated *ability of mankind.*'[37]

While both Marx and Pound are opposed to this domination of money-values, Marx differs from Pound in his refusal to idealize what preceded it. He did not look back to an ideal agrarian medieval society as an alternative to capitalism because although he admitted in feudal landed property

> the semblance of a more intimate connection between the pro-
> prietor and the land than of mere *material* wealth,[38]

he saw in feudalism the whole basis of the capitalist alienation of man from his labour. Refusing to romanticize the fall of the feudal estates, he sees feudal landed property as:

> already by its very nature huckstered land—the earth which is
> estranged from man and hence confronts him in the shape of a
> few great lords. The domination of the land as an alien power
> over men is already inherent in feudal landed property. Indeed,
> the dominion of private property begins with property in
> land—that is its basis.[39]

Pound, with his respect for the feudal system based on landed property, wrongly interprets Marx's attacks on property as really only attacks on Capital:

> Marx attacked 'Capital', the Russian movement has been
> perverted into an attack on Property.[40]

Pound tries to make a clear distinction between capital and property. Property should be concrete. Anything else is capital:

'The nature of property is radically (at the root, in the root) different from the nature of capital. . . . All such phrases as 'capital in the form of' are misleading. Properly understood, capital is liquid. The great division is between whatever is a lien on the other man's services, and what is either completely neutral and passive or constitutes a potential responsibility, whereof the weight lies on the owner. . . . Property does not imply the enslavement of others.[41]

Pound approved of those conservative elements in the U.S. Constitution which guaranteed the rights of property, and several times in the *Cantos* he quotes or refers to Mussolini's 'Programme di Verona', a manifesto of the Fascist party, where a right *to* property is guaranteed, but not the rights *of* property: ' "Alla non della" in the Verona statement.'[42] In other words, he approves of the possession of private property as long as it is used for the pleasure or convenience of the individual owner, but not when it is used to confer on him power over others. The contradiction here is that the possession of *land* is one of the most obvious forms of power over others, and yet Pound approves of landed estates. He eases his anxiety over the permanence of these estates by an appeal to a key phrase in the *Cantos* taken from Jefferson, 'the earth belongs to the living.' Pound follows Jefferson in deciding that no debts should continue beyond a generation, but he says nothing of the continuation of land ownership as such, transmitted on hereditary principles.

Pound's misunderstanding of Marx is significant, not only for the differences between them, but for the similarities, and the way that Pound's misreading of Marx relates directly to his support of Fascism. At one level both Pound and Marx respond to the same shortcomings, both in capitalism and in the study of economics itself. Pound has to go back to the Classical and Canonist writers to find ethical ideas fully applied to economics, and Marx too notes the same shortcomings in modern 'political economy':

If I ask the political economist: Do I obey economic laws if I extract money by offering my body for sale. . . . Or am I not acting in keeping with political economy if I sell my friend to the Moroccans . . . then the political economist replies to me: You do not transgress my laws, but see what Cousin Ethics and Cousin

> Religion have to say about it. . . . . But whom am I now to believe,
> political economy or ethics? . . . It stems from the very nature of
> estrangement that each sphere applies to me a different and
> opposite yardstick—ethics one and political economy another.[43]

This is exactly the dissociation of different areas of life which
Pound is trying to reconcile by means of his 'totalitarian'
paideuma, but the differences between the two men are instruc-
tive. Pound, relying very heavily on organicism, saw any
counterforce in the body politic as unhealthy and cancerous,
and therefore entertained no idea of class struggle as instrument
of necessary change. Indeed, he regarded radical inequalities
with equanimity, while reserving for himself, as artist, the right
to be outside any particular class.

An examination of the difference between Pound's overall
view of history and Marx's shows how he side-stepped the idea
of the need for, and historical inevitability of, real structural
changes in societies. Calling the present system usury or
usurocracy rather than capitalism, he personalizes the issues
and sees history in conspiratorial, rather than economic
determinist, terms. Here we see the crucial importance of
Pound's anti-semitism, which, as W. M. Chace argues, was no
mere personal quirk:

> It was . . . a way to pin down world troubles on one small
> fraction of that world's population. It might have had as one
> source a kind of perverted American Populism . . . but it was
> nourished and made even more perverse by his hostility to seeing
> life in terms of class-structure.[44]

The need then (and in this respect Pound's anti-semitism is
classic) is to find an identifiable and personalized scapegoat
for the breakdown of society, other than the structure of the
society itself, which is felt to preserve necessary order and
hierarchy which would be lost in fundamental change.

In addition, anti-Semitism has the advantage for Pound of
relating very directly to his tendency to polarize actions and
events in terms of good and evil. Whereas for Marx the selfish
actions of a number of individuals make up a larger picture of
a system which is beyond their individual control and under
which they suffer almost the same alienation as those they
exploit, Pound sees the usurers as far too evil and calculating

to be suffering from any psychological malaise as a result of
their own actions and their own system. He sees usurocracy as
an almost irresistible international force which has corrupted
all of European life and culture:

> There has been some vague talk in recent months [1944]
> about an international power, described as financial, but it
> would be better to call it 'usurocracy' or the rule of the big
> usurers combined in conspiracy. Not the gun merchant but the
> traffickers in money itself have made this war; they have made
> wars in succession for centuries, at their own pleasure, to create
> debts so that they can enjoy the interest on them.[45]

The effect of usury, though, is not just financial exploitation.
The corollary of Pound's belief that artists are the antennae of
the race is that art should show the sickness in a society. In
particular, clarity and definition are at risk:

> Discrimination by the senses is dangerous to avarice. It is
> dangerous because any perception or any high development of
> the perceptive faculties may lead to knowledge. The money-
> changer only thrives on ignorance. . . . An instant sense of
> proportion imperils financiers.[46]

Pound's reasons for believing there has been a deterioration
since the fourteenth century are nowhere fully given, and in
particular there is nowhere a clear model of *how* usury affects
the lines an artist draws or the words he uses. In the following
passage, where he goes back well beyond medieval society to
find the high point of civilization, there is the usual *juxtaposition*
of economic malpractice and artistic degeneration, but no
more:

> And against usury
>   and the degradation of sacraments,
> For 40 years I have seen this,
>   now flood as the Yang tse
> also desensitization
>   25 hundred years desensitization
>   2 thousand years desensitization
> After Apollonius, desensitization
>   & a little light from the borders:
>   Erigena,
>   Avicenna, Richardus.
> Hilary looked at an oakleaf
>   or holly, or rowan

> as against the brown oil and corpse sweat
> & then cannon to take the chinks opium
> & the Portagoose uprooting spice-trees 'a common'
>   sez Ari 'custom in trade'.[47]

The common custom referred to by Aristotle is monopoly, (*Politics*, I, 4/5) and the references to the Portuguese and British actions in China to corner the market in spice and opium are examples of this. The 'brown oil and corpse sweat' is a reference to the lack of clarity and light in art represented for Pound by painters like Rubens,

> the metamorphosis into carnal tissue becomes frequent and general about 1527. The people are corpus, corpuscular, but not in the strict sense 'animate', it is no longer the body of air clothed in the body of fire; it no longer radiates, light no longer moves from the eye, there is a great deal of meat.[48]

These two thousand years of usury are referred to in *Guide to Kulchur* as being a record, set out for those who want to know, of the constant effects of usury to destroy true civilization; but again we are given nothing specific:

> You have 2 millenia of history wherein we see usury opposed to the arts, usury at the antipodes of melody, of melodic invention, of design. Usury always trying to supplant the arts and set up the luxury trades, to beat down design which costs nothing materially and which can come only from intelligence, and to set up richness as a criterion. Short curves etc. 'opulence' without hierarchy.[49]

In general, though, Pound dates the decline of art and thought from the downfall of the authority of the Catholic Church, and he is in agreement with Eliot and Hulme in regarding the Reformation as a disaster in its effects on both art and economic thought:

> The Church slumped into a toleration of Usury. Protestantism as Factive and organised may have sprung from nothing but pro-Usury politics. . ... The 'Church' declined and fell on this issue. Historians have left the politics of Luther and Calvin in the blur of great ignorance.[50]

(Luther was in fact firmly in the Canon Law tradition in his opinion on Usury, and his essay 'On Trading and Usury' is hardly distinguishable in attitude from Catholic economic writings, whereas Calvin agreed that certain types of Usury in certain situations were not necessarily sinful. Pound makes no distinction.) He is aware of the new commercial and industrial developments in the economy at this time but refuses to accept the necessity for new ways of expanding and developing credit facilities. Any divergence from the static controlled medieval system must mean a decline, not only in standards of honesty in economic matters, but in the artistic and intellectual health of the community:

> As long as the Mother Church concerned herself with this matter [usury] one continued to build cathedrals. Religious art flourished.[51]

The great achievement of the Catholic Church for Pound was the development of gradations of thought and fine discrimination:

> things neither perfect nor utterly wrong, but arranged in a cosmos, an order, stratified, having relations one with another.[52]

Whereas the effect of Protestantism: 'has been semiticly to obliterate values, to efface grades and graduations'.[53] The use of the word 'semiticly' here, pin-points what so often goes wrong in Pound's analysis of history. He uses the word, in general, not necessarily just to mean Jewish but to stand for an approach to life which is at best unduly individualistic, and at worst murderous in its willingness to create wars and misery for private financial gain—in other words, as here, the opposite of his ideal ordered society with its fine discriminations and gradations, both in art and society. The origins of this use of the idea for Pound may well have been Gaudier-Brzeska's discussion of the characteristic vortices of the past, which Pound summarizes:

> The Paleolithic vortex, man intent upon animals. The Hamite vortex, Egypt, man in fear of the gods. The derivative Greek. The Semitic vortex, lust of war. Roman and later decadence, Western sculpture, each impulse with corresponding effects on form.[54]

Whereas Gaudier-Brzeska is linking the styles specifically with race here, though, Pound broadens the definition of the word—but at the same time maintaining his racial hostility for

Jews—to include manifestations like Protestantism and earlier individualistic excesses.

It's important, given the generalized schema I used earlier, where Usura was opposed to Eleusis, to insist, with Chace, that Pound's use of usury, and his development of a historical scenario like this is *not* metaphorical. To treat the Usura Canto in isolation as a metaphorical account of corruption is to ignore all the detail in the prose writings and the *Cantos* which insists on the *real* conspiracies, the *actual* changes in the value of gold, etc., in order to make Pound's views more acceptable because more generalized and 'poetic'. What makes it difficult to take seriously *other* than as metaphor, though, is the absence in Pound of any method of relating artistic standards to social systems, but it is here that the role of money as *representation* may be relevant. In a way that is never fully articulated by Pound himself, it is representation which is the connecting link between economic malpractice and artistic decline. Lack of clarity and definition (of money, of words, of signs) leads to a distortion of the correct proportions between elements of different value and therefore a confusion about what constitutes value, either in economic or in aesthetic terms.

So far I have tried to show the particular relation between Pound's social and cultural views, his particular paideuma, and his view of money as sign, and agent of transformation, but the particular *form* his economic ideas take, and the terms in which he expresses them, are also closely related to his own historical position, and the ideas he inherits from his background. Pound's treatment of the monetary controversies in U.S. history stops curiously short at the late nineteenth century, and yet this, the period of Pound's own childhood, was the period of the most intense and explicit monetary debate. The terms of this debate account for a great deal of Pound's terminology and for his attitudes towards economic issues in the twentieth century, but their role has been neglected by Pound scholars. As a result I intend to concentrate on this nineteenth-century legacy rather than Pound's encounter with twentieth-century economists, a detailed examination of which is beyond the scope of this paper. It could, in any case, be argued, that it is from the late nineteenth century that most of the direction and impetus of his economic thinking comes.

The consistent thread of opposition to industrial capitalism, as it developed after the Civil War, and the analysis of its defects, became focused by the 1890s in the growth of Populism, and in the final defeat of silver interests in the election of 1896. Much of the strength and flexibility of the critique of capitalism was lost by the progressive concentration on the issue of silver, and Pound explicitly dismisses this as a red herring, another fetishization of metal.[55] If we go back behind the concentration on this single issue, though, it is clear that the basic analysis, and many of the remedies, of groups described under the term Populist are very close to Pound's own. Presumably the stress on the common man, combined with the eventual obsession with silver, account for Pound's neglect of the movement, but it is worth pin-pointing his considerable debt to it.

At the heart of many Populist arguments is a basic opposition between producers and financiers. As the former became poorer the latter tightened their grip, so that the two groups became also describable as debtors and creditors. As the U.S. economy expanded, and the demand for money grew, the effect of holding down the money supply, by linking it firmly to gold, which was fairly inelastic in supply, was to increase the value of money in relation to goods, thereby benefiting the creditors, and those controlling and manipulating the supply of gold. Hence the call for inconvertible paper money, the continuation of the greenback, not redeemable in gold, and the unlimited coinage of silver, which had earlier been legal tender in fixed relation to gold. Because of its increasing quantity, and the hope it offered of an increased currency, silver became regarded as 'soft' or inflationary money, and the call for it was seen as positively immoral by orthodox businessmen and economists, since this new money would have no fixed relation to a real source of value (i.e. gold). For the Populists, though, it had relation to the only real source of wealth and value:

> Labor in its various forms produces the nation's wealth. This is the ultimate truth. The exchange of this wealth constitutes all of the diversified business of the country. The vast throng of busy thousands who produce this wealth also in large measure consume it. If they are now in possession of an ample supply of sound money, they must exchange it for this wealth.
>
> How is it, then, that all men of all classes complain of hard

times, and chiefly of the difficulty of obtaining money with which to gratify their wants or carry on business? Why is it that so much of this wealth cannot be exchanged at all? . . . Is it not that money is enormously valuable as compared with property and commodities? And, as money has value in proportion to the quantity of it out, do not such conditions show beyond question that the monetary circulation is insufficient.[56]

Behind this specific monetary proposal, though, which is so similar to Pound's in the 1930s, is a suspicion and fear of the manipulation of the economy which comes close to belief in a large-scale conspiracy. Bankers and usurers use the gold standard to control the finances of America:

a band of men, with murderous purposes, went—not into the battlefield—but into the very sanctuary of our country, the holy place of government, and there, under the guise of patriot and benefactor . . . plotted the most diabolical scheme of robbery that ever blackened a historic page.[57]

And elsewhere:

Monopoly is eating out the very vitals of our existence. Usury and extortion have fastened their iron jaws upon every industry of the land. . . . We are travelling the same road to death that nations gone before have travelled.[58]

The practice of monopoly is particularly concentrated on gold as a commodity because of its other use as a medium, and the ability of the monopolists to increase the value of any commodity relative to others means that they can control the currency by creating scarcity, and then a relative glut, of gold. Pound takes over this idea in toto, as in the following passage. The reference to the 'common practice' is to monopoly and the creation of artificial scarcity.

> 'All metal as barter'
>   Destutt or whomso,
> 'Pity to stamp save by weight.'
> Always the undertow,
>   gold-bugs against ANY order,
> Seeking the common (as Ari says)
>   practice
> for squeeze.[59]

It is significant that the word 'gold-bug' used here is standard Populist usage, not only to describe monometallists but to imply, as Pound does here, a whole conspiracy manipulating the economy through gaining a monopoly in gold, as in 'the Wall Street, English, Rothschilds gold bug money syndicate', a phrase that could have come from one of Pound's wartime speeches, but is in fact from an 1896 newspaper.[60] Pound's belief that by this century gold has been taken over by the usurocracy who monopolize it, is his main reason for advocating the formation of a new system based purely on the authority of the State rather than precious metals, and it is in this context that he condemns Churchill's return to the gold standard in 1925. He gives as an example the effect it had on Indian farmers who had to pay debts which were suddenly doubled in value:

> 'And with the return of the gold standard' wrote Sir Montague
> 'every peasant had to pay twice as much grain
> to cover his taxes and interest.'[61]

A way of developing these ideas into a whole interpretation of history was available to Pound in Brooks Adams' *The Law of Civilization and Decay*, which he uses in the Cantos and elsewhere. Written at the height of the money controversy in the 1890s, Adams' book offers a wide-ranging account of the movements of money and the effects of concentration of capital, which manages to account for the fall of Rome as well as the decline of modern civilization. Its view of history as large-scale transformations of energy, constantly centralizing and then being dissipated was attractive to Pound, and although he criticizes Adams for treating money as *literal* concentration of energy,[62] he responds positively to the way Adams charts changes in societies in terms of the movement of money. Adams provides the apparent evidence for a conspiracy of bankers working to control the supply of gold:

> These bankers conceived a policy unrivalled in brilliancy, which made them masters of all commerce, industry, and trade. They engrossed the gold of the world, and then, by legislation, made it the sole measure of values.[63]

Although Brooks Adams does not discuss America in the book his brother Henry was in no doubt about its political relevance or effect, warning him that 'The gold-bugs will never forgive you'.[64] Certainly the book was used by Populists, just as Pound used it, as evidence for the long-standing manipulation of debtors by creditors, and Adams expresses the issue succinctly in discussing the English Bullion Committee of 1810, in which, he says

> the struggle for supremacy between the lender and the borrower is brought out in full relief. To the producer, the commodity was the measure of value; to the banker, coin. The producer sought a currency which should retain a certain ratio to all commodities, of which gold was but one. The banker insisted on making a fixed weight of the metal he controlled, the standard from which there was no appeal.[65]

As the 1890s progressed, the broader arguments about the control of the economy and the power of what was becoming recognizable as monopoly capitalism became subsumed under a more specific argument about the shortage of money, and the need to coin silver. This was a denial of the truth of the orthodox view of the time formulated in Say's law, that it was *impossible* for there to be a shortage of purchasing-power in the economy. The rapid increase in production in nineteenth-century America, or the calling-in of loans, and holding-on to excess reserves by banks (as in the Depression of this century) clearly offered instances which invalidated this supposed law. At times there *is* a need to produce more money—though in itself this hardly constitutes a full response to economic imbalances. In a way very similar to the Populists, Pound lets the issue of distribution take over from a larger critique of capitalism, and he quotes with approval a variety of examples of the supply of purchasing-power by unorthodox means. His grandfather, for instance, issued money to his workers:

> No-one, perhaps, has ever built a larger tract of railway, with nothing but his own credit and 5,000 dollars cash than that laid down by my grandfather. The credit came from the lumbermen (and in face of opposition from the big U.S. and foreign steel monopolists) by printing with his brother the paper money of the Union Lumbering Co. of Chippewa Falls, bearing the promise to 'pay the bearer on demand . . . in merchandise or lumber.'[66]

Similarly the small Swiss town of Wörgl issued its own Stamp Scrip money, and even though the big banks suppressed it, it was really completely valid, since it related to goods in existence and was accepted by its users. The issued money gave the people the ability to buy available goods, and at the same time the issuing bank, in this case presumably the Town Council, claimed tax on the money at 12% which increased the town's revenues and therefore its potential public spending:

> Each month every note of this money has to have a revenue stamp affixed to it of a value equal to one per cent of the face value of the note. Thus the municipality derived an income of 12% per annum on the new money put into circulation. The town had been bankrupt, the municipality had not been able to pay the school teachers, etc., but in less than two years everything had been put right and the townspeople had built a new stone bridge for themselves.[67]

The important thing in this context is not Stamp Scrip as such but the issuing of money for the good of the community, corresponding to goods and labour available. Similarly, Pennsylvania, when still a colony issued paper money to the settlers:

> The settlers or colonisers in Pennsylvania and in other colonies irritated by the disappearance of metal money, understood that any other document could be used for book-keeping and as a certificate of what the bearer was entitled to receive in the market. . . . So the governments of several colonies began to lend paper-money for these purposes.[68]

On the whole, though, in spite of these examples of good private money the best guarantee members of a society can have is that the money is backed by the State itself. Sovereignty in the issue of money is the key to all state power. Once it loses this it has lost all effective power, and this is why Pound sees the U.S. Bank War as so crucial to the rest of American history. Instances of shortage of purchasing-power are seen by Pound simultaneously as instances of a conspiracy *and* evidence of an inevitable *structural* imbalance in capitalism, and he uses twentieth-century economists to support this view. Major Douglas's A & B theory, for example, appeared to him an ideal model to explain the breakdown of the system. Douglas argued that the cost of producing something consists of wages and dividends paid out, *and* the cost of reinvestment and overheads. This means that the money paid out to the actual producers of goods is always less than the total cost of the goods to produce, reflected in the price, leading to a permanent disparity between the cost of goods and the purchasing-power of the producers of those goods. The debt to Marx's theory of surplus-value is clear, but the crucial element which needs to be added, to give this simplified theory any sort of sophistication or relation to economic reality is the *rate* of distribution, and this is why Pound becomes interested in Gesell's Stamp Scrip ideas, since increased *flow* of purchasing-power has the same effect in this area as increasing the amount. Keynes' analysis of the situation was similar in many respects, and Pound's hostility to Keynes and to the New Deal seems to be based partly on a premature judgement of Roosevelt's policies, as well as Pound's increasing inability to revise his views as the '30s progressed. Roosevelt's Federally funded works programmes and deficit financing at least should have appealed to Pound, given the similarity to some of Mussolini's programmes.

In general it is clear, though, that *monetary* policy appealed to Pound more than any more substantial social changes, since it allowed him to ignore the real nature of modern societies, and allowed him to equate widely disparate social systems. By emphasizing distribution rather than production he is able to bypass larger political issues, and in this respect Pound fits Galbraith's description of

> a long line of monetary reformers extending to Professor Milton Friedman in our own day who have hoped that their changes would make other and more comprehensive government action unnecessary. They are monetary radicals because they are political conservatives.[69]

In this respect, too, aspects of Populism are relevant to Pound. Populism as Lawrence Goodwyn has argued,[70] ultimately became deflected, by emphasis on the one issue of money, from its broad and longer-standing critique of capitalism, and its ultimate defeat involved a consequent narrowing of the concerns of American politics. I have tried to demonstrate that something similar happens to Pound. His concern for economics, his criticisms of his society and its manipulation of wealth were not in themselves freakish or peripheral, or unworthy subjects for a poet, but his failure to follow through his arguments at crucial points meant that they became increasingly separated both from his other major concerns and from political reality.

NOTES

1. *Selected Prose* (London: Faber, 1973), p. 198.
2. Ibid., p. 200.
3. Ibid., p. 198.
4. See Leon Surette, *A Light From Eleusis* (Oxford: Clarendon Press, 1979) (who even sees economics as leading Pound into anti-Semitism!). Surette's study of the *Cantos* is otherwise perceptive about Pound's economics; though from a different standpoint from my own. The only full-length study of Pound's economics is Earle Davis's introductory *Vision Fugitive: Ezra Pound & Economics* (Lawrence: Kansas U.P., 1968).
5. *Selected Prose*, p. 133.
6. *Sayings of Mencius* (New York: New American Library, 1960), p. 44.
7. Ibid., p. 82.
8. *The Cantos* (London: Faber, 1964), pp. 610–11.
9. R. Lekachman, *The Varieties of Economics* (Cleveland: World Publishing Co., 1962), p. 47.
10. *Selected Prose*, p. 209.
11. Ibid., p. 204.
12. Ibid., p. 210.
13. Ibid., p. 204.
14. Ibid., p. 220.
15. Ibid., p. 218.
16. *Cantos*, p. 124.
17. *Selected Prose*, p. 312.
18. Ibid., p. 260.
19. *Paris Review*, 28, Summer/Fall 1962, 40.
20. *Cantos*, p. 84.
21. Ibid., p. 327.
22. *The Philosophy of Money* (London: Routledge and Kegan Paul, 1978), pp. 120–21.
23. *Cantos*, p. 464.
24. *Guide to Kulchur* (Norfolk: New Directions, 1938), p. 357.
25. *Cantos*, p. 778.
26. *Drafts and Fragments* (London: Faber, 1970), p. 28.
27. *Selected Prose*, p. 264.
28. *Guide to Kulchur*, p. 357.
29. *Cantos*, p. 267.
30. Ibid., p. 227.

31. *Capital* (London: Lawrence and Wishart, 1970), pp. 59–60.
32. *The Order of Things* (London: Tavistock, 1970), p. 254.
33. Ibid., pp. 255–56.
34. Ibid., p. 254.
35. Ibid., p. 176.
36. *Selected Prose*, pp. 316–17.
37. *Economic and Philosophical Manuscripts of 1844* (New York: International Publishers, 1964), p. 168.
38. Ibid., p. 101.
39. Ibid., p. 100.
40. *Impact* (Chicago: Regnery, 1960), p. 263.
41. Ibid., p. 153.
42. *Cantos*, p. 600.
43. *Economic and Philosophical Manuscripts of 1844*, p. 152.
44. 'Ezra Pound and the Marxist Temptation', *American Quarterly*, Vol. 22 (1970), 724.
45. *Selected Prose*, p. 313.
46. *Guide to Kulchur*, p. 281.
47. *Cantos*, pp. 654–55.
48. *Literary Essays* (Norfolk: New Directions, 1954), p. 193.
49. *Guide to Kulchur*, p. 282.
50. *Impact*, p. 241.
51. *Selected Prose*, p. 293.
52. Ibid., p. 120.
53. *Guide to Kulchur*, p. 185.
54. *Gaudier-Brzeska* (Hessle: Marvell Press, 1960), p. 106.
55. *Selected Prose*, p. 149.
56. Norman Pollack, *The Populist Mind* (Indianapolis and New York: Bobbs-Merrill, 1967), p. 323.
57. *A Populist Reader*, ed. G. B. Tindall (New York: Harper and Row, 1966), pp. 57–8.
58. Ibid., p. 25.
59. *Cantos*, p. 608.
60. Quoted in Norman Pollack, 'The Myth of Populist Anti-Semitism', *American Historical Review*, 68 (1962), 80.
61. *Cantos*, p. 504.
62. *Selected Prose*, p. 277.
63. *The Law of Civilization and Decay* (New York: Vintage Books, 1959), p. 282.
64. Ibid., p. xi.
65. Ibid., p. 267.
66. *Selected Prose*, p. 295.
67. Ibid., p. 284.
68. Ibid., p. 138.
69. *Money: Whence It Came, Where it Went* (London: Andre Deutsch, 1975), pp. 210–11.
70. Lawrence Goodwyn, *Democratic Promise: The Populist Movement in America* (New York: Oxford U.P., 1976), pp. 516–17 and *passim*.

3

A Model for Pound's Use of 'Science'

by MARTIN A. KAYMAN

> It seems that the science of one generation is often a fable to the next, and that sometimes the fables of one generation are the science of the next.[1]

1

In his discussion of the complex relation between Pound and Yeats, Imagisme and Symbolism, Herbert Schneidau maintains that whilst Pound rejected the 'mushiness' of Yeatsian Symbolism and spiritualism, he nonetheless retained at the centre of his art some sense of 'metaphysical mysticism'.[2] But:

> The important point to be made is that Pound did not think of mysticism, such as he finds it in the Troubadours, as bodiless transmission of vague visions. . . . Even of mystic visions Pound predicated exactness, precision, definition as the life-giving component.[3]

Schneidau notes terms from a vocabulary of science applied by Pound to terms from mysticism and art. He sees their relation in Pound's writing not as a matter of conflict, but, on the contrary, as one of *predication*.[4] In so doing he draws our attention to the role of that scientific vocabulary not only in Pound's relation to Yeats, but in a larger question of Pound's technique and theory as a whole: in what sense can these sets of values be 'predicated', and what is the effect of their conjunction?

A careful look at Pound's theoretical writings reveals a high incidence of scientific formulations and exemplifications. These have as yet received little attention in print—unless to be referred to as 'little more than a pseudoscientific smoke-screen'.[5] In fact, the question of whether Pound's ideas are 'scientific' need hardly be asked: would they be any more or less true if they were? But it is nonetheless true that holding an idea to be 'scientific' does make a difference—not so much in terms of truth-content as of 'acceptability'; 'since, in our times, there is no knowledge which can claim the status of truth without the mediation of a scientific discourse. Science is (wrongly or rightly) the only way in which knowledge can acquire universal validity for human beings.'[6]

In pursuit of the relation between Pound's poetic practice and his 'ideas'—especially his fascist ideology—the question of 'acceptability' is of considerable importance.[7] There are any number of possible descriptions of that relation: metaphors extended from the domain of politics to that of poetry (*e.g.*, a 'totalitarian' style); models based on the posited 'personality' of the author, or the 'sensibility' of the age; or Walter Benjamin's suggestion that fascism is an ideology in which aesthetics determine politics.[8] But all these are ultimately tautological: the problem is not a matter of elucidating Pound's 'beliefs' in order to show that his fascism was a consequence of his 'fascist' beliefs; but of finding a *third* term to relate the poetry and the ideology—to see how those beliefs come to be inscribed, and particularly how the inscribing *masks* their contradictions and absences. Taking Pierre Macherey's image of the text as a fractured mirror, we must ask 'by what paradox does it make its own blindness visible without actually seeing itself?'[9] That is the question of acceptability: the means by which the ideological masquerades as knowledge, or partiality as 'truth'.

As we shift the reference of 'scientific' ideas into the realm of acceptability, we move in consequence to an area defined not by a contest of beliefs, but by what Michel Foucault calls the 'positivities' of a discursive field.[10] This means that we view 'Science' not as a content of facts, but as a *signifier*, or chain of signifiers productive of certain positive 'knowledge-effects'. The chain determines the values, syntactical and epistemological, of its articulation—as in 'impersonal', 'objective', 'universal', 'economic', 'precise', 'accurate', 'true', 'factual'. It is the ways in which such words and the discursive tactic of their employment intervene in and transform Pound's discourse that concerns us. It is evidently in the effect of subjective values inscribed in a discourse of apparent objectivity—in its concealments and consequences—that we must look to find the answer to Macherey's question and the determination of fascism within Pound's poetic practice. In this the transformation of 'mystic values' into a scientific context must play a large part.

2

Pound's quest for acceptability appears in a general sense in his early development and leads directly to the language of science. From his first important series of articles, 'I Gather the Limbs of Osiris' (November 1911–February 1912) to 'The Serious Artist' (1913) and beyond, Pound reasons from the private, technical attentions of the poet to his social, public authority: how can you best get your reader to share your experience *and* to trust your rendering of it? The answer he gives is 'technique', the rigorous matching of cause and effect in language: 'Technique is the means of conveying an exact impression of exactly what one means in such a way as to exhilarate.'[11] Good technique means that you say what you mean, *and that people listen.*

In the 'untidy . . . empirical age where . . . not a single Accepted Idea from the poet has any more magic', he is no longer an *a priori* source of wisdom, ultimate verities or prophetic insight, but must achieve his authority.[12] This the poet can do because he is a craftsman, and as such—in the course of his job—he is necessarily involved in a rigorous, precise and particular knowledge of the relation between language and human interest. Without this practical knowledge, whatever the social content of his poems, the poet is not acceptable, has no claims or power as a social agent. The technical efficiency of that knowledge depends on the authority which its practice earns him. The quest for 'absolute rhythm' indicates this: a cadence whose attachment to the emotion that he wishes to convey and elicit is necessary and inescapable.

There is furthermore another virtue or faith in the tools of his job, for the poet's matter is not merely a question of stimulus-response, but of ethics: 'Beauty in art reminds one what is worth while . . . You don't argue with an April wind, you feel bucked up when you meet it. . . .'[13] It is then the control and release of the energies on which the poet's craft depends which gives him the right to claim the attention of men of good will, and to occupy a place of validity and authority. So we come to a central claim for art, expressed as a declaration of the relation between *technique* (art) and *knowledge* (science):

> The arts, literature, poesy, are a science, just as chemistry is a science. Their subject is man, mankind, and the individual. The subject of chemistry is matter considered as to its composition.
>
> The arts give us a great percentage of the lasting and unassailable data regarding the nature of man, of immaterial man, of man considered as a thinking and sentient creature. They begin where the science of medecine leaves off or rather they overlap that science. The borders of the two arts overcross.[14]

This association and resolution of the terms of art and of science organizes the quest for acceptability in Pound's discourse and thus the authority which he could claim for his poetry. It also comes to determine many later important notions, expressed in similar conjunctions—for example: 'I can "cure" the whole trouble simply by criticism of style. Oh, can I? Yes. I have been saying so for some time.'[15]

Here are the claims that will underlie the *Cantos*: that the poet is competent to speak on political economy with an authority gained from 'right reason' (Canto 36), and that his 'poetic logic' is viable in those terms.[16] We will seek the 'command' of the poems by locating the authority and the acceptance in the field in which it originated.

We must first note that Pound's general resolution of art and science is *built up of* a whole number of local analogies in which the energies mastered by the poet are linked to energies

82

recognized in science. This applies, for example, to the 'luminous detail' of the 'Osiris' articles: 'These facts . . . govern knowledge as the switchboard governs an electric circuit.'[17] Whilst such associations recur in Pound's discussions of the properties of poetic energies, they also characterize the 'mysticism' of the Troubadours, to which Schneidau referred, as in the distinction between the ascetic and chivalric minds:

> our handiest illustrations are drawn from physics: first, the common electric machine, the glass disc and rotary brushes, and the wireless telegraph receiver. In the first we generate a current, or if you like, split up a static condition of things and produce a tension. This is focussed on two brass nobs or 'poles'. These are first in contact, and after the current is generated we can gradually widen the distance between them, and a spark will leap across it. . . . In the telegraph we have a charged surface, produced in a cognate manner, attracting to it, or registering movements in the invisible ether.[18]

Thus we proceed to general statements about art constructed from the mastery of such energies:

> 'The Art of Poetry' consists in combining these 'essentials to thought,' these dynamic particles, *si licet*, this radium with that melody of words which shall most draw the emotions of the hearer and accord with their import.[19]

The 'art' of poetry becomes a 'science' by the efficient technical use of energies expressed analogically in scientific terms.

Such means of expression do not figure just at the level of poetic technique, however, They are also employed in a more literal way to underwrite a *content*:

> For our basis in nature we rest on the indisputable and very scientific fact that there are 'in the normal course of things' certain times, a certain sort of moment more than another, when a man feels his immortality upon him.[20]

It is through such conjunctions that one of what Pound called the main motifs of the *Cantos*—the '"magic moment" or moment of metamorphosis, bust through from quotidien into "divine or permanent world"'—can appear without detriment to the poem's claim to 'reason'.[21]

But if this 'art' is a 'science', then the terms of 'Science' have been transformed. Pound's science cannot be the mechanical science of nineteenth-century materialism—the dominant discourse of the end of the century; yet it is nonetheless 'Science', a discourse about 'facts' and universal knowledge. We are concerned then with the changes in the discourse of science which *alone* make possible the assertions and associations that Pound makes, and all that follows from them in terms of 'objective knowledge' and 'right reason' in his theory and practice.

The full task would involve a number of studies. What follows deals with the language of energy and its use in a way which I argue provides a model for part of Pound's practice. Firstly, therefore, we turn to the *area* of science to which Pound's own analogies—from electricity, electromagnetism and radioactivity—direct us, to find their place within the general field, and the *use* that may be made of them to authorize as scientific the sort of proposition and association that Pound articulates.

3

Against the background of the Newtonian world-view and the negation of 'spirit' seemingly produced by the materialism of the latter half of the nineteenth century, it was asked whether there could be such a thing as indirect 'action-at-a-distance'. Clark Maxwell 'showed that all known electric and magnetic phenomena could be interpreted in terms of the stresses and motions of a material medium.'[22] In order to establish this *invisible material medium* (space) as a scientific object, it was necessary to discover the finite speed of forces acting in the medium 'at-a-distance'. This was provided by Heinrich Hertz in 1888, with an experiment which showed that the same electromagnetic wave, operating at different frequencies, produced both heat and light:

> he was able to discover the progressive propagation of electromagnetic action through space, to measure the length and velocity of electromagnetic waves, and to show that in the transverse nature of their vibration and their susceptibility to reflection, refraction and polarization they are in complete accordance with the waves of light and heat. The result was to establish beyond doubt the electromagnetic nature of light.[23]

These waves were known as 'Hertzian waves', the energy of

elc ctromagnetism properly identified, and the posited medium they passed through was termed the *Ether*.

During the 1890s, the physicists Edouard Branly, Sir Oliver Lodge and Marconi developed these discoveries in the following way:

> Edouard Branly, physics professor at the Catholic University, observed in 1890 that metal filings, when subjected to 'Hertzian waves', behaved very strangely. Normally, filings do not transmit an electrical current because there are air spaces between them; but when placed within the range of electromagnetic waves, the filings fuse a little together, enough to offer a conducting path to an electric current. . . .
>
> Branly called the little glass tube in which he placed his filings a 'coherer'; it was the first form of detector for electromagnetic waves.[24]

Lodge made his 'coherer' in 1894, using it for the reception of Morse signals. By 1897, with Marconi's developments, the first wireless telegraph station was built near Cardiff.

In the meantime, physicists were advancing into electron theory (1892), X-rays (1895) and radium (1898). As these discoveries were made, each of them gradually and further undermined the solid structure of Newtonian mechanical physics. According to Henri Poincaré, by 1905 the six basic principles of physics had been endangered by the discoveries that physics had itself made.[25] One thus finds, in the midst of the nineteenth century conflict between scientific and spiritual values, a conflict within science itself: the glories of the discoveries of science produced a disconcerting revolution in the very nature of science. Materialist discourses were gradually revealed as being inadequate to the new facts.[26]

Thus, whilst contemporary materialist texts tried to sustain their own products within their own paradigms, those products and the collapsing of the paradigms offered opportunities for new discourses. These could extend even to the point of using the achievements of science to deny Science itself in favour of Idealism or various forms of Vitalism.[27] Thus any sampling of contemporary texts reveals a number declaring the death of Materialism, Mechanism and Science by their own hands, and a number attempting a holding action on their behalf. The possibilities of the new discourses are then radically volatile.[28] Which corresponds to Pound's usage?

The traditional language of Science, through the historical standing of physics, was mechanics, based on the primacy of matter through the association of a finite number of solid elements separated by a neutral space.[29] The theory of the ether, however, with each atom dissolving into electromagnetic force, and the indirect effect of one part of the medium on another, entailed a discourse which spoke in terms of continuous fields and waves of energy.

Thus it is that one finds Heraclitus' axiom often quoted as the centre of science, replacing the prime term of matter with that of energy. The type of physics was moving then problematically from mechanics *towards the space* represented by energetics.[30] However, there were scientific circles where the threat to mechanicism did not necessarily bring a common consternation, but on the contrary a new promise for science. This promise—seen most materially in the technological achievements of the new physics—was not restricted to the immediate problems of the ether. In these circles the language of energetics was extended beyond what was newly constituting science, in order to claim the new area in advance for science; rather than—as in the avowedly Idealist or Vitalist mode—using the revolution on the contrary to claim science for a new mystical agnosticism. Gustave Le Bon, a pioneer of intra-atomic energy, indicated the 'scientific' attitude:

> It is hardly to be imagined that the forces of nature are limited to the small number of those with which we are acquainted. . . . During the last twenty years, science has annexed the Hertzian waves, the X-rays, the cathode rays, the radioactive rays, and intra-atomic energy to the small kingdom of forces known of old. It is difficult to believe that the end of these discoveries is reached; and mighty forces surround us without our knowing it.[31]

Le Bon's point was keenly felt by many other scientists who took the discoveries to represent a breaching of a new 'threshold' in the progress of science, in which Science would transform itself and be saved from intellectual entropy.[32]

The language of energetics also offered the possibility of

86

escaping the materialism/vitalism debate through a third term, which could be used to unify a wider totality of experience for science. As Professor Aliotta summarized it: 'by putting energy in the place of matter, it is possible to construct a philosophical synthesis, which will afford an adequate explanation of all the phenomena of mind and matter.'[33] A look at the use of such discourses in psychology (not least in Freud) indicates the possibilities of this conjuncture of the 'spiritual' and the scientific in energetics.[34]

4

The chief place where this synthesis and extension of energetics occurred with a degree of cohesiveness sufficient to produce an identifiable field of discourse was the Society for Psychical Research (S.P.R.). When the Society was formed in 1882, its founders indicated their debt to the new physics in the announcement of its aims: the investigation of psychical phenomena, such as telepathy, automatic writing, clairvoyance and the 'survival of bodily death' 'without prejudice or presupposition of any kind, and in the same spirit of exact and unimpassioned inquiry which has enabled Science to solve as many problems, once no less obscure nor less hotly debated.'[35] It was their adherence to this ethos—progressive, 'scientific' and sceptical—that distinguished the S.P.R. from the occult and spiritualist groups of the period.

William James, President of the Society in 1896, was a foremost advocate of the S.P.R.'s work, returning frequently to its scientific integrity. Among the many leading scientists active in the Society, James selected one of the founders, F. W. H. Myers, an influential psychological theorist, as preeminently scientific.[36] James argued that Myers' practice went beyond that of orthodox scientists, and 'as a lover of life and not of abstractions' he ranked alongside Cuvier and Agassiz.[37]

In short then the members presented themselves not as 'spiritualists' but as progressive scientists, as indeed many of them were in their fields. In the Society they found a vindication not only of their faith in psychical phenomena, but at the same time of their confidence in the progressiveness of their scientific values. The S.P.R. is not characterized by a body of dogma, but rather as a place of exchange for both faith

87

and epistemology, heterogeneous in detail, but coherent in principle—a coherence which is apparent in their discourse.[38] James defined their common ground when he wrote that the Society has 'bridged the gap, healed the rift that science, taken in a certain narrow way, has shot into the human world.'[39]

It is firstly then as a specific reaction to that 'narrow' science, materialism, that the Society defined itself. William McDougall's comments of 1922 still bear the mark of that definition:

> Science has seemed to many minds to lead more and more definitely to the strictly materialistic view of the world. But if that, as many of us believe, is a mistake, if materialism is not the whole truth, only the further progress of science can make this clear to all. Only by the methods of science can we hope to combat effectively the errors of science.[40]

This singular auto-criticism of science—the invocation of scientific values to save knowledge from a certain science and restore belief to its domain—prevents the researchers from falling back onto 'spiritualism'. As McDougall says, 'the evidence of revelation no longer suffices'. He distinguishes clearly between psychical research on the one hand, and 'revealed religion and metaphysical philosophy' and spiritualists like Conan Doyle on the other, who are opponents of psychical research.[41]

The possibility of placing psychical research as science, but not materialism, spirituality but not spiritualism, is taken from the language of energetics. In escaping materialism, and shifting from the inorganic through the organic to the psychical *within* science, the researchers could claim that their work unified the material and the psychical.[42] By rejecting an exclusive position in any of the 'mind versus matter' debates in favour of a synthetic one, they revealed the partialities of orthodox science and established themselves, as they argued, in the rightful place of science.

This opposition to an exclusive orthodoxy entails an important transformation of the central term 'science'. Sir Oliver Lodge puts the case soberly. He argued, by adducing the evidence of the new physics, that materialism was just a necessary 'abstraction', a working hypothesis for the founding of basic science; and he continued: 'Some of us . . . now want to enlarge the recognized scope of physical science, so as gradually to take a wider purview and include more of the totality of things. This is what the Society for Psychical Research was established for. . . .'[43]

The new physics had revealed the pragmatic limitations of the old; the new discoveries produced a new epistemology and language which opened the field of the psychical to the province of science through a discourse of energy. This replaces materialism as partial knowledge, and hence not now a science in the sense that psychical research promises to be a science ('more of the totality of things'). At the same time, Science, by its inclusion of the psychical, is itself redeemed as a positive, spiritually progressive vision and made available for such use in discourse.

Three things are mutually dependent: the scientificity of psychical research as a practice; the epistemological synthesis of 'mind and matter' in energy; and the scientific existence of psychical phenomena. Each entails and authorizes the other. In terms of the discourse, this correspondingly involves: the availability of a scientific vocabulary to articulate the practice ('psychical research is a science'); the use of a mediating language of energy; and the possibility of assertions of scientific fact ('it is a fact that . . .'). It is this system of relations which defines the discursive tactic of the S.P.R. It is based on a lowest common denominator among its members: *a paradigm of a scientific and not a metaphysical account of non-material phenomena*— 'empirical' but no longer mechanical. And at its heart is the possibility of *couplings* which 'heal the rift' produced by an earlier mechanicist and materialist science, by articulating the scientific existence of immaterial energies. The effects of this may be seen at many levels, the most important of which, for us, is the local discourse: the production of *a scientific discourse of the mystical.*

5

The argument for the very existence of psychical phenomena as scientific objects, and the legitimacy of their investigation— their scientific status in short—repeatedly refers to the same field of science as we discovered in Pound. Basically it was argued that in the past many of the phenomena recently discovered in the field of physics would have been termed 'supernatural', 'miraculous', or 'unscientific'. Sir W. F. Barrett uses the progressive physics—telegraphy, telephony, radium—to argue a principle of gradations: that phenomena, however dark, are continually being brought within the realm of science by its progressive methods.[44]

Here lies the importance of Hertz's discoveries and of what Poincaré termed 'that grand revolutionist of the present time', radium.[45] Radium and the ether substantiated the proposition that there are forces and objects in nature which defy Newtonian explanation but which may nonetheless be deemed scientific by the new science. And Hertz's discoveries, in producing a field of energy and a spectrum of waves, enact the logical principle of the gradations of these forces.

It is sufficient to observe that these discoveries appear frequently as illustrations for the new researchers; and the spectrum becomes a favourite image, especially for Myers.[46] This is elevated into a principle, of bringing 'unlike things together by forming series of which the intermediary terms connect the extremes', 'a procedure', James continues, 'much in use by scientific men'; in which the intermediary terms come from the new physics of energy.[47]

This vocabulary of energy and the ether has a considerable mediatory potential. Consider, for example, the possibilities of an extended scientific vocabulary offered by Barrett's definition of the 'scientific conception' of the 'luminiferous ether':

> a material medium of a wholly different order of matter from any thing known to our senses, and the very existence of which is only known inferentially.

This sort of scientific 'material' is injected into the notion of the spectrum:

> Moreover, modern science has taught us that there are myriads of waves in the ether which are too short or too long to affect our unaided senses.[48]

These tactics provide a scientific language which makes acceptable such notions as 'psychic force' by referring to the same data of science as Pound's 'delightful psychic experience':

> the theory of 'ectenic' or 'psychic force' . . . attributes the phenomena to some extension in space of the nervous force of the medium, just as the power of a magnet, or of an electric current, extends beyond itself and can influence and move certain distant bodies which lie within the field of the magnetic or electric force.[49]

The conceptual substitution of 'ether' for 'space' produces a complete revision of traditional discourses of mental force and communication. Witness Lodge's discussion of 'means of communication':

> Artistic representation . . . is still truly astonishing when intellectually regarded. An arrangement of pigments designed for the reception and modification and re-emission or reflexion of ether-tremors . . . intervene between the minds of painter and spectator.[50]

It is precisely syntagms such as 'ether-tremors' (which here leads to a discussion of telepathy) that open up a scientific vocabulary for the 'energy' of art and mind.

In the case of the more extended psychical phenomena, it is nonetheless most important to note the limits of what is a *metaphorical* principle. This relation between the psychical and the new physics does not entail the claim, for example, that such phenomena belong to the same spectrum as heat and light. The point is not that there is a materialist account of such matters, but that there is a scientific account. Barrett's discussion of telepathy makes this clear:

> The existence of wireless telegraphy and the bridging of vast spaces by messages transmitted in this way naturally suggest that thought might likewise be transmitted by a similar system of ether waves, which some have called 'brain waves'. And there is no doubt the fact of wireless telegraphy has made telepathy more widely credible and popular. . . . hostility to a new idea arises largely from its being unrelated to existing knowledge. As soon as we see, or think we see, some relation or resemblance to what we already know, hostility of mind changes to hospitality, and we have no further doubt of the truth of the new idea. It is not so much *evidence* that convinces men of something entirely foreign to their habit of thought, as the discovery of a *link* between the new and the old.[51]

91

The physicist then rejects an account of 'brain waves' in terms of Hertzian waves, on the scientific ground of the law of inverse squares.

The relation between the two sets of phenomena is then a relation in thought and not in nature. The significance of the metaphors is operated by their relation to the scientific revolution. This is in short a formal relation: the use of 'material' things from the new physics to signify immaterial phenomena within a context of science. It is not so much through an analytic relation of content—'evidence'—that these phenomena enter science; but through a purely analogical, formal relation—'a link'. Such was Pound's tactic as we saw it: the construction of a network of analogy between energies building into a general resolution of the two sets of values.

In this way, the S.P.R. and Pound both use a similar area of science—the new physics and its signification in terms of the transformation of 'science'—according to a similar metaphorical principle—analogical linkage—towards a similar purpose. Both discourses seek to express 'psychical', 'immaterial' human energies of communication in scientific and not metaphysical terms. From these discourses of energy they both gain the acceptability of scientific status for their practice ('poetry is a science'), and their content ('it is a scientific fact that . . .').

What underlines the parallel I am drawing is that on both sides the metaphorical principle builds into a system and is not just incidental. *In terms of their discourses*, and those discourses in terms of their problematic claim to Science, both Pound and the S.P.R. gain the connotative values of Science from the *totalization* of a number of linked signifiers. Thus it is not just that Lodge answers the question 'How does mind communicate with mind?', like Pound, with an analogy from the wireless; it is that he uses this and other instances to build up a claim for scientific status for the whole field of non-material communication.[52] In the same way, Pound's discourse totalizes conjunctions of mental and poetic energies with 'the radiant node', 'a cluster of fused ideas . . . endowed with energy', 'emotional force', and the 'complex' into propositions like: '[the poet] is the advance guard of the psychologist on the watch for new emotions.'[53]

We have looked at the new physics to see how it offered new possibilities of signification for the language of science, in opening the scientific discourse to 'energy' and the ether. We have seen how this allowed for two opportunities for the non-materialist: either the destruction of Science in favour of a loose mysticism, Idealism, Vitalism or spiritualism; or its trans-formation into a new discursive and metaphysical synthesis.

Of the latter, the S.P.R. is the most thoroughly pervaded by that language, and hence in effect defines the area. We have seen how they establish a system of relations in which the three things go together: the availability of the scientific vocabulary, a synthesis of values, and the establishment of a scientific practice and content of 'mysticism'. Thus we have observed how this is based on a particular *metaphorical* use of the new physics.

The fact that Pound employs a similar frame of reference with a similar metaphorical purpose should be clear from the examples at the beginning of this paper. Finally, lest it be argued that this discourse is incidental to Pound's practice, we must turn to some further examples and their place in his art.

6

The conjunction of science, art and psychic energy is used most of all to underwrite a major sense of *form*. The following extract from 'Cavalcanti' expresses many values of Pound's theory and practice, in a way which cannot free itself from the scientific vocabulary (as analogue *and* content) which we have been discussing. Pound is writing about mediaevalism and 'the Mediterranean sanity':

> We appear to have lost the radiant world where one thought cut through another with clean edge, a world of moving energies *'mezzo oscuro rade'*, *'risplende in se perpetuale effecto'*, magnetisms that take form, that are seen, or that border the visible, the matter of Dante's *paradiso*, the glass under water, the form that seems a form seen in a mirror, these realities perceptible to the sense interacting. . . .
>
> For the modern scientist energy has no borders, it is a shape-less 'mass' of force; even his capacity to differentiate it to a degree never dreamed by the ancients has not led him to think of its shape or even of its loci. The rose that his magnet makes in

93

the iron filings, does not lead him to think of the force in botanic terms, or wish to visualize that force as floral and extant (*ex stare*).

A medieval 'natural philosopher' would find this modern world full of enchantments, not only the light in the electric bulb, but the thought of the current hidden in the air and in wire would give him a mind full of forms, *'Fuor di color'* or having their hypercolours. The medieval philosopher would probably have been unable to think the electric world, and *not* think of it as a world of forms.[54]

As with the S.P.R., Pound's account, without the mediation of a scientific reference, would be a more or less undistinguishable piece of anachronistic and subjectivist mystical philosophy.

The notion of form indicated above is moreover much emphasized in accounts of Pound's poetics. Indeed, Donald Davie takes this extract as the basis for his defence of Pound's method. Through 'the reference to magnetism', he connects it to a passage from *Guide to Kulchur*:

> 'I made it out a mouthful of air,' wrote Bill Yeats in his heyday. The *forma*, the immortal *concetto*, the concept, the dynamic form which is like the rose pattern driven into the dead iron-filings by the magnet, not by material contact with the magnet itself, but separate from the magnet. Cut off by the layer of glass, the dust and filings rise and spring into order. Thus the *forma*, the concept rises from death. . . .[55]

Davie distinguishes the *forma* from the concept, and defines his sense of Pound's art:

> the point to be made is that Pound in the *Cantos* characteristically aims at re-creating not the concept, any or all of them, but rather the *forma*, the thing behind them and common to them all. By arranging sensory impressions he aims to state, not ideas, but the form behind and in ideas, the moment before that 'fine thing held in the mind' has precipitated out now this idea, now that.[56]

The *Cantos* rest then on the *forma*, which in turn rests on the 'rose in the steel dust' and its associated images. These are the terms which make the poem's 'mystical' attitude to perception and structure acceptable in rational and 'objective' terms.

Similarly, in Pound's account of the Noh plays, we find, for example:

> The suspense is the suspense of waiting for a supernatural manifestation—which comes. Some will be annoyed at a form of psychology which is, in the West, relegated to spiritistic seances. There is, however, no doubt that such psychology exists.[57]

Pound values this psychology in the Noh as he does in the Troubadours and Cavalcanti. But these real ('scientific') psychic forces of the seance, trivialized in spiritualism, are precisely the territory of the Society for Psychical Research. Thus it is of interest that when Pound comes to ask 'whether there can be a long imagiste or vorticist poem', it is the Noh, with its psychological forms, which seems to provide the first answer.[58]

In all these cases we can trace the metaphor or the assertion back to the application of the new physics to the psychic life, as seen in the discursive practice of the S.P.R.

Now, there is no record of Pound's having had any dealings with the Society. If his ideas were influenced in this area by any contemporary, it is much more likely that his source was Yeats (whose dealings with the Society were mostly with the more spiritistic wing).[59] It is my position, however, that Pound's 'beliefs' are his own, and that ideas like 'delightful psychic experience' or 'the radiant world' require no derivation. But the assertion that such experience has a *scientific* basis, or that it can be expressed in scientific terms, can only be upheld within the paradigm of science located in the S.P.R.

What I am saying is that what distinguishes Pound's, for the want of a better word, 'mysticism' from that of the Symbolist aesthetic with which he was in contact through Yeats, and against which he rebelled, is the coherent scientific model and vocabulary. I am furthermore asserting that this model is only adequate as a scientific form within the paradigm which finds its *precedent* in the Society for Psychical Research.

If we are looking at the question in terms of a fiction of origins, in terms of the derivation and identity of ideas and beliefs, then we must say that Pound had nothing to do with the S.P.R. If, however, we are concerned with the place that his language takes within contemporary limits of acceptability and authorization in discourse, then we must say that in terms of its problematic claim to science, it is *underwritten*—as it were almost literally—by the paradigm and discourse of the Society in its currency and precedent acceptability.

The relation to Fascism is of course by no means direct at this point—although occultism itself has many theoretical and historical relations to that ideology.[60] But it does open a field to us. It can explain how many discursive associations became available for Pound to inscribe under the total authority of 'science'. Since it is a question of 'universal knowledge', it can show how ideas available in only a *partial* way could be expressed in terms of *totality*. The contradictions and absences thus masked must be worked out in Pound's later writing.

If we merely take that large part of Pound's discourse that involves a scientific vocabulary as being more than incidental; and if we view 'science' always in its context and as the least ideologically innocent of terms; then we are at least on the track of a real relation in discourse between Pound's subjective and idealist ideology and its 'objective' significations, and the forms hence adopted.

NOTES

1. A. T. Schofield, *The Borderlands of Science* (London: Cassell, 1917), p. 106.
2. Herbert Schneidau, 'Pound and Yeats: the Question of Symbolism', *Journal of English Literary History*, 33 (1965), 220–37.
3. Schneidau, *Ezra Pound: The Image and the Real* (Baton Rouge: Louisiana State University Press, 1969), pp. 124–25.
4. Unlike Sister Bernetta Quinn, who observes a 'tension' in the *Cantos* where 'the knife-edged clarity for which Pound has ever striven wars against the vagueness of the reverie method'—*The Metamorphic Tradition in Modern Poetry* (New Brunswick, New Jersey, 1955), p. 27; quoted in Schneidau's article (note 2), p. 236. She is here nonetheless testifying to the conjunction of terms from mysticism and science.
5. Hugh Witemeyer, *The Poetry of Ezra Pound* (Los Angeles: University of California Press, 1969), p. 33. The reference here is to the definition of the Image in terms of the 'complex'. A more serious attention is emerging in the work of Ian F. A. Bell—to whom I owe a large debt.
6. Baudoin Jurdant, 'Freud and Science', *Nouslit-Sandwich*, 1, i (Spring 1974), 14. Jurdant continues: 'That is to say that any knowledge (either old or new) which claims universal validity must be mediated by science

in order to satisfy this claim. And it is no use saying that it does not hold for all kinds of knowledge. No knowledge can escape the question of whether it is true or not, and the question itself cannot escape the fact that its relevance must be provided by science and science only.' This 'science' is not of course static or absolute, but rather an ideological function 'whereby truth-values are given to [a] discourse through the mediation of an imaginary representation of what science is.' It may then be useful to bear in mind Michel Foucault's thought on 'Knowledge and ideology': 'In any discursive formation, one finds a specific relation between science and knowledge . . . archaeological analysis must show positively how a science functions in the element of knowledge. It is probably here, in that space of interplay, that the relations of ideology to the sciences are established. . . . They are articulated where science is articulated upon knowledge'—*The Archaeology of Knowledge*, trans. A. M. Sheridan Smith (London: Tavistock, 1972), p. 185.

7. This is especially true in a wider sense of the question of Fascism as a whole; as witness the role of this concept in its various registers in Jean-Pierre Faye's *Langages Totalitaires* (Paris: Hermann, 1972), a detailed study of the process of languages in National Socialism and Fascism. See also his theoretical prolegomenon, *La Critique du Langage et son Économie* (Paris: Editions Galilée, 1973), pp. 45–63, for a detailed study of the concept.

8. Walter Benjamin, 'The Work of Art in the Age of Mechanical Reproduction', *Illuminations* (London: Fontana, 1970), p. 243.

9. Pierre Macherey, *Towards a Theory of Literary Production*, trans. Geoffrey Wall (London: Routledge, 1978), p. 122.

10. Foucault, *The Archaeology of Knowledge, passim* (*e.g.*, p. 126).

11. Ezra Pound, 'I Gather the Limbs of Osiris', *Selected Prose*, ed. William Cookson (London: Faber, 1973), p. 33. These articles first appeared in *The New Age*.

12. Ford Madox Ford, letter to Mrs. Lucy Masterman, 23 January 1912; in *Critical Writings of Ford Madox Ford*, ed. Frank MacShane (Lincoln: University of Nebraska Press, 1964), p. 154.

13. Pound, 'The Serious Artist', *Literary Essays*, ed. T. S. Eliot (London: Faber, 1963), p. 44. These articles first appeared in *The Egoist*.

14. Ibid., p. 42.

15. Pound, *Jefferson and/or Mussolini* (1933; New York: Liveright, 1970), p. 17.

16. That is to say, the syntax of the ideogram and the 'rose in the steel dust'—all expressed in scientific terms. See, for example, 'The Ideogrammatic Method or the Method of Science', *The ABC of Reading* (1934; London: Faber, 1973), p. 26.

17. *Selected Prose*, p. 22. Compare, for example, the rather muddled analogy from electrostatics and radiation which describes the energy of words, ibid., p. 34.

18. Pound, 'Psychology and the Troubadours' (1912), *The Spirit of Romance* (New York; New Directions, 1968), p. 93.

19. Pound, 'The Wisdom of Poetry' (1912), *Selected Prose*, p. 330. Compare, from 'The Serious Artist': 'the thing that matters in art is a sort of energy,

something more or less like electricity or radioactivity, a force transfusing, welding, and unifying. A force rather like water when it spurts up through very bright sand and sets it in swift motion'—*Literary Essays*, p. 49. This can be pursued through the Vo: ' .st period and beyond.

20. Pound, *The Spirit of Romance*, p. 94.

21. Letter to Homer Pound, 11 April 1927, *Selected Letters of Ezra Pound*, ed. D. D. Paige (London: Faber, 1971), p. 210.

22. Trevor I. Williams, *The Biographical Dictionary of Science* (London, 1969). Hitherto the model of 'action-at-a-distance' had been Newtonian gravity, which was instantaneous and direct. The question had largely been prompted by the work of von Helmholtz in optics.

23. *Encyclopedia Britannica* (1947) 11, 525. This conjunction of energy and light is most important for the light-crystal imagery of the *Cantos*—'In the light of the light is the virtu.' The experiment was very similar to that given in Pound's illustration of the ascetic mind quoted above (note 19).

24. Egon Larsen, *A History of Invention* (London: Phoenix, 1961), p. 278.

25. Henri Poincaré, *The Value of Science* (1905), trans. George Bruce (New York: Dover, 1958), Chapter 8.

26. The gradual nature of this revelation must be emphasized; as G. H. A. Cole writes: 'The advent of Maxwell's theory is of the greatest significance in providing a firmly experimentally-based theory of electromagnetism, of complete internal consistency, but which is incompatible with Newtonian mechanics and Galilean relativity. This incompatibility becomes the more apparent the more the experimental implications are explored'—*The Twentieth-Century Mind*, ed. C. B. Cox and A. E. Dyson (Oxford: O.U.P., 1972), 1, p. 267. Similarly, the gradual nature of the recovery must be noted. Einstein's theories (1905–15) have a far from immediate impact at the level which concerns us. It is not until after the First World War that one begins to see popular expositions of the theory in English.

27. Lenin gives a fairly full study of this in *Materialism and Empirio-Criticism* (1908, revised 1920): 'The movement of bodies is transformed in nature into a movement of something that is not a body with a constant mass, into a movement of an unknown charge of an unknown electricity in an unknown ether—this dialectics of *material* transformation, performed in the laboratory and in the factory, serves in the eyes of the idealist (as in the eyes of the public at large, and of the Machists) not as a confirmation of materialist dialectics, but as evidence against materialism: ... "The mechanical theory, as a professed explanation of the world, receives its death-blow from the progress of mechanical physics itself" '—Lenin here quotes the British Idealist James Ward; the translation is that issued by Progress Publishers, Moscow, 1970, p. 269. Good examples of Vitalist arguments are found in the works of Edward Carpenter, especially 'The Science of the Future', *Civilization, Its Causes and Cure* (London: Methuen, 1912), and in those of T. E. Hulme, collected in *Speculations* (London: Kegan Paul, 1924).

28. As Gaston Bachelard observes, in reference to Clark Maxwell's contri-

bution: *'Une telle soudure de deux phénoménologies aussi diverses que l'électricité et et l'optique suggère des significations nouvelles. Autrement dit les phénomènes immédiats, soit optiques, soit électriques, prennent de nouveaux sens'*—*Le Rationalisme Appliqué* (1949; Paris: Presses Universitaires de France, 1975), p. 153. These significations must be determined within both a scientific and an extra-scientific context.

29. Compare Pound's attack on the 'logic' of bricks and mortar in *The Chinese Written Character as a Medium for Poetry* (1920; San Franscisco: City Lights, 1969), pp. 25–6. This text relies heavily on energetics for its rationale.

30. It must be clear that Energetics is not a body of content ready to fill the gap left by a failing Mechanics. It is a competing set of emerging discourses battling over the space. This is important for the possibility of hybrid and pseudo-scientific discourses which occupy temporary positions of validity.

31. Gustave Le Bon, *The Evolution of Forces*, ed. F. Legge (London: Kegan Paul, 1908), p. 350.

32. Entropy was a concept in thermodynamics originally articulated by Carnot and revived in the nineteenth century by Kelvin, Tait and Maxwell. It became a touchstone in the attribution of a negation of 'spirit' to materialism. George Herbert Mead offers a symptomatic response: 'That mechanical conception which science presents has no future—or a very dark one, at best. Not dark in the sense of catastrophies, for those are always exciting; but dark in the very monotony of the picture. The conception of entropy is anything but exciting. Such a universe would answer only to an infinite sense of ennui'—*Movements of Thought in the Nineteenth Century* (1936; Chicago: University of Chicago Press, 1972), p. 156.

33. Professor Aliotta, *The Idealistic Reaction against Science*, trans. Agnes McCaskill (London: Macmillan, 1914), p. 364. I am afraid that I cannot discover the author's given name.

34. In terms of acceptability, the authentically 'spiritual' and the authentically 'psychological' face the same problem in proposing a science of *'l'esprit'*. Freud especially suffered from this entanglement. Whereas Freud and Breuer's *Studies in Hysteria* (1893–95) were read with interest at the Society for Psychical Research in 1893, when M. D. Eder read the first paper on Freud before the British Medical Association as late as 1911, his audience walked out in disgust. Further, since Pound refers to Bernard Hart in the definition of the Image, it is worth noting the latter's presentation of the 'complex': 'The complex may be said to be the psychological analogue of the conception of force in physics'—*Subconscious Phenomena*, ed. Hugo Münsterberg (London and New York: Rebman, 1912), p. 133.

35. Sir W. F. Barrett's advertisement for the Society, quoted in Alan Gauld, *The Founders of Psychical Research* (London: Routledge and Kegan Paul, 1968), p. 138.

36. Myers played a large part in preparing the ground for the acceptance of Freud's theories. He was an expert on hysteria, hypnotism, and the

dissociation of consciousness, and one of the first to posit a dynamic model of an unconscious which he called the 'subliminal consciousness'. See, for example, L. S. Hearnshaw, *A Short History of British Psychology* (London: Methuen, 1964).

Apart from its scholarly founders, Henry Sidgwick, Edmund Gurney, Myers and James, Presidents of the Society included: Sir Oliver Lodge (Professor of Physics and one of the inventors of the wireless), Sir W. F. Barrett (Professor of Physics), Charles Richet (physician and psychologist), Henri Bergson, Sir William Crookes (discoverer of thallium and inventor of the radiometer), and William McDougall (Reader in Mental Science at Oxford, and an influential psychologist). Other important members were: Lord Rayleigh (Nobel Prize winning physicist in 1904), Sir J. J. Thomson (discoverer of gamma rays), and A. R. Wallace. Corresponding members included Hertz, Jung, Freud, Mme Curie and Bernheim, leader of the Nancy school of psychology.

37. William James, 'Frederic Myers's Service to Psychology' (1901), *William James on Psychical Research*, ed. Gardner Murphy and Robert O. Ballou (New York: Viking, 1973), pp. 224–25. In this account, Myers is presented in the same terms as Pound uses to describe his ideal men of science, from Agassiz to Allan Upward and Frobenius.

38. A sense of the heterogeneity of theory can be gained from the following: 'According to Gasparin, psychical phenomena are produced by some fluid; to Sir William Crookes, by psychic force; to Lombroso, by the transformation of force; to Porro, by the action of unknown spirits; Prof. Richet wisely comes to no conclusion. . . . Prof. Flammarion has no theory, but considers that the phenomena must be admitted as facts into the sphere of positive science'—A. T. Schofield, *The Borderlands of Science*, p. 113.

39. James, 'What Psychical Research has Accomplished' (1896), *William James on Psychical Research*, p. 46.

40. William McDougall, 'The Need for Psychical Research' (1922), *Religion and the Sciences of Life* (London: Methuen, 1934), p. 61.

41. Ibid., pp. 55 and 59. Compare also: Lodge—'Those who call themselves spiritualists have an easy and simple faith', *Raymond, or Life and Death* (London: Methuen, 1916), p. 367; Barrett—'the psychical order is not the spiritual order', *On the Threshold of the Unseen* (London: Kegan Paul, 1917), p. xxx. Conan Doyle resigned from the Society and turned critic because of his 'unscientific' spiritism. See, for example, his *The New Revelation* (London: Hodder and Stoughton, 1918).

42. 'As we pass from inorganic to organic, from organic to psychical, the mechanical warp becomes as it were less important and new aspects of Reality find freer expression'—J. Arthur Thomson, *Introduction to Science* (London: Williams and Norgate, 1911), p. 165.

43. Lodge, *Raymond . . .*, p. 371.

44. Barrett, *Psychical Research* (London: Williams and Norgate, 1911), pp. 11–12 and 18. This process also applies to Psychology (p. 32). It is also invoked in our current enthusiasm for the parapsychological: 'The

unthinkable propositions of modern physics make the unthinkable concepts of parapsychology a little less unacceptable'—Arthur Koestler, *The Times*, 21 February 1977, p. 5.

45. Poincaré, *The Value of Science*, p. 96.

46. Barrett offers a useful summary: 'Mr. Frederick Myers has well compared our normal self-consciousness to the visible spectrum of light; beyond it on either side is a wide tract, imperceptible to the eye, yet crowded with radiation. . . . And just as experimental physics has within the present century revealed the existence of ultra-violet and infra-red portions of the spectrum . . . so with the growth of experimental psychology we are beginning to discover the complex nature of our personality, and how that part of our Ego which is below the threshold of consciousness may be led to emerge from obscurity'—Barrett, *On the Threshold of the Unseen*, pp. 122–23.

47. *William Jones on Psychical Research*, p. 217.

48. Barrett, op. cit., p. 101.

49. Ibid., p. 107. For Pound's 'delightful psychic experience', see 'Psychology and the Troubadours', 'Cavalcanti' (in *Literary Essays*) and the 'Postscript to *The Natural Philosophy of Love* by Remy de Gourmont' (*Pavannes and Divagations* (1918; New York: New Directions, 1958)). See also Witemeyer, *The Poetry of Ezra Pound*, Chapter 2.

  Consider, for example: 'The senses at first seem to project for a few yards beyond the body . . . The conception of the body as perfect instrument of the increasing intelligence pervades. . . . Whether it is necessary to modernize or nordicize our terminology and call this "the aesthetic or interactive vasomotor magnetism in relation to the consciousness," I leave to the reader's own taste'—*Literary Essays*, p. 152.

50. Lodge, p. 339.

51. Barrett, *Psychical Research*, pp. 107–8.

52. Lodge, p. 338.

53. Pound, 'The Wisdom of Poetry' (1912), *Selected Prose*, p. 331; see also 'As for Imagisme' (1914), ibid., p. 345. The 'myth' or the 'image' then becomes an 'equation for the human emotions' (*Spirit of Romance*, p. 14; *Literary Essays*, p. 431).

54. *Literary Essays*, pp. 154–55.

55. Pound, *Guide to Kulchur* (1938; London: Peter Owen, 1966), p. 152. See also, Pound, 'Through Alien Eyes, I', *The New Age*, 12 (16 January 1913), for a contemporary exploitation of the same image.

56. Donald Davie, *Ezra Pound, Poet as Sculptor* (London: Routledge and Kegan Paul, 1965), p. 220.

57. Pound, *The Classic Noh Theatre of Japan* (1917; New York: New Directions, 1959), p. 26.

58. Pound, 'Vorticism' (1914), *Gaudier-Brzeska*, (New York: New Directions, 1970), p. 94.

59. Yeats is a difficult case. His main contact with the S.P.R. was James H. Hyslop, a spiritualist who was forced to resign. A full account can be found in Arnold Goldman, 'Yeats, Spiritualism, and Psychical Research',

Yeats and the Occult, ed. George Mills Harper (London: Macmillan, 1975).

60. A useful approach to this question may be found through Theodor Adorno's 'Theses against Occultism', *Minima Moralia*, trans. E. F. N. Jephcott (London: New Left Books, 1974) and Sigmund Freud, *Totem and Taboo* (1912), trans. James Strachey (London: Routledge and Kegan Paul, 1950). Similarly, a study of William McDougall's racism and occultism as it developed through the 1920s would be productive.

4

Pound's Poetics of Loss

by H. N. SCHNEIDAU

A poetics of loss and failure seems to be a Romantic artifact, or
at least to have been available in latent form to all poets since
that time. In any poetics which posits the centrality of loss or
the inevitability of failure, part of the problem must be laid at
the door of a certain historical condition, and we have been
living in that condition for two centuries. A key element in the
background for such a poetics is the problem of the status of
poetry itself: the typical question, though it does not often rise
to direct expression, is whether poetry has not become out-
moded, vestigial, an ornamental relic, to be put away with
other childish things now that we have reached the age of
enlightened scientific opinion. To call one a 'poet' in our era is
to use a very ambiguous epithet. When Pound noted that
Whitman was 'still suspect/ four miles from Camden' he was
pointing to a generic condition.[1] The vigour of assertions
about poetry's value in the writings of Romantics and post-
Romantics has never fully concealed the anxiety: all this time
we have been haunted by the Benthamite question, what is the
use of it? As Pound noted, for many 'poetry' is a synonym for
'bosh, rot, rubbish', and is hopelessly associated with facile
escapism.[2] No reply to that allays all of our nervousness, not
even John Stuart Mill's prescription of poetry as a cure for
depression. Those who assert that poetry can have salvific
powers, from Mill and Arnold to I. A. Richards, can best be
seen as fighting a rearguard action. Wordsworth's fears and

103

misgivings and visions of 'mighty poets in their misery dead', Coleridge's dejection, Keats's whistling in the dark, all seem to have their allotropic forms in later writers: sooner or later all poets are tempted towards alternations of despair and bravado about their very role as poets. The worries about losing the poetic gift often cover a deeper worry about the worth and validity of that gift. Most sharply put, the question becomes a form of the double bind: might it not be that to succeed as a poet is to fail?

Even the commonplace forms of poetic striving may be drawn towards this extreme: for instance, it is usually agreed, to quote a recent essay, that 'much Romantic poetry deals explicitly with a yearning that can find no objectification in the material world and which escapes the poet's powers of expression.'[3] Obviously one of the defining marks of this yearning is precisely that it transcend expression; and although on the one hand we may want to celebrate the power of poetry to somehow suggest such intangibles, as in answering T. S. Eliot's objections to *Hamlet*, the anxious thought arises that capturing these feelings in any form is betrayal of them. By such paths do we eventually come to observe, in Leslie Fiedler's borrowed aphorism about American writers, that nothing fails like success: so applicable that it has become a lurid Hollywood motif.[4] From Rimbaud to Hemingway and Fitzgerald, the notion has box-office appeal; but though trivially exploited, it has roots in a genuine and deep-seated dismay.

The serious worries that combine in various proportions in this complex of dismay include these: (1) Is not any utterance, no matter how comprehensive, at odds with the resistant non-linguisticality of Nature—largely conceived, since the Romantics, in terms of what Hugh Kenner calls the 'silent Newtonian universe'?[5] In spite of such gestures as the 'correspondent breeze' *topos*, the Aeolian Harp symbol, and pantheistic assertions, the Romantics feel keenly the unyielding, ungraspable qualities in Nature; they are haunted by images of the Cartesian gap between mind and matter, and by the consequent de-personifying and dehumanizing of what we call, in a tell-tale phrase, the external world. Only in the post-Romantic era is it necessary, with Ruskin, to disown the pathetic fallacy: to so object to anthropomorphism is to break the last visible threads to the old personified world-image. A growing gap is seen between language and the world, as in Byron's plaintive lines: 'I do believe/ Though I have found them not, that there may be/ Words which are things . . .'[6] This regretful alarm can lead all the way to linguistic nervous breakdown, diagnosed in many writers by such critics as Donald Davie and J. Hillis Miller; Davie points to Hoffmansthal's *Letter of Lord Chandos*, where the young nobleman sees words as balls tossed by an indifferent fountain, arbitrary and detached from meanings.[7] A sudden, emotionally devastating awareness of the conventionality of language, when a naturalistic or organic view is lost or over-thrown, can produce such an aphasic result. But even when the effect is not so extreme, utterances about Nature or the world can seem pitifully inadequate, improvised, after-the-fact: any-thing that is said serves at best to suggest how much remains unsaid, how much one must leave out in order to state or represent anything at all.

(2) Even if a poet avoids the dilemmas of representing or embodying the world in language, and concerns himself with expressing the so-called inner world, he eventually reaches the double bind implicit in a phrase quoted by Cassirer: 'When *speaks* the soul, the *soul* no longer speaks.'[8] Underneath the phrase that language may 'betray our feelings' lurks a suspicion that a certain kind of treachery is inevitably involved. We have learned to associate sincerity with inarticulateness: what would we do with a glib Cordelia? Or Billy Budd? Viewed simply as a practical problem, the project of registering private experiences forces a poet to steer between the ready-made or commonplace and self-defeatingly novel. Of course there cannot be a truly private language, even if an idiom be as individual as a finger-print: how then is a poet to communicate his uniqueness? Is there any certain value in doing so? What gives any poet the right to assume that his experiences are meaningful to others? We have no sure way of defeating the fear that individual feelings may only 'confirm a prison', to borrow Eliot's para-phrase of Bradley.[9] To put it in a larger frame: how can any subjective statement reach out to objective validity? How do we know that one, settling a pillow by her head, will not say 'That is not what I meant at all. Not it, at all?' How can any one monad have anything to say that will be in any way valid for another

105

monad? Coleridge's labours of reasoning to establish the mutual presupposition of subject and object were never wholly convincing, even to himself, though they do demonstrate the intractability of the problem.

(3) From the Romantic Age onwards, poets typically do not begin with a sense of a rich poetic heritage, but rather with a sense of barrenness or decadence that only new creation will vanquish. To such poets the immediate tradition is likely to seem sterile and dispiriting: 'a doughy mess of third-hand Keats, Wordsworth, heaven known what, fourth-hand Elizabethan sonority blunted, half melted, lumpy', wrote Pound of 'the common verse of Britain from 1890 to 1910', and thus of the poetic language he inherited on voyaging to London, 1908.[10] Hence his remark that 'only the mediocrity of a given time can drive the more intelligent men of that time to "break with tradition" . . . the phrase "break with tradition" is currently used to mean "desert the more obvious imbecilities of one's immediate elders." '[11] Here the generalized Romantic fear of failure becomes a specific fear of continuing a decadent progression. From this follows the belief shared by Pound and Wordsworth, and Plato of course, that the public has been corrupted and miseducated, which accounts for their respective urges to replace 'a degrading thirst after outrageous stimulation' with a calm preference for the 'real language of men', or in Pound's case 'to save the public's soul by punching its face'. To achieve these reformations, however, poetry must be purged of all that is 'poetic': for poeticisms are remnants of what has starved the tradition and turned poetry into an affectation. Posturing and preciosity must be rooted out, the stultifying notion of poetry as a relic must be attacked. We have no more use for relics than Chaucer did for those of his Pardoner, and no faith in poetry whose procedures seem enshrined, antiquarian, under glass. As Marianne Moore said, 'I, too, dislike it.'[12] So cloying and stuffy can official reverence for poetry become that the great moderns sometimes turn with relief to *declassé* forms of endeavour, e.g. the stage (in the case of Yeats or Eliot) or the novel (in Joyce's abandonment of his posture of lyric poet). Popular success in such veins manages to assuage many anxieties about poetry, not least because it deflects the Benthamite question about usefulness.

However, worries about the inadequacy of languages feed into the problem of making poetry by eliminating the poetic. Distrust of the marks of official Poetry may easily combine with distrust of eloquence in general, and once again we reach the paradox: if poetry succeeds in being poetic and eloquent, it thereby fails, as Verlaine saw. Pound and Wordsworth asked of themselves very demanding linguistic asceticisms in facing this problem; but we can also see why Romanticism and modernism recurrently yearn for earlier ages when poetry was an organic whole, integrated with society, not the bifurcated project it is now. These nostalgic primitivisms took the well-known forms, for us, of unity of being, dissociation of sensibility, etc., sharing with Romantic versions the evangelistic tinge that leads one to speculate on the powers of religious ideas gone underground: what would these ideas be without the myths of prelapsarian unity and innocence, the metaphor of the stream that is purer close to the source, and other staples of Protestant Christianity? T. E. Hulme had no right to dismiss Romanticism as 'spilt religion', as if the only good religious ideas were those that could be containerized; Hulme's own ideas were certainly a form of spilt or diverted religion, and so were those of his contemporaries.[13] None of the great ambitions of modernism can be fully comprehended apart from their matrix of displaced religious motives, their homage to some form of the sacramental religion of art. Yet all such relationships increased the load of responsibility that poetry had to bear, and in the end they clouded even further the equivocal nature of the epithet 'poet'.

Several famous texts recapitulate the problem in their portrayals of poet-figures. In 'Kubla Khan' and 'The Ancient Mariner' old vatic and bardic traditions are invoked; the poet has great wisdom to impart, and by implication should play a vital spiritual role in his culture, yet he exists in the isolation of a trance, or wanders about as if under a curse, solitary and stigmatized; his power to compel listeners only spreads the stigmata to others. This is the familiar paradox of the 'Romantic Image', but the question is whether the equally familiar Wordsworthian answer to the paradox is adequate.[14] Wordsworth's poet afflicted by doubt and 'the fear that kills'—kills poets that is—finds regeneration by confronting an ancient chthonic creature whose form suggests images of life itself

107

crawling out of the primeval slime, and who is indeed standing in a protozoan pool that springs perhaps from the heart of the earth. Up from the old oracle wells a fountain of discourse that might sound to the godless like a countrified babble, but the poet can hear it as an indivisible stream of the real language of men; the implication is that the poet can revive himself by cross-fertilizing his works with this resolute prose. But not many after Wordsworth have been able to find replenishment from rusticity. Pound endorsed the principles of current speech and cross-fertilization by prose, but for the *Cantos* and his other ambitious poems he required far more exotic infusions. It is simply not enough to record the real language of men.

Pound's own anxieties about language and poetry were most marked in his early career, when he was worried about having something to say. At 15, full of admiration for those who could make words dance or lock themselves into vivid combinations, he decided to be a poet, and further decided that to do so he would have to master all the technical side of the art; for inspiration was in the hands of the gods, but if it struck, one wanted to be ready. Later he discovered that translation had uses beyond those of getting in touch with foreign traditions: 'Translation is likewise good training, if you find that your original matter "wobbles" when you try to rewrite it. The meaning of the poem to be translated can not "wobble".'[15] Surely these are revealing statements, though it must be true that poems in revision are quicksilverish and metamorphic, difficult to confine or control, often resistant to original purposes.

The *Cantos*, in one sense, is a vast elaboration on Pound's advice about translation: in its several incarnations, it became something much more than one man's fulfilment of his undergraduate dream of spinning a mighty opus out of his own entrails. For Pound, the long poem was a model for achievement that would be worth far more than an equally thick book of *Collected Poems*. If an epic could actually be written, it would validate the whole Modernist enterprise, not only because it would show that an impressive result could be achieved, but because it would solve some of the post-Romantic dilemmas about poetry itself. Such an achievement could exploit a poetics of loss and turn it into a magnificent gain; it could take the elegiac possibilities of our poetic heritage and carry them at least some way beyond nostalgia, beyond primitivism. In short, Pound's estimation of epic potentialities far exceeded that of the average admirer of Homer *et al.* The well-known laconic notation that an epic is a poem including history is a shorthand phrase for Pound's belief that such a poem is made of long-preserved and well-filtered traditions of knowledge transcending the mind of one man or even of several. In other words an epic must be a composite artifact, a cumulative if not a collective production, and must have a close and complex relation to the *paideuma*, and the 'gristly roots of ideas that are in action'. In the phrase from Canto 99, it is not 'a work of fiction/ Nor yet of one man'.[16]

We must remember that Pound's ambitions took shape following the great period of disintegrationist Homeric scholarship. He showed no inclination to doubt the existence or the unifying genius of Homer the man, but he did show a strong propensity to believe that the poems were accumulations of knowledge that one man starting from scratch could never have gathered. In the *ABC of Reading*, in his oft-quoted assertions about the poems' accurate geography and anatomy, Pound implied that Homer must have relied on several centuries of accumulated traditions, not only about the Trojan War but about the whole spectrum of culture at the time. The poem, 'the tale of the tribe', preserves in memorable form the lore of a whole *paideuma*, and its 'news that stays news'. The voyaging lore of generations has obviously been assimilated into the *periplum*, the verbal map of land as seen by coasting sailors; the military traditions of a samurai society have been culled for the reports of the battlewounds, 'fit for coroner's inquest'.[17] Though Homer had no easily observable use for such accuracies, somehow the poem demanded the preservation of details whether or not they had anything to do with 'thematic unity'.

Similarly when Pound wrote of Dante's incarnation of medieval learning and belief, or nominated Shakespeare's history plays as the 'true English epos', he implied that in effect they were cumulative rather than original works.[18] (Presumably he read the plays as a continuous typological series, a tactic that yields several kinds of pleasures.) They bespeak the sedimentation of layers of culture and time: they manifest not simply

109

Florentine or Elizabethan politics, although these are important elements, but rather a tangle or complex of accumulated ideas. The poets' role is to make clear the major lines of force in these complexes.

Given the role of disintegrationist notions in Pound's conception of the epic, it follows that he would place little value on the conventional kinds of unity and coherence:

> I suspect neither Dante nor Homer *had* the kind of boring 'unity' of surface that we take to be characteristic of Pope, Racine, Corneille.
>
> The Nekuia shouts aloud that it is *older* than the rest, all that island, Cretan, etc., hinter-time, that is *not* Praxiteles, not Athens of Pericles, but Odysseus.[19]

In the *ABC* he mentions his suspicion that Peisistratus, the Athenian tyrant, was responsible for such unity as the Homeric poems appeared to have. When these remarks are placed next to his defence of William Carlos Williams' apparent 'formlessness', it becomes clear that Pound believed in a 'Mediterranean' tradition of cumulative, heterogeneous, inclusive, polytheistic and polymorphic works, with Homer and Ovid as supreme exemplars; and that this line (terminating in himself and Williams?) continued through the Middle Ages, with Dante, Chaucer, Rabelais and others. Dante at first does not seem at home here, but Pound may have classed Dante's architectonics as a singular *tour de force*. His remarks on medieval culture show that he saw it as latently polytheistic and metamorphic, full of 'pagan survivals' and arcane traditions of occult wisdom. Chaucer was not occult, for him, but was a 'Mediterranean', an Ovidian collector of miscellanies: the best stories, plots, devices, and practices of polyglot medieval literature and culture. Chaucer has as little apparent regard for form as Pound could want: the *Canterbury Tales* inevitably reminds one of a Gothic cathedral. (Leon Surette has recently reminded us that Wordsworth used this comparison for his own work, in the 1814 Preface to *The Excursion*: another link to the *Cantos*.)[20]

For the poetics of the *Cantos*, then, heterogeneity was necessary, *mélange* the obligatory form, because the preservation of cumulative traces required the breaking of thematic and topical unities. More and more it seems that the key to the poem is that reminiscence recorded or confected by Donald Hall, that the form had to be one 'that wouldn't exclude something merely because it didn't fit'.[21] Pound never really believed in fittingness. Hence the texture of the *Cantos*, which has puzzled and even angered so many; it was inevitable that Pound would write a poem that at times seems to consist largely of traced quotations, the echoed words of other men. Not only was he committed to many voices and many sources, he is the poet who even more than others believes in the power of language to shape worlds: an idiom or a style is a state of mind that governs the perception of an environment; the state of public language is the state of public health. These devices and convictions provided Pound with some lightening of the burdens inherent in the term 'poet'. Here the maker can become a catalyst, as Eliot desired; his utterances in these contexts get free of the burden of double binds and paradoxes of the poet whose only source and authority is himself.

Only through programmatic heterogeneity and farraginous inclusiveness was it possible, given Pound's premises, to emulate Homer's 'news that stays news'.[22] His conception of the epic is closely related to his conception of the anthology— Ovid and Chaucer really mediate between them—and both evince what he called, in connection with the *Confucian Odes*, a 'real' or direct 'knowledge obtainable only from such concrete manifestation' of precisely rendered particulars. This is the knowledge that enables one to 'tell a Goya from a Velasquez, a Velasquez from an Ambrogio Praedis', and so on: it is contrasted to textbook or catalogue knowledge by Pound, who scoffs at the latter's supposed 'syllogistic connections'.[23] What Pound seems to mean is very close to E. H. Gombrich's concept of *schemata*, the templates and *gestalten* of perception that we build up in gaining familiarity with any field.[24] All of *Guide to Kulchur*, indeed, is an exposition on schemata that become habitual and effortless, 'part of my total disposition'. The implication is that we cannot read at all without acquiring a usable set of verbal schemata; this would be consonant with the rationale behind the curricula of *How to Read* and similar pieces. But it relates also to the *Cantos*, which proposes so many new and heuristic schemata that it is still not fully assimilated as 'readable'.

111

In Pound's epistemology, knowledge comes only through 'phalanxes of particulars' or 'a rain of factual atoms': details related to each other only in the sense that components of an ideogram are. They cannot, by definition, be homogeneous or unified or syllogistic in the usual sense. Every literary quality that Pound admired, from the juxtaposition of images in *haiku* or Chinese poetry to the swift sequences of detail in Joyce or Flaubert, has its great exemplar in this particularist and farraginous notion of the epic. The 'prose tradition' and the exotic arts of Li Po or Arnaut Daniel or Catullus depend alike on verbal schemata that preserve the 'real knowledge' of the time, through what Pound called elsewhere 'hyperscientific precision'.[25] All these qualities recapitulate in their own ways Homeric accuracies, and are inherent in true epics; and the poet who deals in these structures of knowledge can avoid the dilemmas of speaking solely as himself. When Keats proposed the selflessness that Hazlitt taught him to revere in Shakespeare as an escape from the 'Wordsworthian or egotistical sublime', he pointed the way to many devices for the evasion of these dilemmas, such as the dramatic monologue and Pound's experimentation with *personae*.[26] But Pound was never satisfied with quasi-dramatic developments or any solutions that went no further than ventriloquistic modulation of voice. He needed a poetics that would do away with the subordinating single voice altogether, along with its factitious unities. Here is where he was able to turn to account the potentialities for a poetics of loss which he had inherited.

Pound's interest in the theme of loss is well known. Every serious student of his knows this representative passage from the Cavalcanti essay:

> We appear to have lost the radiant world where one thought cuts through another with clean edge, a world of moving energies . . . magnetisms that take form, that are seen, or that border the visible, the matter of Dante's *paradiso*, the glass under water, the form that seems a form seen in a mirror. . . . For the modern scientist energy has no borders, it is a shapeless 'mass' of force; even his capacity to differentiate it to a degree never dreamed by the ancients has not led him to think of its shape or even its loci.[27]

Is this a nostalgic yearning, a pipedream for time-travel?

Hardly: Pound credits the modern scientist with amazing powers, but laments the wilful ignorance that prevents him from making good use of them. He is concerned that the present may mutilate itself through sheer loss of memory; he has no urge to flee modern vulgarities for capsulized ancient utopias, but is angry at the spectacle of the present depriving itself of its own sources. For the *rêveur* with his mind on the past, the man who according to Wyndham Lewis loved the dead as he never loved anything living, coexisted with the poet whose motto was MAKE IT NEW. Pound repudiated antiquarian interpretations of the *Cantos*, since the poem's aim was to conjoin past and present as in a 'painting with distance in background'. He believed that 'the modern world has lost a kind of contact with and love for the classics which it had, not only in the eighteenth century and in the Renaissance (part snobism), but throughout the Middle Ages, when in one sense it knew much less. And life is impoverished thereby'.[28] Most simply put: the past was always a source of renewal for Pound: hence his conviction that the poem, though a slice through layers of past culture, would speak directly to our condition, specifically against our plagues of warmongering and usury. History was not, for him, a repository of dead facts, but a diagram of potent vectors. His belief in the past was less idealist, less attracted to the 'days that are no more' or 'the light that never was, on sea or land' than were those of some contemporaries.

D. S. Carne-Ross has brilliantly argued a similar point, in holding that Pound at Pisa was fortified by a deep religious belief in the pagan gods: 'Persephone is in that thrusting tip' of the green shoot in spring, and the most recondite of the mysteries can be penetrated if we attend to the world.

What these cantos show is that Pound won through because he felt himself sustained by the powers he had always believed in. He himself went down into the unending labyrinth of the souterrain, a dark night of the soul that left no room for 'poetry', for makebelieve. And he came up again, to look on the eternal elements and a nature once again brilliant with divinity. The army gave him a patch of ground to lie on and he found Demeter there and celebrated the marriage of Heaven and

Earth. It must be the most astounding breach of military discipline since Coleridge joined the 15th Dragoons.[29]

Pound's beliefs were too literal to be really nostalgic; they lack the Platonism that enervates Romantic equations of myth with truth. Pound is not content to wish he could see old Triton blow his wreathéd horn. If for him the gods have not returned, it is because they never left us. A visionary he is, certainly, but not an escapist nor an antiquarian; he has no need to turn away from the grittiest details of quotidian life, for it is in them that the mysteries are manifest. One must, as he said of Ford Maxod Ford, see 'the Venus immortal crossing the tram-tracks'.[30] The gods are not pleasing wraiths but live incarnations.

To take a poetics of loss beyond nostalgia, one does not make fanciful romances out of the shards of culture. On the contrary, one must proclaim and underline loss: for where we can discern and register a loss we frame the possibility for recovery. More important still, Pound was able to visualize loss as a positive means of revelation, with the help of some very important metaphoric schemata. First among these is what I call, in Finnegans Wakish, the manuscrap. Surely one of the most felicitous gestures in all Pound criticism is Hugh Kenner's exposition on 'The Muse in Tatters' in *The Pound Era*, where he demonstrates the rich potentiality that contemplation of fragments of ancient papyrus and parchment had for Pound's thought.[31] His whole sense of language, of the nature of words and of their possibilities in new combinations drawing on unconventional, creative syntactic relation, is a fruit of his attention to the remnants of Sappho and others. Instead of concocting elaborate fantasias to serve as contexts for the fragmentary words and phrases, Pound sought to see them unadorned, as the radiant 'gists and piths' of his probes into the layers of culture. Their fragmentary condition allows us to see them with a new clarity, just as the archaeologist sees the remains of ancient worlds in a defamiliarized way, deducing far more from them than the inhabitants of the lost culture ever could. What we throw out as garbage may be of consuming interest to future archaeologists (or even to the C.I.A. and K.G.B.); such are the powers of concentrated attention. A

114

remnant of bone may allow a forensic pathologist to convict a murderer, or a palaeontologist to establish a link in an evolutionary hypothesis; a voice may leave a traceable print as unique as that of a finger; everywhere we and our artifacts leave traces of significant patterns we have no awareness of, but to see them we must isolate them, magnify patterns of difference, make them into graphic representations.

When Pound does reconstruct a context, as for Sigismondo's letters, he is not recuperating a satisfyingly Romantic fullness of meaning in the way of the historical romance; what he provides is a flash of demotic manifestation, scraps of lost conversation. In the Malatesta Cantos, the abrupt contrasts between soldiers' gossip and 'bear's-greased latinity' do not enable us to fantasize ourselves as Sigismondo or his soldiers, but rather function as twirls of the dial of an imaginary radio that can tune in to history: and this is the principle of the other Cantos too, though the demotics range from vulgar to stately, and even can be purely imaginary, as in the English Chinese of the Seven Lakes Canto. The multiple and fragmentary nature of the voices, never those of wholly recuperated and rounded 'characters', inevitably suggests the radio model: one could even say that Pound has put in a certain amount of squawking.[32] Sooner or later all the voices fade, leaving us to make what we can of their scraps of locutions.

If we can see loss as an erosion or erasure, we can see its heuristic possibilities: and manuscraps enable us to isolate the revelatory tropes, the 'luminous details' of the past, freed from their obscuring burden of conventional contexts and connections. Elsewhere I have asserted that Pound writes with an eraser; if one's epic is a palimpsest (which he began to call the poem towards its end) it can be fully manifest only if erased.[33] In the earlier statement I had in mind Pound's obsessive concentration, his manic drive to eliminate all superfluity and redundancy, to boil all down: *dichten* = *condensare*. For a man who believed that 'great literature is simply language charged with meaning to the utmost possible degree', who strove for 'maximum efficiency of expression', and resolved 'to use absolutely no word that does not contribute to the presentation', whose admiration for Ford Madox Ford and the prose tradition was awakened by trying to take notes on a Ford passage and finding that it couldn't be done in fewer words than the passage contained, writing with ruthless condensation and concentration was an obvious technique.[34] But the model of the manuscrap gave a whole new dimension, a revelatory capacity, to the process. The *usure* of time has worn away many fascinating heirlooms of language, but in doing so it has raised others to prominence, as of bas-relief; the loss itself can free us from our standardized, preconceived notions about them. As Kenner skilfully shows, if one does to a page of Pound or Marianne Moore what time has done to Sappho, one gets a display of distinctive features of each poet's style; one sees why neither page could be by Williams. And the radio figure, the sense of snatches of conversations, keeps us from indulging in nostalgic fantasies of plenitude: when the voices are gone, they are gone, and we stick to what we have heard instead of imaginary completions. So erasure may make us aware of our own 'desensitization', and show us magnified saliencies, unapprehended relations, a host of potentialities that might otherwise remain smothered. Massimo Bacigalupo touches on a similar principle in discussing Pound's theory and practice of translation: it 'discloses layers of meaning that have been concealed by the "closed" readings of which the text has been the object.'[35] Moreover it is the essence of the ideogrammic method to display things out of their normal contexts, as if they were found objects; it creates patterns of meaning not limited to the content of the objects but arising from the relationships among them: meanings not in them but between them, as it were, relationalist not substantialist. 'Relations are more real and more important than the things which they relate', wrote Ernest Fenollosa.[36] The continuity of Pound's poetics from Imagist days onwards is the drive to reveal unseen relations, to display the lines of force in the material. This is facilitated by erosion as another form of concentration. A canto is then a kind of anatomy, a display mechanism that works not like a diorama, or restoration or imagined fullness, but like a diagram suggesting skeletal, paradigmatic lines of force by juxtaposition. In some ways it works by what the computer scientists call 'image enchancement'. Loss and erasure magnify and etch discontinuities, dissociations, and differences in general, thus sharpening the resolution.

116

This metaphor of the manuscrap is not merely my extension of Kenner's insights. In the drafts, the provisional title for what is now Canto 1 was 'Meaning of Odyssey to the Renaissance'. Fortunately Pound eliminated all such flatfooted phrases as blatant and constricting, but its occurrence serves to underline the process I have been reconstructing. Evidently Pound believed that this scrap of the Odyssey was a node of meanings that filiated and ramified throughout the whole of the *translatio studii* which is his basic subject. Translated into an English that recapitulates its own derivation from an Anglo-Saxon world of *comitatus* ethics (which in turn typologically rhymes with the samurai loyalties of the *Odyssey*), the chunk of Andreas Divus's 'crib' displays several aspects of the cultural transformation we call the Renaissance. A scrap of text does duty for a world in change. By the time of the Pisan Cantos, Pound has given up the naïve hope that a 'civilization' or even a 'Risorgimento' could be implicated in his poem, but scraps of text now living only in his memory stand for the lines of force that enable him to survive amid the fragments of the broken ant-hill of Europe. These cantos are shards upon shards, embodying the poetics of loss in a form more poignant than any before. Indeed, buried within these cantos is the anatomy of a pastoral elegy, built on the contrast of the green world of nature, the wasp, the mint, the lizard, etc., with the red-and-white world of man's wars and destructions that recall York and Lancaster.

Of course no one, certainly not Pound, would maintain that his poetics come to fruition everywhere. Even if it was geriatric depression that caused him to dismiss the *Cantos* in 1968 as a 'botch', we know that he had felt misgivings all along, and by 1938 was defining the poem's defects as those 'inherent in a record of struggle'.[37] For many reasons, Pound could never be Homer, nor could he present a version of history that does not seem highly arbitrary when compared with the 'matter of Troy'. History means something different now, and an author has a kind of adversary role to his culture (which Pound deeply enjoyed, though it cost him many years of incarceration) that is nearer the role of prophet than that of bard. These and other irreconcilable necessities prevented Pound's project from being wholly integrated.

What Carne-Ross calls 'slag' does disfigure the poem to some extent, though it is still necessary for an apprehension of the whole. Even the most discriminating archaeologist turns up large amounts of unsightly material, and part of Pound's strategy was not to refine it excessively, to include the dross. As I have indicated, a closed, coherent thematic unity was out of the question in any case. A canto is not so much a part of a poem with a running thread as it is a basic poetic unit on which transforms are made, over and over. In assessing the mixed results we might use the strategy of defining poets by what they have risked, the ways in which they chose to fail if they do so. Wordsworth ran the risks of prosaicism, dullness, repetitive- ness, and occasionally outright silliness. Pound's risks are equally obvious: incoherence and fragmentation due to hetero- geneity, obscurity due to allusiveness (Basil Bunting's com- plaint), impenetrability due to concentration and intolerance of redundancy, 'slag' due to farraginous inclusiveness. These risks were heightened by some personal characteristics, especially a combination of irritability and reticence, as we see in many opaque passages. Whether these outweigh the significant accomplishments is not a matter for summary judgement; other times than ours will render it. We have not yet learned all the schemata of the *Cantos* any more than we have learned those of *Finnegans Wake*, though there have been admirable feats of individual attention. But the histories of music and of art are dotted with works once thought 'unplayable' or offensive, 'a pot of paint flung in the public's face'; many have long since been domesticated. Perhaps it may be so with this poem; perhaps not. For many reasons it seems worthwhile to me to make the effort to assimilate all those schemata, and to continue to trace around the outlines of the blanks in the writing. For although the poem is neither acceptable nor dismissible as a 'monu- mental failure', it transcends the question of its own readability. Like the other great Modernist texts it raises nothing less than our most pressing questions: how does meaning mean? What does representation represent? And what is to be the role of literature in the intense studies of language that must address these questions? Many further inquiries follow from these: why is modern poetry much more than a field of interest for those who 'like poetry'? As Marianne Moore's line indicates, we must embrace our very devaluation of poetry in order to value it fully;

118

what is it about the specific conditions of Western culture, especially in its recent history, that makes this necessary and possible, and that makes all these questions so urgent?

NOTES

1. *The Cantos of Ezra Pound* (New York: New Directions, 1972), Canto 82, p. 526 (hereinafter cited as 82/526).
2. 'The Serious Artist', in *Literary Essays of Ezra Pound*, ed. T. S. Eliot (Norfolk, Conn.: New Directions, 1954), p. 49.
3. Gerald Graff, 'Deconstruction as Dogma', *Georgia Review* XXXIV, 2 (Summer 1980), 407.
4. Leslie Fiedler, 'Some Notes on F. Scott Fitzgerald', in *An End to Innocence* (Boston: Beacon, 1955), p. 175.
5. Hugh Kenner, *A Homemade World: The American Modernist Writers* (New York: Knopf, 1975), pp. 77–85, 93–5; cf. his *The Pound Era* (Berkeley and Los Angeles: University of California Press, 1971), p. 26.
6. *Childe Harold's Pilgrimage* III, cxiv.
7. Donald Davie, *Articulate Energy: An Enquiry into the Syntax of English Poetry* (New York: Harcourt, Brace, 1958), pp. 1–5.
8. Ernst Cassirer, *Language and Myth*, trans. Susanne K. Langer (New York: Harper, 1946), p. 7.
9. *The Waste Land*, 415; cf. Eliot's note to 412.
10. 'Hell', *Literary Essays*, p. 205.
11. 'Notes on Elizabethan Classicists', *Literary Essays*, p. 227.
12. 'Poetry', 1.
13. *Speculations*, ed. Herbert Read (New York: Harcourt, 1924), p. 118.
14. Frank Kermode, *Romantic Image* (London: Routledge, 1961).
15. 'A Retrospect', *Literary Essays*, p. 7. First published as 'A Few Dont's' in *Poetry*, 1913. The information about his ambitions at 15 comes from 'How I Began', first printed in *T.P.'s Weekly* in 1913, also available in *Ezra Pound: Perspectives*, ed. Noel Stock (Chicago: Regnery, 1975), p. [1].
16. 99/708. For the *paideuma*, see *Guide to Kulchur* (Norfolk, Conn.: New Directions, n.d.), pp. 57–8.
17. *ABC of Reading* (New York: New Directions, 1960), p. 43.
18. Ibid., p. 59.
19. *The Letters of Ezra Pound*, ed. D. D. Paige (New York: Harcourt, 1950), p. 274.
20. Surette, *A Light from Eleusis: A Study of Ezra Pound's Cantos* (Oxford: Clarendon Press, 1979), p. 8. For Williams and 'formlessness', see *Literary Essays*, p. 394; cf. pp. 150–55, 180, etc.; also see *ABC of Reading*, p. 92, and my essay 'Pound's Book of Cross-Cuts', *Genre* XI, 4 (Winter 1978), 512.
21. *Writers at Work: The Paris Review Interviews, Second Series* (New York: Viking, 1963), p. 38: see Hall's memoir of how this interview was transcribed in

119

his *Remembering Poets: Reminiscences and Opinions* (New York: Harper, 1977), pp. 134--39.
22. *ABC of Reading*, pp. 29, 44.
23. *Guide to Kulchur*, p. 28.
24. Gombrich, *Art and Illusion: A Study in the Psychology of Pictorial Representation* (Princeton, N.J.: Princeton University Press, 1960): see index s.v. 'schema'.
25. *The Spirit of Romance* (Norfolk, Conn.: New Directions, n.d.), p. 87.
26. John Keats, *Complete Poems and Selected Letters*, ed. C. D. Thorpe (New York: Odyssey, 1935), p. 576 (letter of 27 October 1818, to Richard Woodhouse). Cf. Hazlitt's *Lectures on English Poets*, 'On Shakspear and Milton'.
27. *Literary Essays*, p. 154.
28. *Letters*, pp. 239 and 263.
29. D. S. Carne-Ross, *Instaurations: Essays In and Out of Literature, Pindar to Pound* (Berkeley: University of California Press, 1979), pp. 212–13.
30. From Pound's obituary of Ford (Hueffer) in *Nineteenth Century and After*, CXXVI (1939), 179.
31. *The Pound Era*, pp. 54–75. Cf. pp. 5–6, 51, etc.
32. Pound's remarks on radio suggest that he saw it as a potent, not always beneficent, force. Cf. *Letters*, pp. 342–43, where in the course of decrying its potential for abuse he remarks 'I anticipated the damn thing in first third of *Cantos*. . . .'
33. 'Wisdom Past Metaphor: Another View of Pound, Fenollosa, and Objective Verse', *Paideuma* 5, 1 (Spring/Summer 1976), 24.
34. See *Literary Essays*, pp. 3, 23, 56; *ABC of Reading*, pp. 36, 92; and the obituary cited in note 30.
35. Bacigalupo, *The Forméd Trace: The Later Poetry of Ezra Pound* (New York: Columbia University Press, 1980), p. 183.
36. Fenollosa, *The Chinese Written Character* (Square Dollar, n.d.), p. 72.
37. *Guide to Kulchur*, p. 135.

5

Pound, Merleau-Ponty and the Phenomenology of Poetry

by ERIC MOTTRAM

Plus the luminous eye—Canto 3

Both Pound and Merleau-Ponty expound the exhilaration and the anguish of participating in the totality as their writing articulates its points of control, both political and philosophical—and in Pound's case poetic—towards what is taken to be the writer's responsibility in the twentieth century: his active commitment in its social determinations. Sartre's 1961 memorial essay for his colleague and friend (in *Situations IV,* Paris, 1964, and *Situations,* trans. Benita Eisler, New York, 1966) begins with childhood memory—a position singularly absent in most of Pound's work: 'Our capacity for happiness is dependent upon a certain equilibrium between what we refuse and concede to our childhood.' Childhood is a remembered totality whose 'style of life' the child could not question or enquire into. It is ritual, a spontaneity within 'superintended liberty', a naïvety whose structure—what happened—we partly discover lately when we know we have entered history and our life as an 'unravelling mesh' to which we bring cognition, and begin to ask: 'What can be the values of a human

121

thought about man, since it is man himself who both makes the judgement and vouches for it?' This is a primary point for cogitation in Merleau-Ponty, and in the *Cantos* this essentially phenomenological position appears increasingly as it moves towards Canto 90 where the neoplatonic doctrine of signatures is placed within procedures of perception and conception: 'From the colour the nature/ & by the nature the sign!' But 'Near Perigord' in 1915 already concerns ways of inheriting the past actively—part of that *virtù* which activates the *Cantos*—and 'Provincia Deserta', also dating from 1915, draws attention to the conceptual mind which needs to organize discoveries of motive and action in the past.

For the two French philosophers, the primary pressures of the 1940s, when their attitudes were shaping firmly, the Resistance offered a proper political action. For Pound, the continuations of medieval and Renaissance wars had become the twentieth-century conflict between Capitalism, Fascism and Communism, the three major totalitarian political systems. These men enquired, that is, into the bases of recurrent and fundamental struggle in the West. The Frenchmen experienced the totality of comradeship emerging from combat against the Occupation under Nazism and its collaborators, the French ruling classes. But that friendship included a common recognition of 'key words' and their ambiguity: *phenomenology* and *existence*. The ambiguity lay with the very nature of perception, and action which preoccupied Merleau-Ponty until his death in 1961, but which is also a main energizing impulse in the *Cantos* whose final stages appeared in 1968. For Merleau-Ponty, perception was *one* of the beginnings through which 'our body is surrendered to the world and the world to our body. It is both hinge and anchorage' (the words are Sartre's). But the world is also history. The dynamic interchange of perception and history is the object of Merleau-Ponty's *Humanism and Terror* (1947). Both the French philosopher and Pound enquire continually into how to confront history and nature as they simultaneously envelop us and are under our control. Sartre's paraphrase reads like a summary of Pound's interior action:

> How can we discover the others within us as our profound truth?
> How can we perceive ourselves within them as the law of their

truth? The question is already asked at the level of perceptive spontaneity and 'intersubjectivity'. It only becomes more urgent and more concrete when we replace the historical agent in the womb of universal flux. Work and anxiety, tools, government, customs, culture—how can we 'insert' the person into all this? And inversely, how can we be extracted from that which never tires of spinning, and which incessantly produces him? Merleau had believed he would live in peace. A war had made him a warrior, and he had made war.

The epic existential sense is enforced in the twentieth century in philosophy and poetry which emerges under the urgencies of contemporary catastrophic life. 'Epic is a poem including history', and the philosophy of Merleau-Ponty and Sartre is necessarily epic.

In Canto 85 Pound meditates on the ideogram of total process, both subjective and objective—that concern with process which infuses Merleau-Ponty, Whitehead, Charles Olson and the post-Olson poets including Robert Kelly and the ethnopoetic figures in *Alcheringa*, New Series Vol. 2, No. 2—a record of the first international symposium of ethno-poetics in 1975:

> But if you will follow this process
> not a lot of signs, but the one sign
>   etcetera
>   plus always   Techne. . . .

Peace within process, for Pound, depended on the benevolent despot's ability to maintain stability, the pivot of the total process. He prefers Yong Tching to Locke or Milton in Canto 61; Mussolini correctly cut back bureaucracy to create stable centralism. But, of course, such views were commonplace in the interwar years; strong leaders were to solve government rather than democracy or socialism. Heroes in the *Cantos* are exactly the heroes of the masses and their rulers—kings, emperors and the quasi-republican replicas. Divine right had to be transferred to 'heroic vitalism'. Pound's typical monism is a longing for subsumption in the One. His yearning for peace, within his warrior combativeness and constant intervention, is a ground base in the *Cantos*. Hugh Kenner put it accurately in an essay in *Gnomon* (New York, 1958): 'From the very beginning, Pound's work has been polarized by two implicit themes: the hero in rebellious exile, and the emergence of order from chaos.' His discovery of Adams' *Law of Civilization and Decay* in the 1940s, with its structuring of history by cycle from an economic point of view, confirmed his more intuitive reading of rise and fall in cultures. The *Cantos* is an eminently practical work.

Pound's particularity of information continuously worked towards a poem demonstrating a refusal of what Merleau-Ponty also rejected as 'high altitude thinking' (and both Rilke and Wittgenstein show a repeated understanding of the necessity to criticize any kind of supervisory vision in which the totalitarian authority is rooted), particularly that version which reduces 'hinge and anchorage' to personal anarchism, a kind of enfeebling relativism. Clearly Pound found it hard to reconcile despotism with a refusal of what Wittgenstein termed the urge to the *übersichlich* stance. But dogmatic doctrine is relegated in both men, whatever their engagement in political action, Left or Right. Sartre quotes Merleau-Ponty:

> Every historical undertaking has something of an adventure about it, as it is never guaranteed by any absolutely rational structure of things. It always involves a utilization of chance, one must always be cunning with things (and with people), since we must bring forth an order not inherent in them.

From doctrine arises 'the possibility of an immense compromise, of a corruption of History'. For both Merleau-Ponty and Pound, Christianity presented itself as a unity, a totality, which could not fulfil its promise of integration, neither transcendentally nor as a daily contingency here and now. Pound's 'Religio or, The Child's Guide to Knowledge' (1918) is an explicit catechism which concludes that 'a god is an eternal state of mind' manifest 'when the states of mind take form'. Gods appear 'formed and formlessly' to 'the sense of vision' and to 'the sense of knowledge' respectively. The opening of Canto 91 presents such a vision and knowledge, the elements of Pound's highly mobile phenomenology, in an image of perception and form which is strongly constant throughout the *Cantos*. First, a piece of Provencal song which, roughly translated, provides a phenomenological opening chord: 'with the

sweetness which comes into my heart' (c.f. *Paideuma* 1.2 and
11.2); and then:

> that the body of light come forth
> > from the body of fire
> And that your eyes come to the surface
> > from the deep wherein they were sunken

This characteristic account of the 'forma' can be related to a
passage in *Guide to Kulchur* (London, 1952, p. 152) which com-
bines politics and nature the hand that holds the magnetic
tool and makes the politician's bust is the agent of the total
techne:

> The *forma*, the immortal *concetto*, the dynamic form which is like
> the rose pattern driven into the dead iron-filings by the magnet,
> not by material contact with the magnet itself, but separate
> from the magnet. Cut off by the layer of glass, the dust and the
> filings rise and spring into order. Thus the *forma*, the concept
> rises from death
> > The bust outlasts the throne
> > The coin Tiberius

This in turn can be related to a statement in the *Paris Review*
interview: 'The thrones in the *Cantos* are an attempt to move
out from egoism and establish some definition of an order
possible or at any rate conceivable on earth.' In the *Guide to
Kulchur* passage, the *forma/techne* hold is further related to
Jannequin's 'intervals, his melodic conjunctions', Yeats's 'I
made it out of a mouthful of air', and, broadly, to Arnaut
Daniel and to 'god knows what "hidden antiquity"'. These
elements are reasonably specific where the Canto 91 passage is
alchemic, concerning the *anima* emerging from purification,
parallel to the visionary sight of the raised statue, its eyes
meeting the poet's eyes. As *Psychology and Alchemy* (London,
1953, p. 48, note 1) suggests: 'The sea is a favourite place for
the birth of visions (i.e. invasions by unconscious contents).'
When Pound writes in 'Cavalcanti' (1910–31—*Make It New*,
1934; *Literary Essays*, London, 1954, p. 152) 'the god is in the
stone' as a way of presenting the 'force' for creation, it amplifies
his sense of relationship between vision and *forma*. But in fact
he adds a passage which checks any tendency to separate
unconscious latent image from the created work (he is nearer

Breton's sense of the intimacy of form and unconscious energies):

> The force is arrested, but there is never any question about its latency, about the force being the essential, and the rest 'accidental' in the philosophical sense. The shape occurs.

That is, it occurs phenomenologically. At the end of Canto 74 the *forma/techne* process is again given as the steel rose, prior to a citation of Francesco da Milano, who also appears in the *Guide to Kulchur* passage:

> nec accidens est   but an element
> in the mind's make-up
> est agens and functions   dust to a fountain pan otherwise

The electromagnetic imagery dramatizes the delicacy of the action—'so light is the urging'—in the ordering. The Dante supports here—from *Paradiso* 30 and 31—are not taken up within Christianity, but remain examples of the creative mind in action:

> The whole is fashioned from a radiance
> Shone from above the Primum Mobile
> Which draws vitality and virtue hence. . . .
> So now displayed before me as a rose
> Of snow-white purity, the sacred host
> I saw, whom with his blood Christ made his spouse.

Dante was exiled from the order of his city-state, but not from the order of Christianity, however much heresy the *Divina Commedia* may contain. Both Merleau-Ponty and Pound lived in exile from desired order but would not approach order from dogma, whether Communism or Fascism; Marxism under continual revision for Merleau-Ponty, and for Pound, the American Constitution, even as a guide to check the authoritarianism of Fascism, to judge from his Rome broadcasts, were the limits of contemporary acceptable ideological order. Both men responded to ideological conflict from a phenomenological attitude profoundly within their sensibilities rather than something adopted from outside purely. Both were reluctant to end adventure in dogma, still needing to be active rather than dogmatically philosophic and aesthetic. Order and basis

126

obsessed them in a time of chaos and rigid doctrine. But, as Sartre writes in the memoir, 'we can't go backwards, the gesture cannot be reclaimed, the gentle contingency of birth is changed, by its very irreversibility, into destiny.' We are threatened with a myth of degradation following some supposed Golden Age, and both Merleau-Ponty and Pound resisted such critical criteria against the present. The former asked, in the year Pound was arrested near Genoa, in Spring 1945, 'whether the human venture would founder in barbarism, or whether it would be vindicated by socialism'. Pound under arrest said: 'If a man isn't willing to take some risk for his opinions, either his opinions are no good, or he's no good' (*A Casebook on Ezra Pound*, New York, 1959, p. 5).

Merleau-Ponty's disillusion with the possibilities of Communist socialism in the 1950s turned him towards the bases of his thinking and allegiance. He searched for the nature of 'primordial historicity' (or the 'adventure' of survival and extinction between existence and death) and 'the fundamental'. In the essay 'From Mauss to Lévi-Strauss' (*Signes*, Paris, 1960; *Signs*, trans. Richard C. McCleary, Northwestern University Press, 1964) he projects his thinking through the discourse of anthropology, since comparative studies of societies is a primary phenomenological method by which to ascertain bases. Pound's method counterpointed—explicitly given as a pleasure of the mind in Canto 79—examples of social excellence drawn from European, Chinese, African, as well as American cultures. His desire for archetypes is part of his search for the meaning of a regenerative singular and particular, the One. The failure of America to be truly the New World, the Earthly Paradise haunts him far more than the failure of Mussolini's 'Roma'. Social anthropology with Lévi-Strauss becomes a study of totalities called structures—'the configurations of the perceptual field, whose wholes are articulated by certain lines of force and giving every phenomenon its local value'—'the interacting totality of these systems' rather than the study of 'crystallized ideas'—a search for elementary kinship, exchange and balance, 'a formal infrastructure' at the base of social systems, a set of invariants in a metastructure—and so forth, using Merleau-Ponty's formulations. The *Cantos'* 'periplum' is a parallel adventure for order in what Pound called 'an age of

127

experiment'. His Hell is part of the current world as it inherits the past fatally. His ideal cities are forms of stability or perfect community—Dioce, Roma, the Earthly Paradise.

During the past two decades one group of American poets has extended these concerns into a poetry actively impregnated with anthropology—three examples may suffice here: Jerome Rothenberg's work towards *Technicians of the Sacred* in 1968, the work of Nathaniel Tarn, himself an anthropologist, exemplified in 'The Heraldic Vision: Some Cognitive Models for Ethno-poetics' (Alcheringa, op. cit.), and the kind of poetry Robert Kelly produces in *The Loom* (1975). The relationship with Merleau-Ponty can be established through his realization that we are not, in research, concerned with 'primitive societies' as simple, and certainly not as regressive, models, but as ethno-logical examples of the human praxis:

> We become ethnologists of our own society if we set ourselves at a distance from it. For a few dozen years, since American society has become less sure of itself, it has given ethnologists access to governmental and military agencies.

The resultant problem is not only local to ethnopoetics, or to Merleau-Ponty and Pound, but concerns contemporary struc-turalist semiology, and the problem is a phenomenological one:

> To want to understand myth as a proposition, in terms of what it says, is to apply our own grammar and vocabulary to a foreign language.

So that Freudianism is 'no longer an interpretation of the Oedipus myth but one of its variants'. And Merleau-Ponty cites an observation by the physicist Niels Bohr:

> The traditional differences (between human cultures) . . . in many respects resemble the different and equivalent ways in which physical experience may be described.

That is, the necessity of complementarity is complemented by the erasure of 'the frontiers between cultures'. Merleau-Ponty's immediate concern here is clear from a passage which Sartre quotes in his memorial essay:

> What interests the philosopher in anthropology is just that it

128

takes man as he is, in his actual situation of life and under-standing. The philosopher it interests is not the one who wants to explain or construct the world, but the one who seeks to deepen our insertion in being.

This is the philosophical and anthropological direction of the *Cantos*, except that, unlike Merleau-Ponty, Pound had to bring himself to relinquish a lifelong belief that one system of economics in the hands of one kind of powerful leader would solve society. But it still has to be pointed out that he shared that belief with Eliot, Shaw, Yeats, and the Wyndham Lewis of *The Art of Being Ruled* (1926) and *Hitler* (1931), as against the investigative anarchisms of Brecht, Orwell and Henry Miller. Both Pound and Merleau-Ponty disdain package truths and opt for that penetration into the flow of existential being which Sartre calls 'meditation . . . as endlessly sustained tension between existence and being'. In fact, this formulation could be applied to a good deal of the direction of the American long poem during the past fifty years, through to Enslin's *Synthesis* in 1975.

But this kind of exploration necessitates a description of the unconscious or that which is 'below' history, the sign or the transcendence—there are various spatial terms for it. As Robert Duncan observes in his 1974 interview in *Unmuzzled Ox* (Vol. IV, No. 2, 1976):

> We're constantly imagining what's in the unconscious. But we have no access to it. By the time it appears to us in dreams, it's consciousness. If we can see it, it's conscious.

This is one of the reasons why 'eyes' and 'seeing' become insistent in the *Cantos'* meditations on perception, and in both Zukofsky's *Bottom: On Shakespeare* (1963) and in Olson's *Maximus Poems* (1950–70). 'Consciousness is created', Duncan observes—'Poetics means making something up.' Concern for this interfacial region—the place of *forma/techne*—probably urged Pound to those examinations of the psyche which Martin Kayman explores in his doctoral thesis *Ezra Pound and the Phantasy of Science* (unpublished, York, 1978)—that is, those areas of irrationalism and the analysis of perception in which the image becomes a psychological concept. Dr. Kayman establishes the effect of Bernard Hart's *The Psychology of Insanity*

(Cambridge, 1912) on Pound's ideas of the 'complex', which for Hart meant 'a form of latent energy provoked by experience, operating in memory', and 'triggered by a "stimulus"', or 'a system of emotionally toned ideas'. Complexes are 'causes which determine the behaviour of the conscious stream, and the action which they exert upon consciousness may be regarded as the psychological analogue of the conception of "force" in physics.' It is such ideas that secure, in the *Cantos*, the use of the rose of filings and, in Canto 76, the notion of *atasal*.

Where Merleau-Ponty works so much like Pound, and in ways like other American epic poets of this century, emerges particularly from his sense of the 'mobile of history' in which— the words are again Sartre's—'contradictory truths never fight one another', and which is 'the living sign of fundamental ambiguity'. In dialectical terms, he accepts thesis and antithesis but not synthesis, and prefers the action of a spiral which neither concludes nor builds. The *Cantos*, too, cohere in such a 'mobile', and Pound's last sense of partial incoherence seems to have been forced on him by reactionary critics as much as from his own mistaken belief that the poem ought to have led to some tightening conclusiveness, some synthetic prophecy of Earthly Paradise, exactly that kind of nostalgia from which Merleau-Ponty sought to release himself, in his case, from an infantilism generated in part from a lush paradisal childhood.

The totality of the spiral, unlike that of the circle—the enclosure which dominates so much American writing at least since Emerson's 'Circles' essay—can predict process in Whitehead's sense (and Merleau-Ponty had read Whitehead). What the French philosopher requires is a process of motion and intention which 'changes the positive notation of "immediate data" into a dialectic of time and the intuition of essences into a phenomenology of genesis'. So that the definition of being may include process in time as defined in the *Parmenides*: 'beyond the empirical multiplicity of existent things and as a matter of principle intended through them, because separated from them it would be only lightning flash or darkness' ('Everywhere and Nowhere', *Signs*, p. 156). What then is 'the present moment' in philosophical research, or standpoint for distancing and examination? He avoids 'dialectic' and 'contradiction' in order to be able to say: 'Incarnation and the other are the labyrinth of reflection and sensibility for our contemporaries.' He seems not to have used that kind of definition of event and process available, for instance, to Olson from Whitehead's *Process and Reality*—used, to take one example, in 'A Later Note on Letter 15'—1962—in *Maximus Poems IV, V, VI*, which relates also to Buckminster Fuller's sense of self as verb or motion. Olson writes of Whitehead's 'getting the universe in', as against 'man alone', or history as 'a verb, to find out for yourself:/ 'istorin, which makes anyone's acts a finding out for him or her/ self':

> that no event
> is not penetrated, in intersection or collision with, an eternal
> event

The relevant passage in *Process and Reality* (New York, 1969, p. 26) speaks of 'eternal events' as 'pure potentials for the specific determination of fact' or 'forms of definiteness'—which is like Pound's concept of process in *forma*. 'Nature', for Merleau-Ponty, is a 'decidedly universal' world of encounters, rather than Sartre's 'psycho-chemical perceptions'. But he once spoke of possibly writing a piece emerging from Whitehead's sentence 'Nature is in tatters'. In 'Eye and Mind' ('L'oeil et l'esprit', ed. James M. Edie, *The Primacy of Perception*, Northwestern University Press, 1964) he enquires into the phenomenology of response to nature, through an examination of painting, an enquiry which, for those interested in poetry, frequently parallels the phenomenological notations in Marianne Moore's work, especially in that technique which makes an adventurous encounter out of a mountain in 'The Octopus', by placing multiple information, natural and man-made, at the disposal of what Pound terms the *concetto*, the emergent form of the phenomenological event. Moore's poem holds the mountain as a way into existence and being, experienced together and verbally articulated. And in her poem 'Virginia Britannica' the cultural log is the adventure basis, a work to place with Olson's Gloucester logs and Paul Metcalf's informational processes in our understanding of Americans' obsession with ordering multiple intersecting events.

For Merleau-Ponty, Cézanne's mountain, Mont Ste.-Victoire, is a similar process in painting (*Sense and Nonsense*, Northwestern University Press, 1964, p. 17): 'The picture took on fullness and density, it grew in structure and balance; it came to maturity all at once. "The landscape thinks itself in me", he said, "and I am its consciousness".' Creative perception arises from human complexities—Pound's 'complexes'—of senses and transcendencies. The work of art is a message of interrelationship, 'a process of expressing'—'my gaze wanders in it as in the halos of Being. It is more accurate to say that I see according to it, or with it, than that I *see it*.' The painting is 'autofigurative' among experienced things; it breaks ' "the skin of things" to show how the things become things, how the world becomes the world' (ibid., pp. 18, 164, 181). Pound does cite Cézanne but it is Brancusi who exemplifies, in the *Cantos*, the total process in its creative human form. *Ming*, the total light process, is translated into the Great Crystal in many passages. When it occurs in art—always partly involuntary and partly trained for—it exemplifies, in philosophical terms, the phenomenology of the creative process—as in Canto 85:

> 'One of those days', said Brancusi,
>> 'when I would not have given
> '15 minutes of my time
>> for anything under heaven.'

In Canto 90 'the stone taking form in the air' is part of an ideogram relating Dionysus and his 'great cats', woodlands 'epi chthoni' (around the earth) and their growth principle— 'the trees rise/ and there is a wide sward between them', an altar to the chthonic gods and the Corpus Christi procession, and the resurrection of those energizing forces imaged as gods, as in 'Religio'. These are placed under the aspect of Richard of St. Victor, so that nature, art and love become a single interfacial action, the very process of the phenomenological mobile:

> Trees die & the dream remains
>> Not love but that love flows from it
>> ex animo
>> & cannot ergo delight in itself
>> but only in the love flowing from it.
> UBI AMOR IBI OCULUS EST.

This process of perception, and especially the eye's action, highly resembles Cézanne's eye of perception and its action between nature and art, and the function of the eye in perception in Zukofsky's *Bottom: On Shakespeare*: 'Love, or—if one wishes to explain—the desire to project the mind's peace, is one growth.' But Zukofsky's citation is Spinoza:

> [Love] does not depend upon ourselves, but only on the good and benefit which we observe in the object, and which of course would not have been known to us if we did not wish to love it.

To which Zukofsky adds:

> The basis for written characters, for words, must be the physiological fact of love, arising from sight, accruing to it and the other senses, and entering the intellect. . . . Constantly seeking and ordering relative quantities and qualities of sight, sound, and intellection, the action of words moves also with a craftsman's love. . . . Music implicit in the movement and pitch of the words is accessory to the desired order of sight.

In 'Eye and Mind' Merleau-Ponty also rejects, like Pound and Zukofsky, reductive intellection. Our eye is 'a computer of being', and that phrase may be allowed to reverberate with Andrew Marvell's sense of interface in 'The Garden', where a herb and flower dial, made by 'the skilful Gardner'—the new out of the old, time told in transcience under the eye—is used by the industrious bee who 'computes its time as well as we'. In the Renaissance, art is a science, *techne*, in addition to a *mimesis* (analysed in Agnes Heller's *Renaissance Man*, London, 1978, Chapter 13—'Work, Science, *Techne*, Art'). Sartre beautifully paraphrases Merleau-Ponty's main sense here:

> With these airborne signs [our eyes] will produce an accumulated heap of the heaviest terrestrial mass. Our gaze is no longer content 'to perceive being through the motion of time'. We could say that its present mission was to erect from this motion the ever-absent unity starting from multiplicity. 'Doesn't this unity exist', we will ask. It is and is not, like the dead clothes which haunt the tatters, like Mallarmé's rose, 'absent from each bouquet'. Being is through us who are through it. All of this, to be sure, does not work without the Other. This is how Merleau explains Husserl's difficult affirmation: 'the transcendental conscience is intersubjectivity'. Nothing, he thinks, can see without it being at the same time visible.

The painter is, within this process of perception, 'the privileged artisan, the best witness of this mediated reciprocity':

'The body is caught in the fabric of this world, but the world is made of the stuff of my body'. A new spiral, but more profound than the others because it touches upon the 'labyrinth of incarnation'. Through my flesh, Nature is made flesh. But, inversely, if painting is possible, then the ribs of being which the painter perceives within the thing, and which he fixes on canvas, must designate within himself the 'flexions' of his being. . . . For, as Merleau says, 'culture is advent'. Thus the artist has the sacred function of instituting being within the milieu of men. . . . 'How should we define this milieu where a form burdened with contingency suddenly opens a cycle of the future and governs it with the authority of the established, if not as History?'

This passage illuminates and gives a wide context, and perhaps affords an unexpected continuity within twentieth-century thinking, not only for Pound's metamorphoses of nature and art, but for Hopkins' perception of immanence, Olson's sense of the poet-historian, Ginsberg's perception of divine landscape in 'Siesta in Xbalba', and a good deal more American poetry. As Pound wrote in 1935, 'an epic is a poem including history', but it makes sense to interpret 'history' in Merleau-Ponty's way for the *Cantos* ('An Impact', *Impact,* ed. Noel Stock, New York, 1960, p. 142). Pound's epic initiates and meditates society with the same urgency. In the *Paris Review* interview his relationship with Dante's urgency is clear: 'I was not following the three divisions of the *Divine Comedy* exactly. One can't follow the Dantesquian cosmos in an age of experiment. But I have made the division between people dominated by emotion, people struggling upwards, and those who have some part in the divine vision. . . .' In *The Primacy of Perception* (p. 118), Merleau-Ponty puts his social concerns like this:

Society itself is a structure of structures: how could there be absolutely no relationship between the linguistic system, the economic system, and the kinship system it employs?

His 'labyrinth of incarnation' could be read as a secular version of Hopkins' process in *inscape*, which stems from both Duns Scotus, whom Pound inherited, and from Pater's ideas of form, also deeply influential in the *Cantos:* 'Every moment some form grows perfect in hand or face, some tone on the hills

134

or the seas is choicer than the rest.' Scotus, a Franciscan critic of Aquinas—a factor which appealed to Pound—believed, in the words of Austin Warren ('Instress of Inscape', *Gerard Manley Hopkins*, The Kenyon Critics, London, 1949) that 'the "matter" individuates, while the "form" is generic . . . Scotus insisted that each individual has a distinctive "form" as well: a *haeccitas*, or thisness, as well as a generic *quidditas*, or whatness.' From this structure Hopkins developed—explicitly in his 1871 notebook—'inscape' to mean form, focus, or pattern discerned in the natural world, with a range of meaning 'from sense-perceived pattern to inner form' (John Pick, *A Hopkins Reader*, Oxford, 1953, p. 150). Inscape is 'not mechanically or inertly present, but requires personal action, attention, a seeing and *seeing into*.' Nor is it restricted to nature; it includes men and words. The language of inscape is thus the language of the phenomenological process. (And like Michael McClure in the 1960s, Hopkins was drawn to Anglo-Saxon as a language—he learned it in 1888—that could handle this inscape; see McClure's essay 'Phi Upsilon Kappa', *Kulchur*, Vol. 2, No. 8, Winter 1962.)

But the primacy of perception through inscape for Hopkins was of course Catholic: form is immanence of divine spirit. He wrote in his notebooks: 'God is so deeply present in everything.' The 'felt pattern or design' (Arthur Mizener's phrase in *Gerard Manley Hopkins*, ed. cit., p. 106) is always doctrinally present. Merleau-Ponty did not have this theological limit, and Pound's search for the One to cohere the Work lasted all his life. Olson's Catholicism provided some sense of spiritual continuity throughout the *Maximus Poems*, and Ginsberg increasingly employed Asian religious processes and iconography through to his later allegiance, not to say obedience, to the Tantrist Chögyam Trungpa Rinpoche. And like Merleau-Ponty, Ginsberg at one time found in Cézanne's work exactly the phenomenological interactions between objects and the artistic process he could use in his early poetry (*Writers at Work*, Third Series, London, 1968, pp. 296–97): the sense of 'solid-space objects' and 'enormous spaces' in the canvas, his standing in the actual places from which Cézanne painted Mont Ste.-Victoire, his feeling that Cézanne's transformations related to Plotinian and hermetic changes (which Pound uses in Canto 91 and else-

where and Olson used, partly through *Psychology and Alchemy*, in
Maximus Poems IV, V, VI), the use of geometrical forms to
produce three-dimensionality, and Cézanne's movement from
eye to universality. The relationships to the conclusion of
'Howl', part one, and the methods of the whole poem, are
explicit:

> Apparently he'd refined his optical perception to such a point
> where it's a real contemplation of optical phenomena in an
> almost yogic way, where he's standing there, from a specific
> point studying the optical field, the depth in the optical field,
> looking, actually looking, at his own eyeballs in a sense. The
> attempting to reconstitute the sensation in his own eyeballs. And
> what does he say finally—he said, 'and the *petite sensation* is
> nothing other than *pater omnipotens aeterna deus.* . . .'
> . . . just as Cézanne doesn't use perspective lines to create
> space, but it's a juxtaposition of one colour against another
> colour (that's one element of his space), so, I had the idea,
> perhaps overrefined, that by the unexplainable, unexplained
> nonperspective line, that is, juxtaposition of one *word* against
> another, a *gap* between the two words which the mind would fill
> in with the sensation of existence. . . . The problem is then
> to reach the different parts of the mind, which are existing
> simultaneously, the different associations which are going on
> simultaneously. . . .

Ginsberg then relates Cézanne's record to Blake's seeing *with*
not *through* the eyes, and through that immediacy to the
universe. More obviously, in the poet's work, this process can
be used epically. The work as 'cultural event' in Merleau-
Ponty's sense, draws in History and, with increasing pressure
during the post World War II decades, the physical sense of
participation in the historical process. And that is also the
main source of energetic organization in the *Cantos*, especially
as they reached the period in which Pound believed that after
Mussolini's downfall, his own directed synthesis had even
greater political importance. Of Merleau-Ponty's sense of
history, Sartre writes: 'Reading him at times, it would seem
that being invests man in order to make itself manifest through
him. Didn't Merleau, from time to time, think he perceived
some sort of transcendental mandate "hidden in immanence"
within us?'

Besides the versions of Spirit immanent in Nature which both Hopkins and Pound inherited, it is possible to translate the coherence which this tradition seeks to afford, through physics, as the neuro-chemical structure of existence, the base of being in another mode. Olson's 'Maximus from Dogtown— 11' (1959; *Maximus Poems IV, V, VI*, London, 1968) combines Hesiod's figurative analysis of Creation with universal chemical processes, and Jung's sense of the monogene as both the created and the self-creating principle in Nature with the genetic element in human history, or, in broader summary terms, *Psychology and Alchemy* with *The Secret of the Golden Flower* (cf. 'Ezra Pound, Charles Olson and the Secret of the Golden Flower', Eric Mottram, *Chapman*, Vol. 2, No. 2, Summer 1972). The poem shows Olson's working within those heretic spheres of light, love and spirit which fuse the later *Cantos* especially. In his essay 'Against Wisdom as Such' (*Human Universe*, San Francisco, 1965), he writes:

> I believe that the traditional order of water to fire to light—that is, as of the sectaries, as well as the Ionian physicists, that except a man be born of water and of the spirit, he cannot enter into the kingdom of God—has to be re-taken. Light was the sign of the triumph of love and spirit before electronics. And so we after. So, fire . . .
> Sound
> is fire, As love
> is
>   Light is reductive. Fire isn't. Or—to get rid of any of those false pleasures which paradox and sectaries involve themselves in (are alchemic or gnostic or Lü Tung-Pin, the Guest of, the Cavern) I said to Duncan, 'heat, all but heat, is symbolic, and thus all but heat is reductive.'
>   I asked Duncan if it wasn't his own experience that a poem is the issue of two factors, (1) heat, and (2) time. How plastic, cries Wilhelm, is the thought of 'water' as seed-substance in the *Tai I Chin Hua Tsung Chih*. And time is, in the hands of the poet. For he alone is the one who takes it as the concrete continuum it is, and who practices the bending of it . . .

Duncan himself enters further into the relevance of the phenomenology of contemporary physics. In 'Towards an Open Universe' (ed. Howard Nemerov, *Poets on Poetry*, New

137

York, 1967) he acknowledges Olson's contribution to the processes of 'a physiology of consciousness', 'the totality of the body . . . involved in the act of the poem, so that the organization of words, an invisible body, bears the imprint of the physical man, the finest imprint that we feel in our own bodies as a tonic consonance and dissonance, a being-in-tune, a search for the as yet missing scale. . . . perhaps we recognize as never before in man's history that not only our own personal consciousness but the inner structure of the universe itself has only this immediate event in which to be realized. Atomic physics has brought us to the threshold of such a—I know not whether to call it certainty or doubt.' In the 1974 interview Duncan returns to Olson's observations on his work:

> Charles is talking about conversion of energy in me. He saw a thing in physics and he began to worry: if something is converted, will there be a gain on one side and a loss on the other.

Duncan's sense, years later, is now beyond Olson's theosophical physics, and moves towards another and secular basis:

> Pressed on my world of belief, I would say we must be an event in particles . . . You can't even get interested in language now without finding growing in your imagination the existence of a single human language, something like DNA. There's a huge reservoir of meanings but none of them can be individual.

In Canto 91 the Great Crystal contains water, light and fire as the simultaneous source of primal creative force and its forms, and Pound renews his faith in such an eternal resource: 'That the tone change from elegy'. To this we can add that the electronics of the Earth and *forma* had appeared as early as 'Psychology and Troubadours', printed in *The Spirit of Romance*, whose original version dates from 1912:

> For effect upon the air, upon the soul, etc. the 'lady' in Tuscan poetry has assumed all the properties of the Alchemist's stone . . .
>
> Some mystic or other speaks of the intellect as standing in the same relation to the soul as do the senses to the mind; and beyond a certain border, surely we come to this place where the ecstasy is not a whirl or a madness of the senses, but a glow arising from the exact nature of the perception . . .
>
> Let us consider the body as pure mechanism . . . our kinship to the vital universe, to the tree and the living rock . . . we have

about us the universe of fluid force, and below us the germinal universe of wood alive, of stone alive. Man is—the sensitive physical part of him—a mechanism, for the purpose of our further discussion a mechanism rather like an electric appliance, switches, wires, etc. . . . Chemically speaking he is *ut credo*, a few buckets of water, tied up in a complicated sort of fig-leaf.

Consciousness lies, then, in 'the phantastikon', both reflection and germination in the universe—'as the thought of the tree is in the seed' (Ian Bell's 'The Phantasmagoria of Hugh Selwyn Mauberley', *Paideuma*, Vol. V, No. 3, Winter 1976, concerns Pound's use of 'phantasmagoria', 'phantasmal', 'phantastikon' and 'germinal'). Mind both affects and is transmuted. This chapter of *The Spirit of Romance* works into materials developed poetically forty years later in Cantos 90 and 91, published in 1957. Pound maintained a physical sense of interface with the universe through the phenomenology of perception. But, as this present essay is attempting to show, this is a twentieth-century condition rather than his uniqueness. Its presence in Olson, Ginsberg, Enslin and others is, of course, in part due to his particular formulations. But in Europe, too, contemporaneously, Merleau-Ponty gives this necessity in 'Eye and Mind' (p. 162), again recalling to us Fuller's sense of verbal intersection with nature:

It is by lending his body to the world that the artist changes the world into painting. To understand these transubstantialities we must go back to the working, actual body—not the body as a chunk of space or a bundle of functions but that body which is an intertwining of vision and movement.

I have only to see something to know how to reach it and deal with it, even if I do not know how this happens in the nervous machine. My mobile body makes a difference in the visible world being part of it; that is why I can steer through the visible. Conversely, it is just as true that vision is attached to movement. . . . Each of the two maps is complete. The visible world and the world of my motor projects are each total, parts of the same Being. . . . A self, therefore, that is caught up in things, that has a front and a back, a past and a future. . . . Visible and mobile, my body is a thing among things; it is caught up in the fabric of the world, and its cohesion is that of a thing. But because it moves itself and sees, it holds things in a circle around itself. . . . Vision happens among, or is caught in, things—in that

139

place where something visible undertakes to see, becomes visible for itself by virtue of the sight of things; in that place where there persists, like the mother water in crystal, the undividedness (*l'indivision*) of the sensing and the sensed.

In 1926 William Carlos Williams wrote in 'Paterson', which appeared in *The Dial*, 'Say it, no ideas but in things' and in the final lines:

> They are the divisions and imbalances
> of his whole concept, made small by pity
> and desire, they are—no ideas beside the facts—

In 1946 he presents *Paterson* as a celebration 'in distinct terms; by multiplication, a reduction to one', 'a plan for action to supplant a plan for action; a taking up of slack; a dispersal and a metamorphosis'. And he later remarked to Edith Heal (*I Wanted to Write a Poem*, 1958), 'the idea was a metaphysical conception; how to get that into form probably came gradually' (these principles and their praxis are developed in 'The Making of Paterson', Eric Mottram, *Profile of William Carlos Williams*, ed. Jerome Mazzaro, Ohio, 1971). The related instances in the later *Cantos* are plentiful—for instance, in Canto 76 Merleau-Ponty's water in crystal and Williams' metaphysics of form are imaged as 'the sphere moving crystal fluid', and:

> no cloud, but the crystal body
>   the tangent formed in the hand's cup
>   as live wind in the beech grove
>   as strong air amid cypress

—which Hugh Kenner interpreted in a seminal essay in *Hudson Review* back in Spring 1950, as 'the reality of the *nous*, of mind, apart from any man's individual mind'. In Canto 76, Pound writes:

> spiriti questi? personae?
>   tangibility by no means *atasal*
>   but the crystal can be weighed in the hand
>   formal and passing within the sphere: Thetis,
>   Maya, Aphrodite

—where *atasal* is a classical Arabic term in part meaning close relation but not necessarily divine union (this information comes from a Jordanian student of Helen M. Dennis, Department of English, Warwick University). These formulations are taken up in the celebrated passage in Canto 116, where their confidence is challenged: 'who can lift it?/ Can you enter the great acorn of light?' Canto 76 stands in relation to the idea of water force in 'Psychology and Troubadours'—'the crystalline, as inverse in water,/ clear over rock-bed'—and in Canto 113 Pound is still, so late, able to structure his lifelong belief with astonishing and clear beauty: 'That the body is inside the soul—/ lifting and folding brightness'. The affirmation can be made again in Canto 116:

> These concepts the human mind has attained.
> To make Cosmos—
> To achieve the possible—

But, immediately, this impersonal statement of 'the human universe' is interrupted by political failure—'Muss[olini] wrecked for an error'—and by the possibility that the *Cantos* themselves cannot be entered now, that their time and their possible reader have been lost. But then Pound again affirms those phenomenological perceptions which are the matter of this essay:

> to 'see again',
> the verb is 'see', not 'walk on'.

Coherence, in the terms proposed by the *Cantos* themselves, is the mobility of the poem's perceptions, the perceptive 'palimpsest'. But 'palimpsest' means here more than the counterpoint in Canto 79: it is 'the record . . . a little light/ in great darkness—/ cunculi—'. This record is not static layering, with the mind archaeologizing between datelines; the *Cantos* have in fact the mobility of the *periplum* adventure. With respect to Pound's aged feelings, it must be said that his sense of what his masterpiece had become betrays, here, its marvellous fluidity. His 'eye and mind' worked to the last 'drafts & fragments', even if he, like Merleau-Ponty—and like most twentieth-century artists of any stature—has to admit that the terrestrial paradise falls short, that he is part of a tradition of endless cosmos-making, and that the non-verbal has a coherence the verbal cannot attain. The poet has to be modest to be intelligent. The epic cannot be an inclusive totality. Empson's comment on Milton suggests the modernity of Pound's condition ('All in Paradise Lost', *The Structure of Complex Words*, London, 1951, p. 101):

> [The use of the word *all*] seems to be suited to his temperament because he is an absolutist, an all-or-none man. All else is unimportant beside one thing, he is continually deciding. . . . The generosity of the proud man also requires the word; when he gives he gives all. It is as suited to absolute love and self-sacrifice as to insane self-assertion. The self-centred man, in his turn, is not much interested in the variety of the world and readily lumps it together as 'all'. . . . In a stylist, the word presumes economy of means; it raises the thing in hand absolutely without needing to list all the others. . . .

But, adds Empson, in a note (p. 104): 'Certainly it is hard to know what Milton thought he was doing, but I take it the man was so intensely self-assured that he hardly criticized his work—it had to suit his feelings.' That 'self-assurance' rested on the 'fiction' that guided the epic *through* feelings and scepticism and dogma—'fiction' in the sense used by Pierre Macherey (*A Theory of Literary Production*, 1966; London, 1978, p. 64):

> Fiction, not to be confused with illusion, is the substitute for, if not the equivalent of, knowledge. . . . Fiction is determinate illusion, and the essence of the literary text is to establish those determinations. Thus the *power* of language, settled in the more or less fixed edges of the work, is displaced. To know what a literary text is we must ask: From what new centre is the work of fiction being carried out? It is not a question of a real centre, for the book does not replace ideologically decentred illusion with a permanent centre around which the system of language is to be ordered; the book does not endow this system with a subject. Fiction is not *truer* than illusion; indeed, it cannot usurp the place of knowledge. But it can set illusion in motion by penetrating its insufficiency, by transforming our relationship to ideology. . . . The text begins from where 'life' reaches its formless conclusions; the two terms, then, form a distinct contract; but they are also inseparable, not because they are simply different forms of the same content, but because they constitute an endless dialectical opposition.

That is, in brief, fiction is a form of knowledge which is neither illusion nor science but a conditional knowledge or determinate illusion. Pound's *Cantos* show a man conceiving himself through 'fiction' at the intersection of history and art, as the artist-historian (see 'Henry Adams: Index of the Twentieth Century', Eric Mottram, *American Literary Naturalism,* ed. Y. Hakutani and L. Fried, Heidelberg, 1975), discovering the absolute resisted by his perceptions. In this he confronts the state of twentieth-century science—in the words of J. Robert Oppenheimer ('On Science and Culture', *Encounter,* October, 1962):

> In the sciences, total statements like those that involve the word 'all', with no qualifications, are hardly ever likely to occur. In every extension of knowledge, we are involved in an action; in every action we are involved in a choice; and in every choice we are involved in a loss, the loss of that we did not do. We find this in the simplest situation.

(The radical development of this position is taken by Paul Feyerabend in *Against Method,* London, 1975.) In Pound's terms, in Canto 74, his structure is 'by no means an orderly Dantescan rising'—and, more familiarly, he had no 'Aquinas map'; or, in terms proposed by Macherey, the work has no preplanned subject. This is, in fact, calculated, in spite of Pound's final remorse that his palimpsest has no such armature of idealism or ideology or any kind of dogma. Milton, like Dante, had Christianity, however arbitrary its translations in mid-seventeenth century, with angels copulating and Adam asking questions. So that 'all' is reasonably defined, apart from personal urge towards totality. Pound has no such fiction, and although he compared his method with Dante's unifying his various sources 'by their connection with himself', he does not, say, revert to the theory of Fascism. He requires the accoutrements of the gods, spirit, crystal and that Renaissance region of belief, and edges these into a certain understanding of physics. But the 'all' remains obstinately synthetic and mobile. And the final cantos express his irritation with that as if it were failure. But it is no more failure than is *The Education of Henry Adams.*

Martin Kayman's thesis concludes that since Pound 'lacks a category of fiction', he *confuses* illusion and science, and 'obliterates the distinction between fiction and theory'. Dr. Kayman believes, therefore, that Pound's technique is basically mythic, 'a narcissistic manipulation of the discourse of science'. Perhaps such arguments can be best confronted here by suggesting that they point towards the difference between Merleau-Ponty's philosophical discourse and Pound's poetic discourse—the former is a form of phenomenological logic while the latter is a phenomenolist synthesis.

But the search for a place in which to rest, a base, is common to both writers. In Canto 83, Pound writes: 'HUDOR et Pax/ Gemisto stemmed all from Neptune/ hence the Rimini reliefs' (Duccio's bas-reliefs in the Malatesta Tempio—Pound's meaning can be enhanced from a reading of Adrian Stokes' *The Stones of Rimini*, 1934, pp. 97–9, for example: 'we experience again the potential and actual shapes of the stone in water, changing its form. . . . Agostino's forms never cease to be potential as well as actual . . . they have the quality of apparition which, so far from mitigating the singleness of their impact on the eye, makes them the more insistent and even unforgettable. They glow, luminous in the rather dim light of the Tempio. Their vitality abounds.'). And then: 'the brightness of *'udor'*. In Merleau-Ponty's words:

> Henceforth the irrelative is not nature itself, nor is it the system of seizure of absolute conscience, nor is it even man, but rather this 'teleology' which is written and thought between quotation marks—the joints and framework of a being which effects itself by means of man.

(Some biologists' contemporary creation myth is that men exist to enable the processes of DNA to continue.) In his essay, Sartre, quoting these words, presses a danger here: that even if he denies the absolute to any other 'domain', he still denies it to man. Merleau-Ponty continually collided with the transcendent as he enquired into the immanent—quite as much as Pound did, although perhaps less vulnerably, since he was never imprisoned, nor threatened by madness, and never felt compelled to say under extreme social pressure, as D. A. Levy did (*Collected Poems*, Wisconsin, 1979):

> Lady you have to be realistic
> sending all your poets to the looney bin
> aint helping the profession very much
> your blue hair in the wind
> & yr eyes full of diamonds

144

Or to say with Pound: 'the beauty is not the madness/ Tho' my errors and wrecks lie about me./ I am not a demigod,/ I cannot make it cohere'—that is, the *poet* cannot *make* it cohere, or, in Macherey's terms, fiction 'cannot usurp the place of knowledge'. Sartre asks the crucial question: 'Can dialectical materialism—in whose name many will try to criticize this mediation—do without an ontology?' Merleau-Ponty's answer comes through the great Renaissance sceptic, one of those thinkers through whom the medieval Christian synthesis is undermined, for whom the fiction is not converted into an absolute:

> The explanations which define man as metaphysics or physics are those which Montaigne rejects in advance, since it is still man who 'proves' philosophies and science, and they are explained by him, rather than he by them.

Sartre then takes up the concept of continual creation as those flashes of energy in which form appears, or being is revealed: 'Precisely because he is ceaselessly resumed in this ever-renewed flash of light, there will be a future for man.' This is also the hope within the pressure of despair in the later *Cantos*. For Merleau-Ponty, the hope that 'la virtù' can emerge as courage and virtue together; in Canto 85 the Chinese ideo-gram for process relates to Pound's translation of the Great Digest's introduction—in the poem, 'not a lot of signs, but the one sign', and in the Confucian text (*Confucius*, New York, 1969, p. 21):

> What results, i.e., the action resultant from this straight gaze into the heart. The 'know thyself' carried into action. Said action also serving to clarify the self-knowledge. To translate this simply as 'virtue' is on a par with translating rhinoceros, fox and giraffe indifferently by 'quadruped' or 'animal'.

Since Pound's phenomenalism includes *techne*, the ideogram has to be process plus *techne*. *Virtù* could never be a simple definition for him. In 1910 he writes: '*La virtù* is the potency, the efficient property of a substance or person. Thus modern science shows us radium with a noble virtue of energy.' (In *Paterson*, Book IV, part 2, Williams presents discovery as a form of need and a form of love, the birth of radium and Mme.

145

Curie's pregnancy as 'a luminosity of elements' and as an alchemic change in nature and human nature, or knowledge—with the necessary puns on 'vessel'. In Canto 23, the Curies again appear as searchers for light to illuminate darkness or *materia*.)

In 'The Serious Artist' (1913) Pound writes that the energy in art is like electricity or radio-activity, 'a force transfusing, welding, and unifying. A force rather like water when it spurts up through very bright sand and sets it in swift motion.' Elsewhere he observes that 'energy creates pattern', and that it is the centrifugal energy of the personal vortex which is the artist's *virtù*. Dr. Kayman believes that in this way Pound 'employs the mechanisms of magic *and* sustains the lie of their being truth', adding that 'the narcissistic [imaginary] mechanisms of primitive thought [are] worked up into knowledge.' But it seems at least possible that Pound's phenomenological interchanges between nature and human nature are nearer modern scientific practice than reversion to some simplicistic, nineteenth-century separation of the two. We need here the direction suggested, for instance, by the essays in the *Biopoesis* issue of *Io* (No. 20, 1974, ed. Harvey Bialy).

The artist's *virtù* also appears in his taking of risks. Sartre cites a Chief of Police who summed up public opinion 'by declaring that nothing surprised him'; whereas Merleau-Ponty, like any adventurous philosopher and artist, was 'surprised by everything', 'a child scandalized by our futile grown-up certitudes . . . Nothing seems natural to him':

> But he is not interrogating us. He is too afraid that we will hang on to dogmatisms which will reassure us. He will be this interrogation of himself because the 'writer has chosen insecurity'. . . . The philosophic attitude disappears as soon as astonishment ceases. . . . Every life, every moment, every era—contingent miracles or contingent failures—are incarnations. The word becomes flesh, the universal is only established by the living singularity which deforms it by singularizing it. . . . For Merleau, universality is never universal, except in high-altitude thinking. It is born alongside the flesh, flesh of our flesh. . . . Such is the warning that anthropology—psychoanalysis or marxism—should never forget . . . the flash of light, the singular universalization of universality.

146

So the Work, then, appears as 'a flash of light between two risks' in that 'primordial historicity' he speaks of in 'Eye and Mind', an example of 'virtù without illusion', what Pound calls 'interactive force: the virtù' ('Cavalcanti', *Make It New*):

> A dogma builds on vacuum, and is ultimately killed or modified by, or accommodated to knowledge, but values stay, and ignorant neglect of them answers no purpose . . . . where the thought has its demarcations, the substance in *virtù*, where stupid men have not reduced all 'energy' to unbounded undistinguished abstraction.

There follows one more use of the iron-filings rose. Pound finds no gap between the medieval philosophical sense of the *forma* out of invisible energy and electricity, 'the current hidden in air and in the wire' which produces 'the light in the electric bulb': 'the medieval philosopher would probably have been unable to think the electric world, and *not* think of it as a world of forms. But from his translations and applications of Cavalcanti's poetry, Pound knew his own poetic strength lay in keeping 'virtù' and 'perfection'—the terms of 'Donna mi prega' in his own English—within the senses' 'interactive force', their phenomenological perceptions. The *Cantos* succeeds overwhelmingly in this praxis. But perhaps Pound recalled in his final days his translation of Cavalcanti's Sonnett 23, addressed to Dante:

> Much doth it grieve me that thy noble mind
> And virtue's plenitude are stripped from thee . . .

> . . . *E d'assai tue virtù, che ti son tolte.*

6

'Speaking in Figures': The Mechanical Thomas Jefferson of Canto 31*

by IAN F. A. BELL

> Then stayed the fervid wheels, and in his hand
> He took the golden compasses, prepared
> In God's eternal store, to circumscribe
> This universe, and all created things:
> One foot he centred, and the other turned
> Round through the vast profundity obscure,
> And said, Thus far extend, thus far thy bounds,
> This be thy just circumference, O world.
>
> —*Paradise Lost,* Bk. VII

> These Englishmen are strange people; because they can live upon what they call bank notes, without working, they think that all the world can do the same. This goodly country never would have been tilled and cleared with these notes. . . . By writing they send this cargo unto us, that to the West, and the other to the East Indies. But, James, thee knowest that it is not by writing that we shall pay the blacksmith, the minister, the weaver, the tailor, and the English shop.
>
> —*Letters from an American Farmer,* Letter I

* I am grateful to my colleague Richard Godden for reading an early draft of the present essay.

1

That most potent of scientific instructions, 'Invent', has always carried a double function: to discover and to construct. America, by the second of these functions, was made by a series of words collected under the rubric of the Declaration of Independence, words whose constructive capacity was to mark, above all, the difference of the New World, its distance from the Old. The invention of difference, the 'Novus Ordo Seculorum' in the older language of the Seal of the United States, was predicated on the basis of a beginning grounded in the paradox of all arguments for unity, 'E Pluribus Unum'.[1] Language's capacity for construction was rediscovered by the Enlightenment's facility for synthesizing a primitivist world-view with a materialist science. John Locke, at the beginning of the third book of *An Essay Concerning Human Understanding*, anticipated the lexical concerns of Emerson, Whitman, Fenollosa and Gourmont by stressing 'how great a dependence our words have on common sensible ideas':

> 'Spirit', in its primary signification, is breath; 'angel', a messenger; and I doubt not but, if we could trace them to their sources, we should find, in all languages, the names which stand for things that fall not under our senses to have had their first rise from sensible ideas.

Locke's ideal dictionary at the end of the third book proposed that 'words standing for things which are known and distinguished by their outward shapes should be expressed by little draughts and prints made of them.' The practicable and economical 'true signification' of such expressions would replace 'all the large and laborious comments of learned critics' on the model of natural science:

> Naturalists, that treat of plants and animals, have found the benefit of this way; and he that has had occasion to consult them will have reason to confess that he has a clearer idea of *apium* or *ibex* from a little print of that herb or beast, than he could have from a long definition of the names of either of them.

Pound, composing, in 1933, Canto 31, *Jefferson and/or Mussolini* and the *ABC of Reading*, began the latter with his most famous testament to the naturalist's eye, a story from

Emerson's America, that of Agassiz and the fish. Five years earlier, in, for Pound, the soundest and most impartial account of Jefferson, W. E. Woodward's biography of Washington,[2] we find a tribute to Jefferson's eye:

> As Jefferson travels over the face of Europe a stream of descriptive letters come from him. He is an eye ... a philosophic eye ... he sees everything, the inside as well as the outside of places and political institutions. He learns the languages; he notes the various methods of planting; he fingers little mechanical contrivances and writes about them; he observes that bricks are laid differently in Holland; he talks with peasants; he sends to America vast bundles of new plants and fruits; he studies French cooking and astronomy. He is at home in France, among a people so intellectually vivid.[3]

The most cursory glance through Jefferson's letters or, most obviously, the *Notes on the State of Virginia,* supports the accuracy of Woodward's claims: it was not coincidental that Pound should offer his first acclamation of Agassiz during the period when he was working most intensively on Jefferson. Pound's choice of image for the Jefferson who opens Canto 31 is particularly significant here. He is not the Jefferson of 'humanistic' government, the opposer of the Federalists, the fiscal theorist or any of the other figures more familiar from Pound's prose accounts, but the practical, scientific Jefferson, interested in the building of the Erie Canal, in curious botany, in marine technology; the Jefferson whom Pound oddly refused to designate by the term he employed on behalf of Mussolini: 'Artifex'.

Locke's sensationalist basis for the constructive power of language found expression in Jefferson's materialism, most fully articulated in the later years of his correspondence with John Adams, the years which focused Pound's interest in that aspect of Enlightenment thought deserving to be designated as 'A Shrine and a Monument'. In a letter to Adams of 14 March 1820, for example, he testified to his interest in the work of the French *idéologues* Tracy and Cabanis to offer material accounts of seemingly immaterial phenomena (work which, through its later formulations in Havelock Ellis, Samuel Butler, Edward Carpenter, Remy de Gourmont and Allen Upward, was to be decisive for the distinctive strategy of Pound's own materialism[4]):

And they ask Why may not the mode of action called thought, have been given to a material organ of peculiar structure? as that of magnetism is to the Needle, or of elasticity to the spring by a particular manipulation of to [*sic*] the steel. They observe that on ignition of the needle or spring, their magnetism and elasticity cease. So on dissolution of the material organ by death it's action of thought may cease also. And that nobody supposes that the magnetism or elasticity retire to hold a substantive and distinct existence. These were qualities only of particular conformations of matter: change the conformation, and it's qualities change also.[5]

It was inevitable that a stress on the constructive potential of words in an age which valorized the materialization of the world should rely on a resistance to the metaphysical, the abstract, and on a testimony to the vitality of words beyond the dictionary. A philosophy of sensation emphasized both the shaping energy of language conceived empirically and the scientific impossibility of the immaterial. In the space of a single letter to Adams of 15 August 1820, Jefferson drew attention to these two propositions, considering, first, the nature of language in a way that anticipated Whitman's hopes for a new vocabulary commensurate to a new world:

I am a friend to *neology*. It is the only way to give to a language copiousness and euphony. Without it we should still be held to the vocabulary of Alfred or of Ulphilas; and held to their state of science also: for I am sure they had no words which could have conveyed the ideas of Oxigen, cotyledons, zoophytes, magnetism, electricity, hyaline, and thousands of others expressing ideas not then existing, nor of possible communication in the state of their language. What a language has the French become since the date of their revolution, by the free introduction of new words! The most copious and eloquent in the living world. . . . Dictionaries are but the depositories of words already legitimated by usage. Society is the work-shop in which new ones are elaborated.[6]

Words themselves thus had an intimate connection with the sensations viewed as forming the basis of knowledge: in the next paragraph, Jefferson responded to the doubts expressed by Adams in an earlier letter (of 12 May 1820) concerning the ancient problem of Matter and Spirit:

On the basis of sensation, of matter and motion, we may erect
the fabric of all the certainties we can have or need. I can
conceive *thought* to be an action of a particular organisation of
matter, formed for that purpose by it's creator, as well as that
attraction is an action of matter, or *magnetism* of loadstone. When
he who denies to the Creator the power of endowing matter
with the mode of action called *thinking* shall shew how he could
endow the Sun with the mode of action called *attraction*, which
reins the planets in the tract of their orbits, or how an absence
of matter can have a will, and, by that will, put matter into
motion, then the materialist may be lawfully required to explain
the process by which matter exercises the faculty of thinking.
When once we quit the basis of sensation, all is in the wind. To
talk of *immaterial* existences is to talk of *nothings*. To say that the
human soul, angels, god, are immaterial, is to say that they are
nothings, or that there is no god, no angels, no soul. I cannot
reason otherwise: but I believe I am supported in my creed of
materialism by Locke, Tracy, and Stewart .... Rejecting all
organs of information therefore but my senses, I rid myself of the
Pyrrhonisms with which an indulgence in speculations hyper-
physical and antiphysical so uselessly occupy and disquiet the
mind.[7]

Jefferson's translation and popularization of the work of the
French *idéologue* Destutt de Tracy indicates the clearest articu-
lation of Jefferson's materialism whereby mental operations
themselves were considered within the framework of natural
history and the sensationalist epistemology of Locke.[8] It is
within the *Idéologue* philosophy, for example, that we find a
metaphor from Pierre-Jean-Georges Cabanis which approxi-
mates to the more familiar physiology of Gourmont: 'The
frequently quoted statement that the brain must be considered
an organ specially made to produce ideas, as the stomach is
made to digest, leads on to the sensational formula that the
brain secretes thought as the liver bile.'[9] Jefferson himself
responded with enthusiasm to the neurological physiology of
Pierre Flourens' *Recherches sur le Système Nerveux dans les Animaux
Vertébres* ('the most extraordinary of all books') in a letter to
Adams of 8 January 1825:

He takes out the cerebrum compleatly, leaving the cerebellum
and other parts of the system uninjured. The animal loses all its

152

senses of hearing, seeing, feeling, smelling, tasting, is totally deprived of will, intelligence, memory, perception etc. yet lives for months in perfect health, with all its powers of motion, but without moving but on external excitement, starving even on a pile of grain unless crammed down its throat; in a state, in short, of the most absolute stupidity. He takes the cerebellum out of others, leaving the cerebrum untouched. The animal retains all it's senses, faculties and understanding, but loses the power of regulated motion, and exhibits all the symptoms of drunkenness. . . . Cabanis had proved, from the anatomical structure of certain portions of the human frame, that they might be capable of receiving from the Creator the faculty of thinking. Flourens proves that the cerebrum is the thinking organ, and that life and health may continue, and the animal be entirely without thought, if deprived of that organ. I wish to see what the spiritualists will say to this.[10]

Pound's choice of a practical, scientific image of Jefferson to begin Canto 31 clearly belongs to the materialist, sensationalist philosophy that Jefferson espoused in his letters to Adams. In some senses it was an odd choice, partly because, revealingly, Pound evinces only an oblique acknowledgement of this image in his other readings of Jefferson. It should be evident, however, as I have suggested elsewhere,[11] that this particular aspect of the Enlightenment temperament was especially congenial to a body of critical prose which articulated its positions through a whole series of metaphors derived from a similar understanding of scientific materialism; a materialism that shared Enlightenment science's resistance against the tyranny of metaphysics through an urge to naturalize seemingly non-material processes, to displace the dualism of mind and body by advocating an inclusive, synthetic system of study which was grounded in individualistic sensation and a materialist epistemology. Jefferson's version of the programme advanced by Cabanis and Flourens to resolve mental functions through the activities of the nervous system lies comfortably within the field of Pound's critical pronouncements during his London years: as Locke's theory of sensations naturalized thought for Jefferson, so the glandular theories of, in particular, Gourmont and Louis Berman technologized the human personality.[12] The virtues of such mechanical readings of the world and of man's place within it were obvious: they suggested a unity of knowledge unfragmented by metaphysics or spiritualism; they offered possibilities for a more realistic egalitarianism, enabling Jefferson to speak strongly against what he referred to as 'tinsel-aristocracy'; they celebrated man's active power as a maker, a constructor, thereby placing his own destiny in his own hands as it became possible to recognize his liberation through the machine, both human and non-human, from the dictatorship of nature's imprisoning circle; at the level of language, the burdens of abstraction and representationalism were displaced by concrete words with a positive function for action. Of all these Enlightenment ambitions, the most dominant was the sanction of progressive liberty achieved by measuring the world through the available branches of material science; Jefferson wrote to Adams on 28 October 1813 about the evils of European notions of aristocracy and concluded:

> But even in Europe a change has sensibly taken place in the mind of Man. Science had liberated the ideas of those who read and reflect, and the American example had kindled feelings of right in the people. An insurrection has consequently begun, of science, talents and courage against rank and birth, which have fallen into contempt. It has failed in it's first effort, because the mobs of the cities, the instruments used for it's accomplishment, debased by ignorance, poverty and vice, could not be restrained to rational action. But the world will recover from the panic of this first catastrophe. Science is progressive, and talents and enterprize on the alert. Resort may be had to the people of the country, a more governable power from their principles and subordination; and rank, and birth, and tinsel-aristocracy will finally shrink into insignificance, even there.[13]

Within such a system, even a state as amorphous as happiness became mathematically calculable:[14] meritocratic liberty so conceived was inextricably linked to the control of mechanism. One of the reasons for Pound's choice of a scientific Jefferson at the beginning of Canto 31 resurrects exactly this paradigm: the initial function is one of resistance to nature's own control, the natural cycle of *Ecclesiastes* in the opening tag ('Tempus loquendi,/ Tempus tacendi'). The mechanically minded Jefferson proposed to refuse the determinancy of that cycle by the construction of a man-made world; initially

154

through his campaign for the Erie Canal, an image carefully selected by Pound to register science's technological role. And when Pound repeated the image some thirty-seven lines later (as Jefferson himself repeated the point in a later letter to Washington[15]), he took the opportunity of placing it within the context of Jefferson's views on meritocracy:

> . . . turn through the Potomac . . . commerce of Lake Erie . . ./ I can further say with safety there is not a crowned head/ in Europe whose talents or merits would entitle him/ to be elected a vestryman by any American parish.

Pound was able to repeat the equation between liberty and technology partly because of a willingness, in the early 1930s, to restore earlier Republican virtues. The mechanistic vocabulary of construction which expressed this willingness drew some of its strength from the similar vocabulary employed to face the crises of his London years, years filled not only with Pound's own scientific discourse but also with the mechanical lines of Lewis, Wadsworth, Etchells, Roberts, Nevinson, Bomberg, Epstein and Gaudier-Brzeska, with the polemics of, in particular, Hulme and Lewis whereby metaphors of mechanism fought against the chaotic threat and monotheistic representationalism of things organic or natural. Pound, in 1916, writing about Dolmetsch's musical instruments and the 'joys of pure form' considered as 'inorganic, geometrical form', thought of 'the best art' as 'perhaps only the making of instruments'.[16] A year later, on behalf of a different medium, he declared 'The Camera is Freed from Reality',[17] thinking of the lesson remembered by Alvin Langdon Coburn:

> The Vortoscope, he [Pound] said, freed photography from the material limitations of depicting recognisable natural objects. By its use the photographer can create beautiful arrangements of form for their own sake, just as a musician does. . . . It was not until just before World War I that I began photographing musicians, though I had long been very interested in music, especially in connection with the Pianola. I have a theory that there is a certain relationship between the Pianola and the camera, for in each case the mechanical rendering frees the artist from certain technical difficulties so that he is able to concentrate on interpretation. My Pianola was specially constructed for me

in April 1914, and as I often wanted modern music—Debussy, Ravel, Scriabin, Stravinsky—not commercially available, I sometimes cut rolls with a perforating machine made for me by a camera manufacturer. I was very interested in the patterns made by the holes punched in the paper and found that the patterns of Bach were especially beautiful. I also experimented with the sounds made by patterns conceived merely visually.[18]

Aesthetics focus wider cultural issues here. A canal operates as a system of communication (one of Jefferson's most insistent points) and exchange, and, in 1917, the fourth instalment of Pound's 'Provincialism The Enemy' quoted Kipling's maxim that 'Transportation is civilization' to claim 'A tunnel is worth more than a dynasty.'[19] By the time of 'Ecclesiastical History' in 1934, Pound had fully integrated the liberty of technology with its cultural function of exchange, glossing his proposal that 'The SOURCE of value is the CULTURAL HERITAGE' as 'The aggregate of all mechanical inventions and correlations, improved seed and agricultural methods, selected habits of civilized life, the increment of association.' The values consequent upon such a heritage would be, like the literal metaphor of the canal itself, 'in large part STATAL values' and would 'exceed the boundaries of private ownership at many points'.[20]

It should be clear that at this point we are beginning to figure the familiar image of Jefferson in Pound's prose. *Jefferson and/or Mussolini* took its impetus from Mussolini's 'passion for construction', the need to view him as *'artifex'*, a view which followed one of Pound's personal testaments to the value of communication and exchange on the model of the Erie Canal: 'I have never believed that my grandfather put a bit of railway across Wisconsin simply or chiefly to make money.'[21] And Jefferson was a man who 'used verbal formulations as tools', a lawyer and a law scholar who 'used legalities and legal phrases as IMPLEMENTS'.[22] Pound was, of course, careful to try and offset the machine-like determinism of the vocabulary from mechanism and construction ('Jefferson saw machinery in the offing, he didn't like it, he didn't like the idea of the factory'), and he proposed: 'If you are hunting up bonds of sympathy between T.J. and the Duce, put it first that they both hate machinery or at any rate the idea of cooping up men and making 'em all into UNITS, unit production, denting in the individual man, reducing him to a mere amalgam.'[23] Such a proposal elided the less overt technology implicit in the physiology he himself learned from Gourmont and Louis Berman, or Jefferson learned from Cabanis and Flourens. The tactic of *Jefferson and/or Mussolini* was thus one of concealment, stressing the agrarian operations of both men; Jefferson's rice was matched by Mussolini's wheat, they exhibited a shared 'sympathy with the beasts', and unless Mussolini's concern was seen for an 'Italy organic' (further domesticated as 'composed of the last ploughman and the last girl in the olive-yards'), then 'you will have a great deal of trouble about the un-Jeffersonian details of his surfaces.'[24] This modification of one order of metaphor by a further, less obviously determinant, order is in itself revealing: the *Directio Voluntatis,* for Pound, Jefferson's major characteristic, was encoded *via* Pound's reading of Confucius and Dante as a further means of concealment. It is impossible to see such a notion as innocent of the machine-like energies expressed in any number of Wyndham Lewis's fictional characters, or of the mechanical/organic complex of Lawrence's Gerald Crich and/or Rupert Birkin. The latter was a complex figured from the nexus of the broad historical transition whereby the initial paternalistic character of industrial capitalism's early phase became deformed into the perverse liberties released by the exercise of pure force conceived within a similar problematic of the technology applicable to the worlds of both the machine and the organism. Lewis, for whom nature *had* to be mechanized, wrote strikingly in 1919:

> Life, simply, however vivid and tangible, is too material to be anything but a mechanism, and the sea-gull is not far removed from the hydro-plane. . . . every living form is a miraculous mechanism, and every sanguinary, vicious or twisted need produces in Nature's workshop a series of mechanical gadgets extremely suggestive and interesting for the engineer, and almost invariably beautiful or interesting for the artist.[25]

For Lewis, this mode of perception was the product of the 'all-inclusiveness of the direction of our thought', itself engendered by 'the all-inclusiveness of our knowledge'.[26] The literal making of the world in a mechanistic sense was thus reliant upon an epistemological system conceived as all-embracing,

157

matching the ambitions for a unified system of knowledge shared by Enlightenment materialism and the Correspondence theories of Emerson and Agassiz. It is here that we need to site the strategy of Pound's willingness during the early 1930s to revive the revolutionary possibilities of Jefferson's America. This willingness was not an act of nostalgia but a refusal to lose 'our own revolution (of 1776–1830)': as he replaced 'culture' with the anthropological 'paideuma', so Pound viewed the Jefferson-Adams correspondence not as the frozen permanence of a 'monument', but as the technological 'still workable dynamo', arguing for 'The possibilities of revival, starting perhaps with a valorization of our cultural heritage, not merely as something lost in dim retrospect, a tombstone, tastily carved, whereon to shed dry tears or upon which to lay a few withered violets.'[27] The image of Louis Agassiz, the other major figure in Pound's pantheon during the early 1930s, is crucial here because of his function as a focus of interest for specific sources of money during the latter half of the nineteenth century. These sources were concerned to restore, in their turn, the older republican values of wise government by wealthy and powerful men who advertisedly believed in the idea of selfless service to the nation and in the intelligent concentration of resources for general amelioration. Agassiz attracted patronage not from the men of the Gilded Age, Jay Gould, Jim Fiske, or Andrew Carnegie, but from older money, made during the early period of the republic: it was John Amory Lowell, for example, who first enticed Agassiz to America, and Henry Adams followed his courses at Harvard. In the words of Edward Lurie, from whom I draw the information for this present argument, such men as Lowell, Francis Calley Gray, Nathaniel Thayer and John Anderson, 'seized the opportunity by supporting nature's study and appreciation, to protest materially against the shabbiness of America, and the new populism of their age.'[28]

Agassiz's name meant, above all, for his own time and for Pound, radical and exciting innovations in education: rarely had a teacher of natural history experienced such extensive and popular appeal. It was partly his own glamour as well as the intricate unity which his observant eye perceived throughout the whole of the natural world, that rendered him so appropriate for the élitist America (Pound's term was 'responsible'[29])

158

described in Jeffersonian and Emersonian terms by the Brahmin
George William Curtis:

> In America . . . New England has inspired and moulded our
> national life. But if New England has led the Union, what has led
> New England? Her scholarly class . . . men of strong convictions
> and persuasive speech, who showed their brethren what they
> ought to think and do. That is the secret of leadership. It is not
> servility to the mob. . . . Leadership is the power of kindling a
> sympathy and trust which will eagerly follow. . . . As educated
> America was the constructive power, so it is still the true
> conservative force of the Republic. . . . Take from the country . . .
> its educated power, and you would take . . . from national action
> its moral mainspring.[30]

Clearly, Curtis's notion of cultivated, constructive leadership,
could easily take its place in Jefferson's letters, Emerson's
essays (most obviously 'The American Scholar') and Pound's
diptych of Jefferson and/or Mussolini. And all three items of
debate find their ideological resource through a vocabulary of
natural science and technology, ratified by ambitions for a
unified epistemology. Lurie provides a good summary of
Agassiz's role here:

> By analogy, it was as if Agassiz had become a natural history
> money depository which would transform wealth into the moral
> equivalent of the virtues of love, work and fellowship. Americans
> could thus feel strong and renewed by giving succor to an Agassiz
> adventure in furtherance of the good olden virtues of closeness to
> nature, sacredness of fact, and truth through beauty. This was
> the chemistry that linked the mechanic at his Lyceum lectures
> with the men who paid money to make Agassiz's addresses
> possible.[31]

Revealingly, Pound omitted an appropriate opportunity
explicitly to conjoin Agassiz and Jefferson in the second stanza
of Canto 31. The lines '. . . flower found in Connecticut that
vegetates when suspended in air . . ./ . . . screw more effectual
if placed below surface of water' reverse the order of their
occurence in Pound's source, Jefferson's letter to Ezra Stiles of
17 July 1785, and omit Jefferson's interest in morphology: 'I
thank you for your information as to the great bones found on
the Hudson river. I suspect that they must have been of the

same animal with those found on the Ohio; and, if so, they could not have belonged to any human figure, because they are accompanied with tusks of the size, form and substance, of those of the elephant. I have seen a part of the ivory, which was very good. The animal itself must have been much larger than an elephant.'[32] Here, in a more primitive form, was one of Agassiz's most famous activities: the discerning of an entire structure on the basis of a few remains considered comparatively, a zoological principle which found its analogy in Pound's 'luminous detail' and the *kulturmorphologie* of Leo Frobenius.

2

Pound's situation in the early 1930s, the period in which fascism's resistance to the impositions of late capitalism became more explicitly articulated, was one of distinctive disablement. He found himself caught between the Enlightenment promise of science's liberating potential, the promise of a control over nature as a necessary precondition for human freedom, and the practical consequences of science in the forms of technology as instruments for capitalist production. We need to avoid the seemingly obvious corollary of this situation, that control over nature may all too easily be translated into control over social relationships, since, although it clearly contains some truth, it suggests too reductive a reading of history and of the disablement of Pound's art. By attempting to revive the liberating potential of science and constructive technology to combat the threat of the factory system, the 'masses', and a debased currency, Pound failed to recognize that the valorization of technology which such a revival advocated was a prime characteristic of industrial capitalism itself. Pound's value-system was based ultimately on a particular notion of constructive work: his celebration of Confucius, Malatesta, Jefferson or Mussolini, was famously a presentation of the hero as a man who gets things done, by his *directio voluntatis*, by his sense of 'responsibility' to his fellow-man. The problem here was two-fold: first, Pound was unable to differentiate within this system in terms of specific social formations (hence we have the curious role of Lenin in *Jefferson and/or Mussolini*, and the virtual substitution of

Lenin for Jefferson in Canto 74 at the point where we find the reversal of the Latin tag which introduced Jefferson in Canto 31), and second, the notion of constructive work became a value in and for itself, exhibiting no cognisance of its object or its result. Science itself, in the technological role demanded by industrial capitalism in its advanced stage, as Habermas has argued, became transformed and naturalized into a major channel of production.[33]

Towards the end of fascism's most virulent and obscene attempts to reconstruct capitalism in its own grotesque image, Adorno and Horkheimer produced a response to the legacy of valorized technology left by the Enlightenment, a response which is illuminating for the revivalist hopes of Pound at the beginning of the period and the characteristics of his disablement which achieve significant expression in the tactics of Canto 31. They began by reiterating the view of the Enlightenment as a system of rational and scientific knowledge for the purpose of liberating man from the chaos of fate, chance and nature itself: 'The program of the Enlightenment was the disenchantment of the world; the dissolution of myths and the substitution of knowledge for fancy.'[34] The purpose of 'disenchantment' was to appropriate power and control for man as the supreme subject in the world; Adorno and Horkheimer quoted Bacon to demonstrate the core of the scientific attitude: 'the sovereignty of man lieth hid in knowledge . . . now we govern nature in opinions, but we are thrall unto her in necessity: but if we would be led by her in invention, we should command her by action' (pp. 3–4). Whereas myth established man's empathy *via* 'animism' with the natural world, a form of partnership, science predicted dominance, reconstructing nature into a system whereby meaning was possible only within the structures of man's readings. Such readings became accommodated very clearly within the contradictions of late capitalism:

> The concordance between the mind of man and the nature of things that he had in mind is patriarchal: the human mind, which overcomes superstition, is to hold sway over a disenchanted nature. Knowledge, which is power, knows no obstacles: neither in the enslavement of men nor in compliance with the world's rulers. As with all the ends of bourgeois economy in the factory and on the battlefield, origin is no bar to the

161

dictates of the entrepreneurs: kings, no less directly than businessmen, control technology; it is as democratic as the economic system with which it is bound up.

And technology was 'the essence of this knowledge': 'It does not work by concepts and images, by the fortunate insight, but refers to method, the exploitation of others' work and capital. . . . What men want to learn from nature is how to use it in order wholly to dominate it and other men' (p. 4).

The scientific metaphors of Pound's prose had sought a new materiality as a new realism for the world, a materiality which then became available for a view of economics founded on a demand for a return to so-called 'real' value for money. In this context, in 1933, he quoted 'eight of the most significant lines ever written' from Jefferson's letter to Crawford of 1816:

> . . . and if the national bills issued be bottomed (as is indispensable) on pledges of specific taxes for their redemption within certain and moderate epochs, and be of *proper denominations* for *circulation,* no interest on them would be necesary or just, because they would answer to every one of the purposes of the metallic money withdrawn and replaced by them.[35]

Pound's insistence on 'real' money was impelled in great part by Jefferson's agrarianism and the 'hard money' of Jackson revived by the Populists during the Gilded Age, best exemplified by Bryan's 'Cross of Gold' speech of 1896. He was, of course, writing in the wake of the visible decline in the value of 'hard money' dramatized in the events of 1929. These events succinctly demonstrated the obvious evils of a capitalist economy characterized by speculation, the stock market and paper money: paper feeding off paper. Paradoxically, such immateriality was the direct consequence of the valorization of technology and the structures of alienation and distance at all levels of social life which formed the corollary of that valorization. The simple symbolism of coinage, itself a perversion of the system of production and exchange, became yet further perverted, in the system of bourgeois economy, by the more complex symbolism of paper money which mimed exactly the dissociations of that economy designed to perpetuate a world constituted by the fake materiality of commodities.[36] To put it another way, for Adorno and Horkheimer 'the canon of the

162

Enlightenment' which promised a 'schema of the calculability of the world', led inevitably to abstraction as a result of a particular ambition: 'In advance, the Enlightenment recognizes as being and occurrence only what can be apprehended in unity: its ideal is the system from which all and everything follows' (p. 7).

The abstraction consequent upon the numerology in Enlightenment science gave rise to a distinct figure: 'Bourgeois society is ruled by equivalence. It makes the dissimilar comparable by reducing it to abstract qualities', engineering equations which 'dominate bourgeois justice and commodity exchange' (p. 7). In magic and in myth, the uniqueness of things made them unavailable for exchange as commodities; the 'specific representation' of uniqueness ('what happens to the enemy's spear, hair or name, also happens to the individual') was not possible in science where 'specific representation' became a form of 'universal interchangeability (p. 10). Science dealt not with uniqueness but with specimens whose meaning was wholly encoded by what the specimen (interchangeable, having the reproducibility characteristic of commodities) could be made to allude to: the building of an entire skeleton from a single bone, to take a familiar example. It is through the figure of equivalence that we witness again the contradiction of Enlightenment science's ambition for control: 'The doctrine of the equivalence of action and reaction asserted the power of repetition over reality', but 'in the name of law repetition imprisons man in the cycle—that cycle whose objectification in the form of natural law he imagines will ensure his action as a free subject.' Here, the prime casuality may be seen as the elimination of difference:

> The principle of immanence, the explanation of every event as repetition, that the Enlightenment upholds against mythic imagination, is the principle of myth itself. That arid wisdom that holds there is nothing new under the sun. . . . merely reproduces the fantastic wisdom that it supposedly rejects: the sanction of fate that in retribution relentlessly remakes what has already been. What was different is equalized. (p. 12)

The echo from *Ecclesiastes* 1:9 here ('there is nothing new under the sun') reminds us of the figure for equivalence which begins Canto 31, drawn from *Ecclesiastes* 3:7–8, the most famous figure for nature's unified system of balance and repetition. Adorno and Horkheimer show clearly how the Enlightenment view of nature, whereby numbers have a capacity for equalizing, denying difference, through abstraction, pertains to the world of commodities:

> Abstraction, the tool of enlightenment, treats its objects as did fate, the notion of which it rejects: it liquidates them. Under the levelling domination of abstraction (which makes everything in nature repeatable), and of industry (for which abstraction ordains repetition), the freedom themselves finally come to form that 'herd' which Hegel has declared to be the result of the Enlightenment.

This abstraction is thus a function of dominance peculiar to the capitalist period (p. 13) and of the balance insisted upon by Enlightenment thinking, that 'figure of the scales' which for Barthes is characteristic of bourgeois thought whereby 'reality is first reduced to analogues; then it is weighed; finally, equality having been ascertained, it is got rid of.'[37] Adorno and Horkheimer argue that since bourgeois society is 'ruled by equivalence' (p. 7), the 'bourgeois ideal of naturalness intends not amorphous nature, but the virtuous mean' (p. 31). Nature itself can only be conceived as figural, as a constructed system.

The disavowal of difference endemic to the insistence on repetition in Enlightenment science and to the insistence on reproducibility in bourgeois economics is crucial for Pound's poetics, primarily, of course, because the functions of abstraction, the denial of uniqueness and the impossibility of dissociation are the very functions he is avowedly determined to resist, substantially by the metaphors of technology which, as I have tried to suggest, are themselves inevitably infected by their contradictory effects in the world of commodities. Pound's advocation of the principle he applied to Allen Upward, of the 'constructive individual', can be seen as a visible contradiction: the uniqueness of individuality sanctioned by the mythic temperament, to which the early poetry and prose of his London years in particular so strongly testify, simply cannot function within the commodity system. The double contradiction here lies in the fact that Pound is willing both to demystify myth *via* the new materialism prescribed by technology, and to maintain the importance of the individual articulated as supreme subject against the masses conceived as the maleable object of his desire and as a chaotic threat through their uniformity. Such doubleness has, as I shall suggest later, consequences for the disablement of language with which Canto 31 plays.

Here, we may note, finally, how Adorno and Horkheimer recognized the ultimate effect of the Enlightenment's urge to mathematize the world, the internal technologizing of the human body itself, along the lines of the physiology that Jefferson learned from the French *idéologues* and Pound from Gourmont and Berman:

> . . . enlightenment is as totalitarian as any system. Its untruth does not consist in what its romantic enemies have always reproached it for: analytical method, return to elements, dissolution through reflective thought; but instead in the fact that for enlightenment the process is always decided from the start. When in mathematical procedure the unknown becomes the unknown quantity of an equation, this marks it as the well-known even before any value is inserted. . . . In the anticipatory identification of the wholly conceived and mathematized world with truth, enlightenment intends to secure itself against the return of the mythic. It confounds thought and mathematics. In this way the latter is, so to speak, released and made into an absolute instance. . . . Thinking objectifies itself to become an automatic, self-activating process; an impersonation of the machine that it produces itself so that ultimately the machine can replace it. Enlightenment has put aside the classic requirement of thinking about thought. . . . Mathematical procedure became, so to speak, the ritual of thinking . . . it establishes itself as necessary and objective: it turns thought into a thing, an instrument—which is its own term for it. (pp. 24–5)

The human body and the arena of its social relations thus become conveniently harmonized in the most intimate fashion with the dominant forces of industrial production, and domination itself in a commodity society 'has become objectified as law and organization' (p. 37). As industrialism objectified the spirit to resist animism's spiritualization of the object, so human behaviour could only be valuable as a function of the commodity market:

165

Automatically, the economic apparatus, even before total planning, equips commodities with the values which decide human behaviour. Since, with the end of free exchange, commodities lost all their economic qualities except for fetishism, the latter has extended its arthritic influence over all aspects of social life. (p. 28)

The choice of 'arthritic' to describe these effects is a good one because it gestures towards that 'paralysis' which so concerned Joyce and which may be offered as integral to the crisis of language's impoverishment during the modernist period, since sensuous experience, the major canon of value from Pound through to Hemingway, becomes impossible in the reified world of commodities. Or, rather, it is required to be repressed as reminiscent of the animism, the compact with nature, that Enlightenment technology and bourgeois production are designed to resist. Instinctual life has to become fixed, paralysed, as too chaotic for the unity of a mathematized world and the efficiency of the factory production-line. In the process, as Paul Connerton has noted, 'Imagination atrophies in the struggle.'[38] Arthritis, paralysis, atrophy, are useful terms for elaborating the disablement of Pound's art in the linguistic tactics of Canto 31.

3

The most obvious, and the most important, point to be made about the language of Canto 31 is that, with the exception of some six lines, none of it is Pound's, but is taken from the correspondence of Jefferson and, to a lesser extent, Adams.[39] It is characterized by two features: its literal repeatability (with the attendant question of difference) and its autoreflection, its sense of itself as having been made.

Locke closed his discussion of language, 'Of Words', the third book of *An Essay Concerning Human Understanding*, by insisting on the clearest lesson of sensationalist lexicography: that ambiguity should be avoided above all else, that we 'should use the same word constantly in the same sense'. This was to claim that the truth of words lay in their permanence, their impermeability. It was a claim which was resurrected in the debates

about language during the American Renaissance. Diagram-
matically, the issues of these debates may be sited in the work of
two men: Alexander Bryan Johnson's *A Treatise on Language: or,
The Relation which Words Bear to Things* (1836) and Horace
Bushnell's 'Preliminary Dissertation on the Nature of Language,
as Related to Thought and Spirit' (1849). Johnson, disturbed
by language's increasing independence from the physical
world, argued that words only achieved meaning through their
empirical relation to things, whereas Bushnell argued that it
was precisely the ambiguity of words, their indirection and
opposition, which made meaning possible.[40] This clash had
considerable resonance for Pound, and not merely by the
agency of his debt to this period of American literary history
through Emerson and Fenollosa. Adorno and Horkheimer
expressed it in rather different terms:

> Just as hieroglyphs bear witness, so the word too originally had a
> pictorial function, which was transferred to myths. Like magical
> rites, myths signify self-repetitive nature, which is the core of the
> symbolic: a state of being or a process that is presented as eternal,
> because it incessantly becomes actual once more by being
> realized in symbolic form. Inexhaustibility, unending renewal
> and the permanence of the signified are not mere attributes of all
> symbols, but their essential content. (p. 17).

Together with this monotheistic view, they offered language as
a dialectic, the source, as with Bushnell, of its generative
powers: 'When the tree is no longer approached merely as
tree, but as evidence for an Other, as the location of *mana*,
language expresses the contradiction that something is itself
and at one and the same time something other than itself,
identical and not identical.' It is here, of course, that the
notion of difference, so firmly refused by Enlightenment science
and the industrial production-line, is crucial: 'everything is
always that which it is, only because it becomes that which it is
not' (p. 15).

This clash of linguistic positions is not offered as a system of
alternatives but as the field of play in which we may detect the
disablement of Pound's situation in 1933, displayed by his
manipulation of both camps. The familiarity of his materialism
and his concern for precision should not be allowed to obscure

167

his engagement with the generative powers of language's
capacity for contradiction and displacement, an engagement
which, as Joseph Riddel has shown in two exceptional essays,[41]
articulated itself by means of the same metaphors from scientific
materialism. For Pound, Riddel argues, 'proper naming . . .
defines by distinction, by relating differences.'[42] Clearly the
fixity of language incapacitated this generative potency: an
incapacity characterized by the Russian linguist Volosinov in
1930 as 'abstract objectism' on behalf of the Enlightenment
idea of language as 'a system of conventional, arbitrary signs of
a fundamentally rational nature':

> The idea of the *conventionality, the arbitrariness of language,* is a
> typical one for rationalism as a whole, and no less typical is the
> *comparison of language to the system of mathematical signs.* What
> interests the mathematically minded rationalists is not the
> relationship of the sign to the actual reality it reflects nor to the
> individual who is its originator, but the *relationship of sign to sign
> within a closed system* already accepted and authorized. In other
> words, they are interested only in the *inner logic of the system of signs
> itself,* taken, as in algebra, completely independently of the
> ideological meanings that give the signs their content.[43]

Volosinov presents rather too reductive a case by omitting the
physiological character of Enlightenment mathematics and its
consequence for internal technology (the more revealing aspect
of the Enlightenment temperament for a reading of the totali-
tarian impulse and the complex of Pound's advocation of
Jefferson during the same historical period), but he offers an
accurate acknowledgement of the paradox within materialist
epistemology in its inevitable abstraction. Science, of course, is
never grounded in social or historical facts: in itself it is an
ideological apparatus with a function to deny its ideological
status through its refusal of society and history as a means of
siting itself in an arena of practical, constructive objectivity.
The particular incapacity suggested by Volosinov's 'abstract
objectism' was given a more complex reading in Adorno and
Horkheimer's version of the debate about language with which
we began: 'As a system of signs, language is required to resign
itself to calculation in order to know nature, and must discard
the claim to be like her. As image, it is required to resign itself to

mirror-imagery in order to be nature entire, and must discard the claim to know her' (p. 18). Again, if we allow such a statement to remain within a system of alternatives, we simply discount it as too reductive. It is important to recognize here the potential paralysis of language, considered as a means of getting about in the world, in the face of these demands. The issue is complicated and clarified by the monotheistic notion of representation which hangs over it.

Pound's impulse was always to resist monotheism in all its forms, including the dictatorship of language considered as a system of fixed empiricism; his view of Christianity's use of the Bible, for example, has been well expressed by Jean-Michel Rabaté: 'The unique god of monotheism is at best a workable substitute, such as "canned goods" on the market. The Bible cannot be used as "reading matter", since to borrow from a central bank is the economic equivalent of bowing down to a central god: both result in the same oppression or usury.'[44] Pound wanted not to fix the usage of words within a determinant system, but to see how they worked in particular situations; he introduced his discussion of Jefferson in 1933 thus: 'I don't propose to limit my analysis to what Tom Jefferson *said*. I don't propose to limit my analysis to what Tom Jefferson recommended *in a particular time and place*. I am concerned with what he actually did, with the way his mind worked both when faced with a particular problem *in* a particular geography, and when faced with the unending problem of CHANGE.'[45] So Pound's organic metaphors from materialist science, paradoxically, should be seen as strategies for displacing notions of representation by their attention to difference; Riddel has argued convincingly:

> The originality of language lies in its secondary function, its irreducible power of displacement. Thus the doubleness of Pound's origin, whether nature or brain, names creation as a play of forces which has no beginning and end. Brain is not a creative force, but neither is nature. Creation is never the expression of a prior 'subject' or origin, of a self-presence. Creation is repetition. . . . Pound deconstructs the 'subject' in order to celebrate the true power of the creative principle.

Riddel's proposal of secondariness assumes that notion of

repetition (in the form of revision) which always marks differ-
ence. Pound's organic metaphors, situated in the field princi-
pally articulated by Gourmont, Upward and Carpenter, signal
a system of production whereby 'the cycle of the eternal return
as repetition and difference displaces the metaphor of the
eternal return as a repetition of the same.' What this displace-
ment questions are precisely the ideas of 'representation' of its
corollary 'subject': 'Secondariness becomes an originary force.
By bringing into question the idea of representation, it dis-
places the metaphors of the centre and circumference, or
inside and outside, with the metaphor of a theatre of meta-
morphoses ruled by chance, play, desire, and therefore chaos.
Art becomes an endless labyrinth, a staging of differences, a
kind of rebus.'[46] Language, here, thus becomes man's tool, an
instrument for construction, whose characteristic is detach-
ment, 'the mark of his displacement and repetition in and of
nature'.[47]

Riddel acutely demonstrates how the metamorphic propen-
sity of Pound's temperament, invariably suggesting occasions
for his organic metaphors, refuses, by its sustaining of differ-
ence, the tyranny of monotheism. By comparison with the
mythic method of Eliot which sought the unity of stability, a
totalizing centre, Pound's tendency was to disclaim the authority
of history and the myth of primordial originality, be it located in
sacred text or privileged event. Pound's 'gods' are 'changelings
who do not stand behind and effect changes but are in them-
selves multiple forces' and his 'now' is 'not a present of fulfilled
presence, but a place of *praxis*, of production or translation'.[48]
To put it another way, these discriminations propose how
Pound's use of myth and of the past did not share the nostalgia
that characterized Eliot's usage and, consequently, how the
totalitarian nature of their respective politics may be differ-
entiated. Compare Eliot's well-known testament to the past in
'Tradition and the Individual Talent' with Volosinov's sense of
the appropriation of the past during the period virtually
contemporary with Pound's growing interest in Jefferson:

New aspects of existence, once they are drawn into the sphere of
social interest, once they make contact with the human word and
human emotion, do not coexist peacefully with other elements of

existence previously drawn in, but engage them in a struggle, re-evaluate them, and bring about a change in their position within the unity of the evaluative purview. This dialectical generative process is reflected in the generation of semantic properties in language. A new significance emanates from an old one, and does so with its help, but this happens so that the new significance can enter into contradiction with the old one and restructure it.

While Eliot's testament eased itself into cultural acceptability with all the blandness of a distanced idealism, Volosinov, thinking in terms of the expansions under late capitalism, offered a view of language's ruptures that came much closer to Pound's sense of generation:

> There is nothing in the structure of signification that could be said to transcend the generative process, to be independent of the dialectical expansion of social purview. Society in process of generation expands its perception of the generative process of existence. There is nothing in this that could be said to be absolutely fixed. And that is how it happens that meaning—an abstract, self-identical element—is subsumed under theme and torn apart by theme's living contradictions so as to return in the shape of a new meaning with a fixity and self-identity only for the while, just as it had before.[49]

The historical conditions informing Volosinov's view, those, essentially, of a commodity society, precipitated a more radical reading of the familiar modernist wish to revitalize language (in Hemingway's phrase, to cleanse all the dirty words) which pointed succinctly to the occasion for that wish, an occasion of paralysis and disablement deeply relevant for the strategy of quotation in Canto 31. The occasion to which Volosinov referred was, again, a re-reading of a familiar modernist concern, the possibilities for an authentic voice: the 'categorical word', the word 'from one's own mouth', the '*declaratory* word', argued Volosinov, remained 'alive only in scientific writings'. Here, all other verbal activity amounted to piecing together 'other persons' words' and 'words seemingly from other persons'.[50] Explicit quotation itself is a means of drawing attention to words as constructions, as ready-made objects whose process of manufacture is prior to present use: it is, as it were, an extreme version of the fate of language in Volosinov's account,

171

miming by its own procedure the characteristic of inauthenticity that Volosinov noted. This inauthenticity 'bespeaks an alarming instability and uncertainty of the ideological word' which Volosinov figured as 'the stage of *transformation of the word into a thing*, the stage of *depression in the thematic value of the word*'. Needless to say, Volosinov's 'thing' is the static version of Fenollosa's science, paralysed by the commodity values it had been the design of the transcendentalist ideology to resist, and featured by the impossibility of 'the word with its theme intact, the word permeated with confident and categorical social value judgement, the word that really means and takes responsibility for what it says.'[51]

From the conditions outlined by Volosinov, we may see again the contradictions of Pound's enterprise which reveal themselves significantly in the production of Canto 31. The Enlightenment demythologization of language, whereby myth and magic were replaced by materialist science, put an end to, in Adorno and Horkheimer's account, the 'superstitious fusion of word and thing' so that words and their referents were distinct yet inseparable. The technology which made this possible demanded a voice for its own effectiveness, found most obviously in the advertising slogans whose simplicity and repetitiveness displayed the easy move between technology and psychotechnology, procedures for manipulation expressed through the production-line and the bill-board. The linguistic paralysis, as Adorno and Horkheimer described it, which mimed the paradox of Enlightenment materialism as it developed towards the world of commodities, expressed itself through a fossilized meaninglessness at the expense of sensuous experience:

> the result is that the word, which can now be only a sign without any meaning, becomes so fixed to the thing that it is just a petrified formula. This affects language and object alike. Instead of making the object experiential, the purified word treats it as an abstract instance, and everything else (now excluded by the demand for ruthless clarity from expression—itself now banished) fades away in reality. (pp. 163–64)

Such repression was inevitable within the apparatus of technology partly because of the process of privatization (in which Pound's ideal of the 'constructive individual' plays an obvious role) whereby man became increasingly isolated from his environment and from the shared community of meaning that accompanied it.[52] This can be read in terms of the problems of authenticity that Volosinov described and in terms of the linguistic efficiency and concision that Pound had always advocated as the basis of his poetics, an efficiency articulated through a whole series of metaphors derived from applied technology (ranging from his reading of Hudson Maxim in his London years to the loose-leaf book-keeping system of the 1930s). Recently, Wylie Sypher has given a good account of the specific kind of distance predicated by a technological view-point, a distance which results from technology's adherence to methodologies and which has consequences for privatization and for linguistic economy by its 'parsimony':

> In a general sense one might call it a psychology of thrift, a control that is a mode of precaution, privation, or repression, a mentality expressing itself in its sparest and most impersonal form in engineering, the choice of methods that most economically yield the designed results. A law of parsimony worked in aestheticism as it did in science.[53]

Privatization and economy were explicitly paired in Canto 31 by Pound's selection of the quotations which constitute the poem wholly from correspondence, not from public or published papers; a selection designed to yield, in Pound's familiar slogans, a 'phalanx of particulars', a range of 'luminous details'. And since Canto 31 began with considerations of time, in the language of *Ecclesiastes* ('Tempus loquendi,/ Tempus tacendi') and in one of the rare instances of his own language ('Said Mr. Jefferson: It wd. have given us time'), it is worth remembering that against, in Fredric Jameson's phrase, 'the quantified and instrumentalized clock time of the world of work', experienced under late capitalism, was proposed the Bergsonian notion of 'lived' time, inevitably private and marginalized, 'a privatizing response, in its valorization and mystique of an authentic, personal temporality to be cultivated in opposition to the inauthentic time of factory space.'[54] The complex of privation and privatization thus figured in temporal terms, the paralysis of word and object that we have been discussing. The earlier world of Jefferson had no such recognition available to it: indeed it was strongly characterized by the very wish to internalize technology by mathematizing time along with all the other immaterial aspects of life, as witnessed, for example, by Jefferson's enthusiasm for the work of the astronomer David Rittenhouse in constructing working mechanical models of the universe itself.[55] For Jefferson to ask for time, in the version of Canto 31, was to ask for mechanical control, the control evidenced in the re-making of nature through the items of scientific interest that inscribe Pound's choice for beginning the poem.

4

What constitutes Canto 31 is its array of ready-made linguistic objects in the form of the quotations Pound chose as its programme. If nothing else, these objects strike us by precisely their own objectivity, their status of having been made, and by their signification (allusion is the wrong word) of an overwhelmingly concrete world. They operate as items of material and mechanical notation both in the themes they offer on behalf of an Enlightenment temperament and in their own roles as semantic occasions. Such solidity, employed, for the first time in the poem's sequence (and further in its strategies of beginning, in the commencement of another stage of its progress as the poem moved from the Renaissance of Malatesta to the 'Nuevo Mundo' of Jefferson and Adams, mimed by the ceremony of the ancient language in its opening and closing lines, and the new possibilities of 1776), cannot be innocent of the paralysed solidity characteristic of the world of technology and commodity that was late capitalism's valorized figuration of Enlightenment materialism. And paradoxically, as I have tried to suggest, it was to resist such a world that Pound invoked its own materialism. It is within this paradox that we may determine the condition of disablement which is the province of the poem.

In the vocabulary of literary criticism, Pound's composition of Canto 31 was metonymic, and the work of Herbert Schneidau[56] and Max Nänny[57] has displayed how metonymy may be seen as a main component of much of Pound's innovatory practice. Here, I want to stress that in the case of Canto 31

Pound employed metonymy to the extent that we have to consider it not merely as a compositional feature, but as a part of the poem's very theme. It is, indeed, the major articulation of the poem's autoreferentiality, its display of its own manufacture. Nänny has noted that Pound 'tends to prefer icons and indices to verbal symbols'[58] and this is exactly the effect of Pound's metonymy, to use his 'indices', his 'luminous details' as icons, not to claim sacred or metaphysical values, but as a means of refusing such values by the objectivity of his 'particulars'. Part of the office of this objectivity is to attempt to engage an impossible authenticity; Nänny notes that Pound's habit of quoting 'original' words 'is above all an attempt at assuring ear-witness, first-hand authenticity of statement'.[59] This is to rely on the myth that the oral is prior and somehow more real, immediate or whatever terms seem appropriate, than the written, but inevitably the fact that Pound sought his material from correspondence (sited, as it were, between the oral and the written) and not from public papers does suggest that it was a myth he was willing to play with. And, of course, Canto 31 opens with speech, but it is in a language that is no longer spoken and, furthermore, is deliberately ceremonial. I want to suggest, shortly, that the opening three lines of the poem involve a kind of joke whereby Pound attempted to release his writing from the forms of disablement discussed in the present essay, but here we may note provisionally how any spontaneity that may accrue to the oral as against the written is heavily modified by the ontology of quotations as ready-mades and by their initial thematic concern with the technological re-making of nature by Enlightenment science. Schneidau has rightly argued that Pound's ideogrammic method is metonymic and, crucially, that it 'cannot depend on analogy' since it is a practice of one 'who grasps words literally but not metaphorically'.[60] Such literalness would seem to propose a further kind of authenticity whereby objects and words are perceived and offered exactly for what they are: their literalness makes no further (symbolical, metaphorical or allegorical) demands.

We do, however, need to recognize that in Canto 31 it is an authenticity used to inform the poem's concern with its own practice of presentation: Fredric Jameson has shown how the machine-like metonymy of Wyndham Lewis serves not so much to displace metaphor but to conceal it in order to demystify the process of creation (which has always relied on the Aristotelian valorization of metaphor) by the 'unnatural or artificial re-doubling of "nature" by its expression, or by language'.[61] The redoubling process is particularly apparent in Canto 31 where the poem is constructed wholly by a series of synecdoches themselves extracted from material that is already written. Here, the function is to draw attention to the mechanics of creation, as the machine which is Thomas Jefferson is jerked through his dislocated routine (the extracted quotations which, on the page, form no identifiable text of their own) by Pound in the role of engineer. Pound's project here was in part a con-tinuation of the programme of his earlier criticism which adopted the vocabulary of technology to offer the artist's constructions as commensurate with any other comparable system of work or production, allying the artist to the ordinary business of practical living.[62] In Canto 31, Pound elaborated this demystification: the natural world suggested by the open-ing tag from *Ecclesiastes* was not only resisted (in its cyclical form) and remade by Jefferson's mechanical constructivism; it also posited a source of plenitude no longer available in that remade world. Words themselves could no longer seek a resource of richness, fecundity and organic guarantees from the metaphors of a world that, in truth, had never existed and would have to content themselves, through the doubled con-tradiction of their own insistent solidity whereby they exhibit the disparity between event and presentation, with an ack-nowledgement of their secondariness. Jameson has well expressed the characteristic of this secondariness in the case of Lewis:

> Since there exists no adequate language for 'rendering' the object, all that is left to the writer is to tell us how he would have rendered it had he had such a language in the first place.
> There thus comes into being a language beyond language, shot through with the jerry-built shoddiness of modern industrial civilization, brittle and impermanent, yet full of a mechanic's enthusiasm. Lewis's style is thus a violent and exemplary figure for the birth of all living speech and turns to its own advantage the discovery that all language is a second-best, the merest substitute for the impossible plenitude of a primary language

that has never existed. In this sense all speech must settle its accounts with the optical illusion of a natural language if it is to be delivered from a terrorized reduction to silence.[63]

Pound plays explicitly with this secondariness in his opening to the poem:

> Tempus loquendi,
> Tempus tacendi.
> Said Mr. Jefferson: It wd. have given us time.

His reversal of the original order of the Latin, his deliberate translation of two of its words ('Tempus' and 'loquendi') and his equally deliberate refusal to translate its final word ('tacendi') demonstrate a humorous awareness of his play. Not only had Mr. Jefferson never 'said' anything of the kind,[64] but the 'It' is given no reference and, within the humour of Pound's refusal to translate 'tacendi', silently inscribes the vacant place for its meaning, its context for what might have been. The silence of 'It' mimes the virtual silence of Pound's own speaking voice for the rest of the poem. Translation inevitably displays the doubleness of its function, the doubleness that enables Pound's game in these lines, but in the penultimate stanza, he points to its more debilitating aspect in 'A tiels leis . . . en ancien scripture, and this/ they have translated *Holy Scripture*. . . .' Pound's source, Jefferson's letter to Adams of 24 January 1814, was a lengthy diatribe against those who 'extend the coercions of municipal law to the dogmas of their religion, by declaring that these make a part of the law of the land.' Jefferson selected Finch's mistranslation of Prisot's *'ancien scripture'* as 'holy scripture' (further perpetuated by a lengthy and impressive list of the legal misreadings which followed) to point the fraudulent way in which the principles of religion were invoked on behalf of the common law. The activity of mistranslation demonstrates vividly the secondariness of language, and acquires its particular potency here in a context so central to the distrust of monotheism shared by Jefferson and Pound.[65] Pound adds to its potency by inserting a line of his own after the quotation (apart from the opening three lines of the poem itself, and two later lines which are merely directional, this is the only occasion on which he offers us his own voice): 'and they continue this error.' His point is to be taken literally in two senses, referring to the repetitions of the original mistranslation listed in Jefferson's letter, and to Pound's sense that they continue in his own time, yet a further prison for the contemporary world. This is a prison both of ideas and of words, in that meaning suffers from both perversion in the example of mistranslation and the immobility of silence in the absence of any reference for Jefferson's 'It', inevitable consequences of the problems of evaluation in the 'instability and uncertainty' that Volosinov detected as characteristics of language in 1930.[66]

Pound attends to the question of meaning as part of his play with language's secondariness in the cipher he quotes from Jefferson's letter to Madison of 2 August 1787: 'This country is really supposed to be on the eve of XTZBK49HT.' The secrecy of the cipher, at one level, matches the secrecy of Jefferson's reiteration of Adams' proposal for repaying America's debt to France by borrowing from Holland.[67] But as a linguistic event, it further incorporates the meaninglessness of its arithmetical status (in which its figuration as 'o' signifies the silence of its nothingness) and of its status as an arbitrary collection of characters. A cipher bears, of course, a close resemblance to a hieroglyph, and as Joseph Riddel has accurately noted, Pound belonged to a notion of the poet as Egyptologist, one 'who descends into the crypts in order to read the secret language of hieroglyphs', who descends 'not to retrieve a meaning lost or buried in past forms, but to effect a new writing, a pro-jecting and con-jecturing of old signs that is the "beginning" of writing.'[68] Paradoxically, it is through their very secrecy and initial meaninglessness that ciphers draw attention to themselves as pieces of writing since they are wholly free from the determinants of organized grammar. In this sense, they have their own naturalness, of a chaotic kind, for their arbitrariness declares itself unbounded by any law. The arbitrariness of the cipher also recognizes itself as a doubled displacement: like any signifier, it displaces what it signifies which itself (some more organized word) has displaced its appropriate object. And Pound stresses this doubleness by a further act of translation. In the Lipscomb and Bergh edition of Jefferson's *Writings* that he used, no cipher as such was given, but a row of asterisks in place of the 'unintelligible' cipher Jefferson had originally used:[69] a pure case of constructing something out of nothing which took

178

the form of a nonsensical filling of the gap in Jefferson's text. Indeed, it was doubly nonsensical because Pound did not possess the code whereby the cipher could be retranslated back into organized language. Since we are concerned, in Canto 31, with so few words that are Pound's own, the cipher is central to his play with language's secondariness in the particular context of the technology with which *Nuevo Mundo* prepares itself to begin.

The literary counterpart to this technology, metonymy, marks a mechanical inventory; in Jameson's phrase, 'a step-by-step dismantling of the body's gestural machine'.[70] It is a means of deconstructing the world, of providing its synecdoches with a larger burden of meaning than they were designed to carry. As with any machine, too great an over-loading instigates break-down, an explosion of energy. The cipher is the ultimate paradigm for this process: its arbitrariness literally dismantles organized language to display in naked form the displacement and secondariness that characterize language's translations, removing words entirely from the community of communication. Its energy is visible as the joy of freely playing with the keys of a typewriter expresses itself in a typographical dazzle, a cacophony of characters, alphabetical and numerical, to snub the paralysis of the world as market-place, a world which sought its beginnings in the libertarian potential of Enlightenment mechanics in order to begin again, to re-translate and re-make by acknowledging the secondariness of words. The random distribution that characterizes the field of the cipher makes it, as it were, the appropriate expression of the voice which offers the interrupted commencement of the *Cantos* as a whole: the voice of the con-man, the joker, of Odysseus in the non-originating persona of 'No-Man', the paradoxical silence which successfully exploits and deconstructs the confinement of organized discourse.

NOTES

1. Since much of the following essay will be concerned with a range of metaphors for construction and technology in the field of Pound's debt to the Enlightenment, we should remind ourselves of the perceptive readings in Forrest Read, 'The Mathematical Symbolism of Ezra Pound's

Revolutionary Mind', *Paideuma*, VII, 1 and 2 (Spring and Fall 1978), 7–72, elaborated in his *'76. One World and The Cantos of Ezra Pound* (Chapel Hill, 1981), where Read discusses Canto 31 on pp. 200–8.

2. Pound's acknowledgement to Woodward is in *Jefferson and/or Mussolini* (1935; New York, 1970), p. 78.

3. W. E. Woodward, *George Washington. The Image and the Man* (1928), p. 222.

4. See my *Critic as Scientist: The Modernist Poetics of Ezra Pound* (1981), particularly Chapter V.

5. *The Adams-Jefferson Letters*, ed. Lester J. Cappon, 2 vols. (Chapel Hill, 1959), Vol. II, p. 562. Hereafter cited as 'Cappon'.

6. Ibid. Vol. II, p. 567. Pound drew attention to Jefferson's view when he wrote of 'T. J.'s moderate precept of style, namely that any man has the right to a new word when it can make his meaning more clear than an old one' ('The Jefferson-Adams Letters as a Shrine and a Monument', in *Selected Prose*, ed. William Cookson, 1973, p. 123).

7. Ibid., Vol. II, pp. 567–69.

8. The clearest summaries of Jefferson's materialism are given in Adrienne Koch, *The Philosophy of Thomas Jefferson* (1943; Chicago, 1964), pp. 54–88, and Daniel J. Boorstin, *The Lost World of Thomas Jefferson* (1948; Boston, 1960), pp. 111–50.

9. Koch, op. cit., p. 83.

10. Cappon, Vol. II, pp. 605–6. cf. Koch, op. cit. pp. 98–9, and Boorstin, op. cit., pp. 117–18.

11. See my *Critic as Scientist*, ed. cit., *passim*.

12. See ibid., pp. 211–14.

13. Cappon, Vol. II, p. 391. Needless to say, Jefferson's proposal of a 'natural' aristocracy to supplant hereditary aristocracy neatly demonstrates part of the contradiction of Enlightenment arguments for egalitarianism.

14. See Gary Wills, *Inventing America. Jefferson's Declaration of Independence* (New York, 1978), p. 164. Wills's discussion of the Declaration as 'A Scientific Paper' (pp. 93–164) is one of the most suggestive that we have of such accounts.

15. Pound took both citations of the Erie Canal from two of Jefferson's letters to Washington: the first dated 14 August 1787, and the second dated 2 May 1788. (*The Papers of Thomas Jefferson*, ed. Julian P. Boyd, 19 Vols., Princeton, 1955, Vol. XII, p. 36, and Vol. XIII, pp. 124, 128. Hereafter cited as 'Boyd'.)

16. *Gaudier-Brzeska. A Memoir* (1916; New York, 1970), p. 127.

17. *Pavannes and Divisions* (1918), pp. 215–55.

18. *Alvin Langdon Coburn. Photographer. An Autobiography*, ed. Helmut and Alison Gernsheim (1966), p. 104.

19. *Selected Prose of Ezra Pound*, ed. cit., p. 169. Richard Sieburth has rightly commented on this passage: 'Wealth for Pound, be it literary, cultural or economic, was always based on the principle of *exchange:* it is perhaps his deepest affinity with Enlightenment humanism' ('Ideas Into Action: Pound and Voltaire', *Paideuma*, VI, 3 (Winter 1977), 381).

20. *Selected Prose*, p. 63. As early as 1912, Pound had recognized the contra-

diction of any notion of liberty based on property: 'So far as I can make out, there is no morality in England which is not in one way or another a manifestation of the sense of property. / A thing is right if it tends to conserve an estate, or to maintain a succession, no matter what servitude or oppression this inflict' ('Patria Mia', *New Age,* XI, 19–XII, 2; *Patria Mia and the Treatise on Harmony,* 1962, p. 38).

21. *Jefferson and/or Mussolini* (1935; New York, 1970), pp. 33–4.
22. Ibid., pp. 62, 65.
23. Ibid., p. 63.
24. Ibid., pp. 40, 63, 34.
25. Wyndham Lewis, 'The Caliph's Design', in *Wyndham Lewis on Art,* ed. Walter Michel and C. J. Fox (1969), pp. 155–57.
26. Ibid., p. 158.
27. 'The Jefferson-Adams Letters as a Shrine and a Monument', in *Selected Prose,* p. 117.
28. Edward Lurie, *Nature and the American Mind* (New York, 1974), pp. 46–7.
29. See *Jefferson and/or Mussolini,* ed. cit., pp. 19, 39, 103, and 'The Jefferson-Adams Letters', loc. cit., pp. 122, 128.
30. Quoted in Lurie, op. cit., p. 48.
31. Ibid., pp. 48–9.
32. Boyd, Vol. VIII, pp. 299–300.
33. J. Habermas, *Toward a Rational Society* (1971), pp. 100–7.
34. Theodor Adorno and Max Horkheimer, *Dialectic of Enlightenment* (1947), trans. John Cumming, 1979, p. 3. All subsequent references will be included in the main text.
35. *Jefferson and/or Mussolini,* ed. cit., pp. 116–17. Pound repeats the quote in 'The Jefferson-Adams Letters as a Shrine and a Monument', loc. cit., p. 122.
36. We may note the extent of the irony implicit in this contradiction. It can best be illustrated with reference to one of Pound's major sources for his view of Jefferson, Woodward's biography of Washington, where Woodward described Hamilton's role in the establishing of the First Bank of the United States. Woodward saw Hamilton's interest as an attempt to ally proprietary interests on the side of Government, an establishing of, in Jeffersonian terms, a 'tinsel aristocracy' as opposed to a 'natural' aristocracy. The vituperative tone of Woodward's description strongly anticipates Pound's view of Hamilton at the end of Canto 62 as 'the Prime snot in ALL American history': 'The loudly aggressive business element was for him. Every possessor of a mushroom fortune made by buying depreciated paper believed in him. All the little toads that hop around the roots of the money-tree, hoping to pick up something for nothing, were Hamiltonians. . . . High finance in America was born at that time. Speculation became the chief activity of the day. Land gave way to money. Paper fortunes came into existence . . . wealth created through sleight-of-hand tricks with paper and ink' (Woodward, op. cit., pp. 354–55). Hamilton had been unable to introduce a property qualification into the suffrage for the Senate and the Presidency, and the founding of

the Bank provided a means of slipping through the back door: henceforth, 'he managed to identify the idea of Government with that of property so thoroughly that it has never been disentangled' (p. 355). The result instigated what Pound saw as the 'main line of American conflict for the first half of the last century' in the 'fight between public interest and the interests' (*Jefferson and/or Mussolini*, ed. cit., p. 79). Not only Jefferson's views on currency and debt, but his attitude towards a further, related, form of 'paper', the injustice of primogeniture, opposed the Hamiltonian position; Woodward wrote: 'He thought that one generation had no right to bind another generation, either collectively or individually. A practical acceptance of this point of view would put an end to one of the major evils of capitalism; for capitalism's principal hold on civilization lies in its capacity to enslave each new generation by documents representing obligations that were incurred by previous generations' (p. 223). Jefferson deliberately omitted 'property' from the list of 'unalienable Rights' established by the Declaration of Independence, partly, one suspects, because he was aware of the increasing difficulties of maintaining a Lockean view of property (whereby property is earned by labour and limited by the use a man has for the products of that labour) and could foresee the ways in which wealth would become alienated from labour, its proper source of value, and be more and more confined to a minority at the expense of others. His fears were realized with the establishing of the National Bank. Pound, taking Marx as his model in 1933, found the labour theory of value to be incomplete in the face of technological expansion and resisted any nostalgia for a notion of labour that, in Jeffersonian terms, was more applicable to a pre-capitalist, agrarian society. (See, for example, *Jefferson and/or Mussolini*, ed. cit., p. 36.) Jefferson himself acknowledged a similar position late in his life when he noted in a letter of 1816 that, whereas previously, 'to the labor of the husbandman a vast addition is made by the spontaneous energies of the earth on which it is employed . . . to the labor of the manufacturer nothing is added', the present situation demanded 'We must now place the manufacturer by the side of the agriculturalist' (quoted in Stephen Fender, *The American Long Poem*, 1977, p. 105).

Simultaneously, however, Jefferson insisted on a naturalistic view of money; in a letter to Adams of 21 March 1819, praising the work of Tracy, he wrote: 'The evils of this deluge of paper money are not to be removed until our citizens are generally and radically instructed in their cause and consequences, and silence by their authority the interested clamors and sophistry of speculating, shaving and banking institutions' (Cappon, Vol. II, pp. 538–39). Pound cited Tracy towards the end of Canto 71 in exactly this context: '. . . Gold, silver are but commodities/ Pity, says Tracy, they ever were stamped save by weight/ They are commodities as is wheat or is lumber.' Pound's source was a letter from Adams to John Taylor (the author of *An Inquiry into the Principles and Policy of the Government of the United States* (1814), and, arguably, the clearest contemporary exponent of Jeffersonian principles) of 12 March 1819: 'Silver and gold are but commodities, as much as wheat and lumber . . . [Tracy's] chapter "of money" contains the sentiments that I have entertained all my life-time. . . . It is to be desired, that coins had never borne other names than those of their weight, and that the arbitrary denominations, called moneys of account, as L, s., d., &c., had never been used. But when these denominations are admitted and employed in transactions, to diminish the quantity of metal to which they answer, by an alteration of the real coins, is to steal. . . . A theft of greater magnitude and still more ruinous, is the making of paper money; it is greater, because in this money there is absolutely no real value; it is more ruinous because, by its gradual depreciation during all the time of its existence, it produces the effect which would be produced by an infinity of successive deteriorations of the coins. All these iniquities are founded on the false idea, that money is but a sign' (quoted in Frederick K. Sanders, *John Adams Speaking*, Orono, 1975, pp. 502–3). Money, whatever its shape, is of course 'but a sign' within an industrial economy. The confusions between natural products (wheat, lumber), gold/silver, and paper, lead precisely to the contra-dictions evident in the valorization of a 'natural' abundant basis for money in a world of advanced technology. The urge to naturalize money that Pound reiterated from Jefferson and Adams was a token of resistance to the paper of the speculators, but whereas commodities for the Enlightenment were enabled to retain a measure of productive inno-cence, no such possibility was available in the commodity society of later capitalism. The materiality of the former became debilitatingly technolo-gized by the latter to the point of abstraction.

37. Roland Barthes, 'Myth Today', *Mythologies* (1957; trans. Annette Lavers, 1972), p. 153.
38. Paul Connerton, *The Tragedy of Enlightenment* (Cambridge, 1980), p. 67.
39. See Robert M. Knight, 'Thomas Jefferson in Canto XXXI', *Paideuma*, V, 1 (Spring/Summer 1976), 79–93; Stephen Fender, *The American Long Poem* (1977), pp. 94–109; George Kearns, *Guide to Ezra Pound's Selected Cantos* (Folkestone, 1980), pp. 80–92.
40. I am paraphrasing the opening gist of an excellent article by Philip F. Gura, 'Language and Meaning: An American Tradition', *American Literature*, LIII, 1 (March 1981), pp. 1–21.
41. 'Pound and the Decentered Image', *The Georgia Review*, XXIX, 3 (Fall 1975), 565–91, and 'Decentering the Image: The "Project" of "American" Poetics', *Boundary 2*, VIII, 1 (Fall 1979), 159–87.
42. Riddel, 'Pound and the Decentered Image', loc. cit., p. 575.
43. V. N. Volosinov, *Marxism and the Philosophy of Language* (1930; trans. Ladislav Matejka and I. R. Titunik, New York and London, 1973), pp. 57–8.
44. Jean-Michel Rabaté, 'Pound's art of naming: Between Reference and Reverence', a paper delivered to the 'Seventh International Ezra Pound Conference' held at the University of Sheffield 11–14 April 1981, and to be published in a collection of papers from the Conference, edited by Philip Grover for the AMS Press, New York. I am extremely grateful to

Professor Rabaté for permission to quote from the typescript of his paper.
45. *Jefferson and/or Mussolini*, ed. cit., p. 11.
46. Riddel, 'Pound and the Decentered Image', loc. cit., pp. 570–71. It is not solely in Pound's organic metaphors that we can see the dispersal of 'subject' which Riddel suggests: the notion of the 'periplum', for example, presents a famous instance of Pound's unwillingness, literally, to see the world from the point of view of a centred map of stability.
47. Ibid., p. 573.
48. Ibid., pp. 576–78, 581.
49. Volosinov, op. cit., p. 106. Pound and Jefferson refused the valorization of history that we find in Eliot. In Canto 31, Pound cited Jefferson's use of the Maison Quarrée of Nismes as a *working* model for the State of Virginia's capitol building, and chose as his opening quotation from Jefferson the latter's view that modern rather than antique dress would be most appropriate for a statue of Washington. Pound was being rather playful here: Woodward's biography gave details of the pomp and circumstance of Washington's drives to Congress, ceremonies which were abolished by Jefferson's presidency (Woodward, op. cit., p. 352), and amongst the titles by which Washington first wanted to be addressed was 'His Mightiness the President of the United States' (p. 348).
50. Ibid., pp. 158–59.
51. Ibid., p. 159.
52. See Connerton, op. cit., p. 79.
53. Wylie Sypher, *Literature and Technology. The Alien Vision* (New York, 1971), p. xvi. Fredric Jameson's recent investigation into an area directly germane for our present concerns, the machine-like sentences of Wyndham Lewis, offers a similar comment: 'In modern times . . . all creative and original speech flows from privation rather than from plenitude: its redoubled energies, far from tapping archaic or undiscovered sources of energy, are proportionate to the massive and well-nigh impenetrable obstacles which aesthetic production must overcome in the age of reification' (*Fables of Agression. Wyndham Lewis, the Modernist as Fascist*, Berkeley, Los Angeles and London, 1979, p. 81).
54. Fredric Jameson, *Fables of Agression. Wyndham Lewis, the Modernist as Fascist* (Berkeley, Los Angeles and London, 1979), p. 134.
55. See Wills, op. cit., pp. 100ff.
56. Herbert Schneidau, 'Pound, Olson and Objective Verse', *Paideuma*, V, 1 (Spring/Summer 1976), 15–29.
57. Max Nänny, 'The Oral Roots of Ezra Pound's Methods of Quotation and Abbreviation', *Paideuma*, VIII, 3 (Winter 1979), 381–87; 'Context, Contiguity and Contact in Ezra Pound's *Personae*', *English Literary History*, XLVII, 2 (Summer 1980), 386–98.
58. Nänny, 'Context, Contiguity and Contact in Ezra Pound's *Personae*', loc. cit., p. 389.
59. Nänny, 'The Oral Roots of Ezra Pound's Methods of Quotation and Abbreviation', loc. cit., p. 382.
60. Schneidau, 'Pound, Olson, and Objective Verse', loc. cit., p. 19. Pound's

literalness lends further weight to the insistently objective, factual world of the poem (figured most explicitly in the 'tobacco' stanza) and, again, we see here the contradiction in the use of such an overwhelmingly materialist view. Schneidau, in a later essay, has commented on behalf of Joyce's Dublin that 'It goes beyond those rationales for realism that were produced by the insinuation of scientific method into narrative techniques. On the other hand, it may have to do with the development of a renewed sense of the reality of history', but this 'reality' is inevitably paradoxical; Schneidau continues by noting Joyce's irony: 'Far from implying a guarantee of metaphysical "truth" behind the work, the germs of fact opened vistas of disparity between event and representation' ('Style and Sacrament in Modernist Writing', *The Georgia Review*, XXXI, 2 (Summer 1977), pp. 435–36). To see the 'disparity between event and representation' as a play of irony for Joyce cannot be transferred to the case of Canto 31 where the very solidity of its world disables its language as Pound struggled to refute the materiality of a commodity society with the allied materiality of his own practice. His methods of constructive precision and economy, designed to stress the reality of things, were exactly those of the late capitalism and its consequences in reification he so hated.

61. Jameson, op. cit., pp. 28–9. Jameson obliquely reminds us of the liberation promised by technology when he notes that 'the mechanical, the machinelike, knows an exaltation peculiarly its own' (p. 25) where a machine is 'less a thing than a center of radiant energy' (p. 82). Prior to Lewis, the case of Henry Adams offers the most apposite example.

62. See my *Critic as Scientist*, ed. cit., p. 74.

63. Jameson, op. cit., p. 86. I should make it clear that I do not consider Lewis's exercise to be exactly comparable to Pound's but that their respective ideologies of language share some general features.

64. By this I mean that I, in company with those comentators who have substantially annotated the poem by means of Jefferson's correspondence (listed in note 39 above), have been unable to locate its source. In a poem so constructed, the absence of this source is a matter of more germane importance than merely the incompleteness of a scholar's list or faulty memory on the part of Pound.

65. Cappon, Vol. II, pp. 421–25. Jefferson's attack on the tyranny of lawyers who so perverted civic justice by invoking faked religious sanctions (pp. 422–23) was followed by an equally violent attack on that other monotheistic institution, the banks (pp. 424–25). The letter concluded with a postscript admiring William Barton's recent biography of 'our good and really great Rittenhouse' who 'as a mechanician . . . certainly has not been equalled' (p. 425). The range and strength of this configuration of interests, by no means, of course, rare in Jefferson's correspondence, informs the weight of Pound's concern with translation in the poem itself, and, I would suggest, enables us to see his selection from this particular letter as an especially vibrant moment in the field of Canto 31.

66. Volosinov insisted on the inadmissibility of a disjuncture between

referential meaning and evaluation: 'The separation of word meaning from evaluation inevitably deprives meaning of its place in the living social process (where meaning is always permeated with value judgement), to its being ontologized and transformed into ideal Being divorced from the historical process of Becoming.' This, in part, proposes again a problem of authenticity, since by 'evaluation' Volosinov intends 'the expression of a speaker's individual attitude toward the subject matter of his discourse' (op. cit., p. 105). In other words, authenticity may only be gauged in the context assumed by an exchange between two or more voices, a condition of interchange, through the generative powers of language's indirection and ambiguity, which offers the socially hazardous possibility of revision. In the third line of Canto 31, the condition of such dialogue is explicitly refused: Jefferson's 'It' is irredeemably paralysed as a non-dialogic moment (figured by the absence of its context) which responds to the enclosure suggested by the preceding ceremonial language from *Ecclesiastes*. (I am particularly appreciative of a conversation with Richard Godden on this point.)

67. Boyd, Vol. XI, pp. 662–64. The cipher itself is used on p. 664 and belongs to a code which Jefferson used extensively at the end of the letter. The early correspondence between Jefferson and Adams also contained occasional coded passages. The secrecy of a cipher, whereby its reference is available only to those who know the code, suggests ciphers as the most appropriate expressions of the privatization consequent upon technology.
68. Riddel, 'Decentering the Image: The "Project" of "American" Poetics?' loc. cit., p. 163.
69. See Fender, op. cit., pp. 98, 99.
70. Jameson, op. cit., p. 31.

7

'Neo-Nietzschean Clatter'— Speculation and/on Pound's Poetic Image

by JOSEPH N. RIDDEL

> Nietzsche in Basel studied the deep pool
> Of these discolorations, mastering
>
> The moving and the moving of their forms
> In the much-mottled motion of blank time.
>
> His revery was the deepness of the pool,
> The very pool, his thoughts the colored forms,
>
> The eccentric souvenirs of human shapes,
> Wrapped in their seemings, crowd on curious crowd,
>
> In a kind of total affluence, all first,
> All final, colors subjected in revery
>
> To an innate grandiose, an innate light,
> The sun of Nietzsche gildering the pool,
>
> Yes: gildering the swarm-like manias
> In perpetual revolution, round and round . . .
>   —Stevens, 'Description without Place'

There has never seemed to be a 'question' of Nietzsche for (modern) American literature. At least not in the sense of 'question' or problematic which Jacques Derrida has called the 'Question du style' (or 'Eperons', in English, 'Spurs'). Put another way, while there are admittedly thematic traces of Nietzsche woven throughout the text(ure)s of modernist style, the question of Nietzsche as influence is generally identified in historical banalities, as a precursor of contemporary nihilisms and pessimisms. If Harold Bloom's appeals to Nietzsche's rhetoric of interpretation transcend this banality and transform it into a viable poetics, Bloom nevertheless situates Nietzsche's 'discolorations' in a history of influences that transcribes the American scene of writing, Nietzsche being a 'poet' whose 'father' is Emerson and whose influence in turn reinvents the Romantic crisis poem in the style of modernism. Which is to say, Nietzsche intervenes in and breaks the illusion of philosophy's priority to poetic vision, and retells in his own fictions of 'perpetual revolution' the poetic origins of the self/world.

Tracing Nietzsche's 'traces' through modern literature would be a formidable and not altogether rewarding task—a grand tour, as Bloom might say, of the turnings of certain tropes, and of misreadings. On the surface of it, Nietzsche is either the putative father of every pessimism or the herald of every (fascistic) self-overcoming. This thematized Nietzsche, of course, remains the philosopher indicting the modern (the Romantic), and inditing in the margins of literature the radical critique of western intellectual entropy. This Nietzsche appears variously in Shaw and Mencken, as well as in Proust and Spengler, and often in the most naïve forms, as for example in Scott Fitzgerald's youthful romances of the exiled and repressed young artist. The nostalgia of this version of modernism is a commonplace and a somewhat irrelevant consequence of the very historicism Nietzsche so vigorously deconstructed.

We do know that many of the most prominent American poets had more than a passing interest in Nietzsche, though just what they appropriated (and miscomprehended) is difficult to isolate. Perhaps the innocence of, if not antagonism toward, philosophy which characterizes so much modernism (apparent at the same time in efforts to adapt philosophemes to poetic truth-utterances) is the best index to the 'question' of Nietzsche's influence upon modernist poetry. Hart Crane's youthful reflec- tion, 'The Case against Nietzsche' (1918),[1] which defends the philosopher against the political insinuations of 'Prussianism', does little more than suggest the way Nietzsche was read (as an ethical thinker, even when an antagonist of predominant morals) by the poets—in Crane's case as a 'mystery', like a voice of 'Great Indra', a prophet of self-overcoming and recuperated wholeness. Wallace Stevens, who in the late 1930s and early 1940s collected Nietzsche's texts—and even read some of them, evidently—would deny any influence while reflecting it in both his themes and tropes.[2] And Ezra Pound, who is indigenously American in his rejection of philosophy and especially German metaphysics, very early recognized Nietzsche as one of those nineteenth-century thinkers who 'made a temporary commotion' and whose 'prose style' was an intervention and disturbance in a world of received ideas.[3] One could perhaps trace Pound's interest in Nietzsche to A. R. Orage's little book on the philospher's aesthetics,[4] but this is of little help in reading the tone of 'neo-Nietzschean clatter' which surrounds his Mauberley. Is it the popularization and common gossip of intellectuals who threaten his fragile integrity or simply the image of an age in perilous change?[5] At least one can say that Pound seems to owe little of his right-wing politics or economics to Nietzsche, something that one cannot say with absolute surety about Stevens. But if these two very different poets—who serve our two most canonical critics, Hugh Kenner and Harold Bloom, as mutually exclusive titular fathers of the modernist 'era'—seem to share only an admiration for Mussolini, it is necessary to look elsewhere than politics or economics, or to a history of ideas, for the modern problematic they share.

Indeed, to say that they share modernism, whether or not it is the contemporary scepticism derived from this or that philosophy, is to put the issue in terms of the same questionable historicism that permits canon formations of a 'Pound era' or a 'Stevens era', since it is the tendency of literary studies, according to Paul de Man, to describe the 'structure of meaning' as preceding and standing outside the linguistic (and rhetorical) elements they necessarily inhabit.[6] More precisely, to pursue de Man's critique, which is directly related to the 'question' of Nietzsche and the problematic of philosophy he locates in language, the poets do not so much follow Nietzsche as repeat him innocently, since neither poet nor philosopher can take the 'detour or retreat from language'[7] into historiography or psychologism that is common among students of literature. Nietzsche, then, according to de Man, raises in the most acute and deconstructive way the 'perennial question of the distinction between philosophy and literature'[8] which the poets cannot avoid, even though they must ask the question differently, or pose it, this question of where the one crosses the other, as it were, in-versely.

De Man's rhetorical analyses of Nietzsche's deconstructive rhetoric inaugurates a reversal of the 'retreat from language' in critical discourse by turning to that almost forgotten moment in Nietzsche's canon in which the question of rhetoric is first raised. Not surprisingly, he finds that moment in the earliest texts, and not simply the early texts on rhetoric but even before that, in *The Birth of Tragedy*, which poses the question in terms of a narrative or genetic structure that both grounds and undermines its own argument: an argument that must be told as a story of literary origins and therefore an allegory which reveals the allegoricity of literary history. If it is not feasible to summarize, let alone repeat or amplify, de Man's exhaustive critique of Nietzsche here, it is no less impossible to double it in regard to the literature—or poetic theory—which Nietzsche putatively influenced. Nevertheless, the question de Man raises, in a most complex and sophisticated way, is anticipated in the modern poets' need to return (or simply turn) to questions of language: of referentiality, objectivity, precision, or adequation, and hence metaphor, of a language which resists its own ontological claims of being both medium and message. This is not to say that the return to language is unique or exclusive with what is called modernism, or that modernism employed in this way is a meaningful historical and metaphysical category. The apparent self-reflexivity of modern literature (which usually implies its particular inheritance from Romanticism) has been interpreted both as a sign of its weakness (of solipsism, of entropy) and its strength (its formal strength, its effort toward purifying language), even to the point that modernism's obsessive references to its own strategies are viewed as coherent poetic statements about its own coherence, statements that overcome their own figural status and stand as revelatory of 'poetic' language in all its privilege or truth. On the other hand, a certain other notion of modernism, its putative return to concreteness or objectivity, has been interpreted as an overcoming of Romanticism and a recuperation of classical precision, a style of 'attention' in which reference becomes not only sufficient to its object but synecdochal, a kind of 'thing-itself' or 'symbol', and 'poem itself'. This is another version of self-reflexivity, of both internal and external adequation of word and thing. These modernisms resolve the Romantic irony which de Man finds most poignantly elucidated in Nietzsche's athetic rhetoric, an irony which in de Man's reading resists every effort of resolution or overcoming.

It is inconceivable to de Man that literature can resolve what perplexes philosophy, especially when one marks the irreducible literariness (the figurality and rhetoricity) which inhabits all metalinguistic utterances and puts them in question. Similarly, an exploration of poetry, and particularly that poetry which appears to make metapoetic statements, must entertain the same ironic resistance to reductions of meaning or monological readings. It is this kind of 'reading' which led Jacques Derrida to the unhistorical but remarkably salient statement (in *De la grammatologie*) that it was not only Nietzsche but Mallarmé, and more significantly for our purposes here, Ezra Pound and Ernest Fenollosa, who began, if began has any meaning here, the undoing of the western *épistémè* by disrupting its grammatological illusion of erasing writing (or in de Man's terms, of erasing rhetoricity).[9] Though appearing to give historical names and privilege to this belated beginning (again), Derrida like de Man after him resists the historical argument that would associate deconstruction with modernism (or post-modernism), but associates it instead with literature (or poetry) in which is (always ready) inscribed the self-reflexive illusion and its undoing, or grammar (and its metapoetic statements) and rhetoric. If as Derrida suggests, Pound and Fenollosa, along with Mallarmé, recuperate an originary (graphic) poetics, they do not properly recuperate anything, but interrupt certain fictions of closure and offer a glimpse of the indeterminate demarcation between language and 'reality', which rather than expelling the outside or otherness from language allow some indefinite element of the 'other' *in* and thus disallow our coherent readings which are based on the precise demarcation, that fiction of the poem which depicts, expresses, objectifies, or unveils truth or 'being'.

Returning poetry to the linguistic problematic, a poet like Pound cannot be read as having completed the historical (traditional) model he seems everywhere to have privileged, if only as an eccentricity. No more than a poet like Stevens, who is variously read as continuing the Romantic tradition and providing a severe internal critique of it, can be read as a poet who completes the project of metaphor to erase or abyss the 'abyss' that opens between 'us and the object' and hence to provide, in the poem, the 'thing itself' and not 'ideas about' it.[10] If what follows seems thematic rather than rhetorical in its reading of the problematics of modernism, its insistence on the 'neo-Nietzschean clatter' of Imagist poetics does certainly reject the notion that Nietzsche's themes are modernism, in order to argue that the Nietzsche in-habiting modernism is a philosopher never yet 'read' by the poets but one who has 'read' the poets. That is, a Nietzsche which inhabits the rhetoric of poetry and disturbs its speculations, who *figures* in its illusions of self-reflexivity and at the same time *fractures* its self-reflective moments.

2

If any one term can be said to be a watchword of modernist (American) poetics, and especially of that strain most concerned with 'tradition', it is 'objectivity'. For critics like Hugh Kenner it has become a valorized notion of a certain decorum of poetic style, most clearly exemplified by Ezra Pound and after him Louis Zukofsky, but also in a certain sense by Eliot as well as Williams and Marianne Moore. The ideal of objectivity, of an adequation of word to 'thing' which produces a 'precision' and even thing-ness of the word, has been fulfilled in modern literature in a tradition developing from Flaubert through the

'Pound era' and thus never seemed in question to Kenner. On the contrary, it validates the 'poetic' and 'style' as synonyms to 'truth', of 'law'. On the other hand, when a poet like Charles Olson, who is presumably in the 'tradition', argues that one must finally substitute for the ideal of 'objectivism' the idea of 'objectism', because the former simply functions as a dialectical contrary to 'subjectivism', far from affirming an ontological advance towards a purified 'use' of language, he opens instead the question of 'style' which Pound's Imagist/Vorticist theory had exacerbated. Which is to say, the inventive potential of Pound's theory for a return to objectivity in poetry lies not in his overcoming of linguistic mediation (a retreat, and *retrait*,[11] of/ from language) but in his *turn* towards it, in his uncovering of a problematic of language that poetry has always entertained.

In two very different yet similar senses, the experiments of American modernist poets—whether ee cummings' typographical play or Hart Crane's Gnosticism—sought its origins in some ideal concreteness yet self-transcendence of the 'word'. The word, then, was tied, onto-theologically, to the Biblical Word, fallen, as it were, or derived from some transcendental signified. Only Pound's theory seemed to divest itself, fundamentally, of metaphysics and theology, even if it argued that it was a critical as well as a stylistic movement. Imagism, in one way or another, however, infiltrates the poetry of Stevens as well as Eliot, Crane as well as Williams, and not necessarily as a prescription by which the poets learned to write. If I tend to argue here that in some curious way theory precedes and directs a practice that demolishes theory, I am arguing neither historically nor structurally. But I am questioning the curious procedure of a 'method'—what Derrida has called the 'Pas' of method,[12] the methodical *step* that is at the same time *no* method, or the undoing of method—which I believe Pound's Imagist revolution surreptitiously instigates, perhaps against its will.

Let me begin again, then, with the minimum prescription of the Imagist revolution, as Pound noted in a letter to Harriet Monroe concerning the irreducible element of style: 'Objectivity and again objectivity, and expression: no hindside-beforeness— no straddled adjectives . . . Every literaryism, every book word fritters away a scrap of the reader's patience . . . Language is

made out of concrete things' (L, 49).[13] 'Go in fear of abstrac-
tions,' he wrote in an early essay setting forth the tenets of
Imagism, 'the natural object is always the *adequate* symbol' (LE,
5; also 9). Moreover, the 'natural object' is itself denominated
most precisely in natural speech, so that the ideal of *adequation* is
an ideal of language in its original, primordial, or poetic state.
Pound here recounts a condensed but familiar history, of
language's organic and cratylitic development which is con-
taminated by history and technology, by accumulating dis-
persal and abstraction. Language is subject to usury, wearing
out, but also to an unusurious excess that leads to imprecision,
to a multiplication of meanings which violate some ideal of a
proper word for each thing or idea. Periodically, the poet or
poets come to restore the economy of original adequation,
which is not, however, the extravagant ideal of one word for one
thing, but the economy of a word which inscribes the 'law' of
nature. What Pound calls the 'tradition' in a sense anticipates a
repetition, the periodic birth of an original poet who comes to
restore a general economy by exposing the usuriousness of an
epoch which has grown exhausted, or en-tropic.

Along with Fenollosa, Pound sometimes tells this story of
repeated intervention, of return and cure, in geological meta-
phors, and thus as a spatial rather than temporal history during
which language has accrued layers of distancing abstraction,
the word being effaced by accumulations and not substitutions;
so that the poet, like the archaeologist, must peel away or unlayer
language back to its primordial inscription, which is to say its
poetic nature: 'Poetic language', according to Fenollosa, in that
influential essay called *The Chinese Written Character as a Medium
for Poetry,* 'is always vibrant with fold on fold of overtones and
with natural affinities' (CWC, 25).[14] The primordial, then, is not
simple, but a manifold which has been distorted by the unfold-
ing, or logical linearization, of western grammar. 'The sentence
form was forced upon primitive man by nature itself', he insists;
yet, curiously enough, 'Nature herself has no grammar' (CWC,
12, 16). In nature 'there are no negations' (CWC, 14). The
sentence form of a primitive or natural language, then, is not
devoid of time. On the contrary, it is fundamentally temporal.
But it cannot close. It can only be, purely if not simply,
repetitional.

194

'Natural' language, then, is already poetic or irreducibly figural, and adequate to the 'law' or 'force' (mis-named nature) which engenders it only in the sense that the 'law' is figuration or trope. Nature cannot, strictly speaking, be a proper name but only a principle of transition or transformation. Nature is not things—there are no copulas in nature, Fenollosa insisted—but the relation of things, of difference. Hence nature is a 'transference of power', or verbal, that is metaphorical, and the metaphorical could only be defined as the reinscription of the verbal in the nominal, the irreducibility of the verbal to the nominal, or the temporal to the spatial. Western grammar had driven out the verbal and temporal in order to achieve its abstract categorical stabilities. It is this curious recovery of metaphor, or return to metaphor, the re-turn of metaphor in and into modernist poetics, which I want to explore in regard to what Ezra Pound called the 'new method' of poetry.

From a relatively early series of essays, collectively titled 'I Gather the Limbs of Osiris', to his publication of Fenollosa's essay, or for a decade and even longer, Pound elaborated the paradoxes of a now-familiar modernism: that poetry is an instrument or method for recuperating an originary poetic language. This primordially poetic language is natural and objective only in the sense that it is originally rational or logical. Poetry, then, is at once original and repetitional: 'A return to origins', he writes, 'invigorates because it is a return to nature and reason. The man who returns to origins does so because he wishes to believe in the eternally sensible manner. That is to say, naturally, reasonably, intuitively' (LE, 92). Indeed, each of the previously mentioned essays posits within nature a more essential nature, or a language impounded, as it were, within language, a 'force' or 'process' like Hegel's Spirit, of which nature is the going-out-of-itself or exteriorization. In the 'Osiris' essays he named this natural language, which is adequate to this 'force', 'Luminous Detail', and advocated a 'new method of scholarship' based on the way this detail was identified, selected, and deployed in relation to other detail. This method demanded a genius for recognizing certain privileged facts among others, and a strategy for reinscribing this detail into 'fields' or contexts where the luminous highlights all the rest: 'Any fact is, in a sense, "significant", or "symptomatic",' he

argued, 'but certain facts give one a sudden insight into cir-
cumjacent conditions, into their causes, their effects, into
sequence, and *law*' (SP, 22—my italics). That Pound confers
upon this detail the valorized name of solar light, and defines it
at once in metaphors of nature and metaphors of science
(technology), is characteristic, as he says, of the modern.

The mixture of metaphors not only intimates that in any
originary sense language is irreducibly a technic and instru-
mental, but that any notion of the natural already depends on a
structure of language. Not simply a grammar, however. What
Pound calls 'luminous' or valorized detail (sometimes 'fact') is
already a metonymic substitution and a grammatical disloca-
tion, so that one cannot think of his redeployment of this detail
as simply a re-grammatization—for example, as the notion of
parataxis substituting for or displacing a hypotactic order.
When Pound accepts Fenollosa's view of poetic language as a
weave of verbal and nominal, the one irreducible to the other in
the 'abstraction' of ideogrammatic writing—and a writing,
moreover, which like nature can have no strict grammar—he
promotes a 'method' which at the same time suspends and
undoes method. The reinscription of the verbal into the
nominal undoes the grammatico-logical order and suggests the
priority of the figural, which is also the trope. Pound's Image is
a trope of trope. To speak of his 'style' as metonymic rather than
metaphoric, in Jakobson's sense, is to misplace the thrust of his
'method', then, since it is precisely the undecidability of the
Image (as a medium of transference or a substitution) that
confirms its irreducible linguistic, graphic, and rhetorical
nature. In this sense, Pound's new method surreptitiously
recovers the rhetoricity of poetry which in other contexts he so
aggressively denounces, though here rhetoricity must be under-
stood in de Man's and Nietzsche's sense and not as the ab-use
(in the moral sense) of language for psychological deception.
The same Pound who vigorously denounces rhetoric in poetry
is most assertive of the pedagogical and persuasive function of
poetry.

Though committed to an orderly, and even classical, ter-
minology, Pound struggled towards redefinitions that demanded
he break or disrupt the very decorums of his discourse as if from
the inside of that discourse. We might say now that his recog-

nition, along with Fenollosa's, that nature has no grammar is a recognition that every epistemological moment is a linguistic moment, which de Man describes as the figural or rhetorical intervention (or reinscription) into the grammatical and logical order. Thus nature's symmetries are inhabited or disturbed by the anamorphic, the verbal 'law' which Pound calls, somewhat in the sense of Nietzsche, 'force' and energy.

Pound therefore defines 'Luminous Detail' as 'interpreting detail'; and in the Fenollosa essay, at a point where its author is arguing that 'Metaphor, [poetry's] chief device, is at once the substance of nature and language', Pound adds his own footnote, distinguishing true from false metaphor: 'true metaphor' is 'interpretative metaphor or image', and its function, in contrast to 'untrue, or ornamental metaphor', is transformative. Poetry and nature, then, can only be thought on the model of language, and language is a transformational (or translational) field of energies. Nature is not only a field of analogies, but an alogical resistance to any effort to understand it grammatically and logically. In Pound's proposed 'new method', which links poetry to scholarship, thereby indicating the critical thrust of poetry, luminous or interpretative detail cannot be some creative, unitary presence or singular energy which it is the poet's genius to recover from language or through language. On the contrary, the originary is metaphor itself, and metaphor maintains relations by multiplying analogies, therefore resisting any reduction of analogy to a unified field theory. When introduced or reinscribed into a field of detail, luminous detail at the same time organizes and disturbs that field, like the return of some devalorized and unabsorbable entity. The interpretative does not function like Eliot's catalyst, which ideally promotes a reaction without becoming a part of it. On the contrary, the interpretative interferes and agitates, setting off a translative or substitutive movement. The 'luminous detail' functions at the same time as a centre and an excess, as what Derrida calls the uncanny logic of the supplement.

Pound read Ovidian metamorphosis as an irrepressible de-positioning or de-grammatization, as an overthrowing of the morphic or structural rigidity from the inside. Metamorphosis could be identified with nature, then, and most clearly understood as a certain model of a language or metaphor. Metaphor

197

not only transports or carries over from one structure to another, but, like nature, branches and multiplies. It is a *law* of fecundity or super-abundance, an economy of excess. The organic metaphor, then, cannot be read in a sentimental or theological way, as the circle of determined return. Metamorphosis breaches and overflows its boundaries. It is marked by violence and excess. Art, therefore, is metaphor and metamorphic, hence, as he argued in his first book, *The Spirit of Romance*, 'interpretative' (SR, 87). Pound's 'Credo' for Imagism insisted that the Image, itself a figure for the poem, was a play between the visual and the abstract, and thus between the figural and the grammatical, the one resisting a reduction to the fixture of the other. To produce poetry, the poet introduces that which interferes or disturbs, but that which in itself does not totalize or order. For example, the Ovidian Dionysus in Canto 2, a translation and appropriation of Dionysus, out of Golding's translation, becomes not only a figure of literary interference, but a figure of figure, Dionysus being that which inhabits any grammar or system (the ship on which he is transported) but cannot be reduced to it. Dionysus entangles and becalms the ideal of a completion of the voyage, and in his delay produces by resistance the most vigorous transformations of meaning while at the same time permitting an excess of metamorphic possibilities, all those Protean expansions of story and trope. Thus, in the 'Credo' of Imagism: 'A man's rhythm must be interpretative' (LE, 9). As in *Gaudier-Brzeska*, which remains the programmatic text for Imagism, Pound calls poetry the 'language of exploration', employing once again his favourite metaphor for metaphor: interpretative or explorative metaphor functions like an electric circuit, by transformations, leaps, reversals, and resistances, a figure he had earlier employed in *The Spirit of Romance*, where poetry is compared to 'an electric current' which 'gives light where it meets resistance' (SR, 97); and in the 'Osiris' essays, interpreting detail is said to 'govern knowledge as a switch-board governs an electric circuit' (SP, 23, also 24).

In the same spirit, he both praises modern scientists for achieving precision of definition and damns them for having reduced nature or 'energy' to 'unbounded undistinguished abstraction' (LE, 154). The scientist, he argues in an essay on Cavalcanti, where he is also promoting his theory of 'interpretative translation', fails to understand 'energy' as other than a 'shapeless "mass" of force', and insists that if scientific language could come to 'visualize that force as floral and extant (ex stare)' or in 'botanical terms', it would be able to give 'shape' and 'loci' to its thought (LE, 154). Visualization, the exteriorization of force into form, is not simply a movement from invisible to visible, but is ex-pli-cative, an unfolding. At which point he offers as example an early version of a metaphor that will recur in the *Cantos* as the primary figure for poetic ordering—the 'rose in the steel dust', the figure of the floral pattern generated by an iron magnet held under a glass on which iron filings are sprinkled. The language of nature (verbal) must be reinscribed into the abstract language of science (nominal); but at the same time, a language of nature becomes sentimental unless the precisions of scientific abstraction are in turn reinscribed into botanic figures: 'We might come to believe that the thing that matters in art is a sort of energy, something more or less like electricity or radioactivity, a force transfusing, welding, and unifying. A force rather like water when it spurts up through very bright sand and sets it in swift motion. You may make what image you like' (LE, 49). Whatever the image, it is a double inscription, of the figural (at the same time confused with the natural or organic) into the grammatical. The Image, then, is irreducible to a singular notion of language, or to univocity. Nature is 'interpretative metaphor' and metaphor is natural only if both are thought of in terms of a violence or a resistance, a repetition that intervenes upon itself. Thus what Aristotle meant by the 'apt use of metaphor', says Pound, in perhaps his most favourable reference to the philosopher, was that it provided a 'swift perception of relations' and that 'use' must be understood as a 'swiftness, almost a violence, and certainly a vividness. This does not mean elaboration and complication' (LE, 52). 'As language becomes the most powerful instrument of perfidy,' Pound writes elsewhere, 'so language alone can riddle and cut through the meshes' (LE, 77).

As we might expect, Pound's formulations of the new poetics of Imagism, of 'making it new', is less radical in conception than in its strategy of attack. In this respect, the celebrated theorist of 'tradition'—he used the notion earlier and more provocatively than Eliot—can be read as under-mining the way criticism today seems to understand it: as the valorization of the cultural continuity of the west. If language is to be used to cut through the 'meshes' and 'perfidy' that language has constructed, then it is necessary for us to explore Pound's argument in terms quite incompatible with his own concise simplifications. To repeat, it is Pound's strategy, never directly spelled out, that is the clue to 'making it new'. The very notion of periodicity that characterizes his sense of tra-dition is a notion of repeated discontinuity and a discontinuous repetition, the style of a creative period being the sign of a resistance to and reappropriation (transcription) of the style of a previous period. If every major style, as Paul de Man has argued in another context, is in a sense a 'modernism',[15] the modernism of the ideogrammic method would be an *always already* modernism. The non-linguistic inhabits language from any conceivable beginning and disturbs its illusions of self-presence.

But Pound's strategy needs to be defined more exactly than his broader cultural generalizations allow, and to this end I want to turn to a short essay which has not attracted much critical attention. In 1922, he published a translation of Remy de Gourmont's *Physique de l'Amour,* under the title *The Natural Philosophy of Love,* to which he added a translator's 'Postscript'. A long-time admirer of Gourmont's prose (though not necess-arily the letter of his thought), Pound had published a year earlier, in a text called *Instigations,* an essay on that part of Gourmont's work which he found most crucial for the modern writer: Gourmont's concern with 'modality and resonance in emotion' which distinguishes man from all other biological species, the 'right of individuals to *feel* differently' (LE, 340). Pound was particularly attracted to a cluster of Gourmont's non-fictional texts on biology, love, and aesthetics, which Pound lauded as instigations or provocations, as the 'dissocia-tion' rather than syntheses of ideas. A decade later, in an introduction to the second edition of Pound's translation, Burton Rascoe would also discount the intellectual rigour of Gourmont's biologism as bad science or research, but celebrate his 'defense of sensuality' which Rascoe called an 'extenuation of Nietzsche's "Transvaluation of Values"' (NPL, xvii).

Gourmont's 'principal philosophical concept', according to Rascoe, maintained that 'intelligence is anti-natural and the result of a long process in defeating the elementary purpose of nature which is the "perpetual return to unity" through fecundation and birth' (NPL, xi–xii).

Pound has little to say of this 'philosophy' of the ever-deflected return in his translator's postscript except to remark at one point that the biological theory was consistent with the great geological speculation of the nineteenth century upon the 'rapidity of the earth's cooling, if one accepts the geologist's interpretation of that thermometric cyclone' (NPL, 303). Pound, indeed, found in Gourmont an 'instigation' or a resistance to the nihilism of this unidirectional and levelling theory, without however denying the larger truth that everything was indeed cooling or moving towards random dispersal. In Pound's formulation, as a 'body approaches the temperature of its surroundings', its cooling speed decreases, just as the larger body it inhabits, the earth, remains warmer still than its surroundings. Pound is playing with a notion of resistance and prolongation which would be elaborated decades later by cybernetics to explain that, while man lived within the inevitability of the general theory, because he was not an isolated but an open system he composed a resistance to the very entropy to which he was at the same time subject. And Pound, as if to anticipate Norbert Wiener, found man's resistance to lie in the efficiency of the machines, the tools which were almost literally projections of his body and which made possible an efficiency and economy of delay: 'The invention of the first tool turned his mind,' Pound says of man; 'turned, let us say, his "brain" from his own body' (NPL, 304).

The 'Postscript' refines a theory of poetic invention, as resistance, out of this 'turn' of mind—this trope which produces trope. Pound's opening sentence modulates Gourmont's biological theory into a theory of language; or at least, of the Image: 'it is more than likely', he writes, speculating upon a passage from Gourmont's text, that 'the brain itself is, in origin and development, only a sort of clot of genital fluid held in suspense or reserve' (NPL, 295). Perhaps it is more than coincidental that this passage owes less to Gourmont's physiological intuitions than to a section of Nietzsche's *The Will to Power*

201

which bears the indexical heading, section 805, 'On the genesis of art': 'That making perfect, seeing as perfect, which characterizes the cerebral system bursting with sexual energy . . .: on the other hand, everything perfect and beautiful works as an unconscious reminder of that enamoured condition and its way of seeing—every perfection, all the beauty of things, revives through contiguity this aphrodisiac bliss. (Physiologically: the creative instinct of the artist and the distribution of semen in his blood—) The demand for art and beauty is an indirect demand for the ecstasies of sexuality communicated to the brain.'[16]

Like Nietzsche, as we will see in a moment, Pound's deconstruction of a genetic theory of poetic making begins in a double displacement: if the image is an 'ejaculation' of nature, nature is a play of images, the 'power of the spermatozoide': or in other words, language is a metaphor for physiology, and physiology for language. Again, of the play between the figural and the grammatical. And if the 'turn' of mind is poetry, and poetry an 'upspurt of sperm', we hardly have to appeal to the double sense (or non-sense) of the *seme* irrupting at the inside of semen which we have learned to call, in a word which belongs to no one language, *dissémination*.[17] Pound accentuates, then, the discontinuity of origin and image: 'I am perfectly willing to grant that the thought once born, separated, in regard to itself, not in relation to the brain that begat it, does lead an independent life . . .' (NPL, 301). But if this discontinuity suggests, on the one hand, a pattern of thermodynamic dispersal, and perhaps an en-tropy, it also suggests the economy of a 'suspense or reserve'. Pound's metaphor of the seminal 'brain' is a figure for the poetic 'reserve' he elsewhere calls 'tradition', of the always already play of images. Thus, when Pound turns to the figure of dreams or dreaming to project his notion of poetic making, we must recognize the 'reserve' of dream images not as archetypes of some poetic universal unconscious, but as a 'textual' reserve.

If the poet dreams, it is because he nods, or by a chance that is also a strategy, disturbs the orderly and coherent structure of literature's great house so that new and unexpected affiliations or rhymes occur or are produced: 'Do they [dreams] not happen precisely at the moments when one's head is tipped; are they not, with their incoherent mixing of known and familiar images, like the pouring of a complicated honeycomb tilted from its perpendicular? Does this not give precisely the needed mixture of familiar forms in non-sequence, the jumble of fragments each coherent within its own limit?' (NPL, 299–300). 'We have the form-making and the form-destroying "thought"', he continues, and while he wishes to think of poetry as the first, as constructive, it is precisely this disorientating dreaming, this 'turn' of mind from itself, that he celebrates as the 'interpretative' or deconstructive process of poetry. Poetic construction involves a deconstructive intervention, a re-turn of metaphor, as it were, but a return which may also appear as a withdrawal. The 'ideogrammic method', as we will see, involves more than the appropriation and re-articulation of other texts, but puts a new stress on the strategies of allusion, reference, quotation, citation and re-citation, translation, incorporation and inscription, in which the re-turn of figure, or the re-inscription of figure into figure produces the effect of metaphoric withdrawal, of the effacement of figure; so that for a moment, at the moment the non-linguistic re-invades language, one senses the return of the 'object', or in Pound's terms, a coherent field of relations, or an Image. Thus when Pound finds what Kenner calls 'subject rhymes' running through widely disparate texts and fragments of texts, and rearticulates not only different literary texts but different orders of texts (literary, historical, mythical), he does not so much reveal an underlying order or cultural law affiliating all texts to the poetic impulse, as he reveals the disturbing metamorphic work (form-making and form-destroying) of language. Pound's Image, then, is what I have called elsewhere a 'machine' of repetition; and its very name, as we will see, signifies the re-turn of metaphor. But first I want to swerve from poetic theory to philosophy, or to the breach in philosophy where Pound situates literature.

3

Derrida's linkage of the 'names' of Pound and Fenollosa with Nietzsche and Mallarmé was made, as I suggested earlier, necessarily in a language of historical priority and influence that denies or undermines such conceptions. Even the suggestion that what Pound and Fenollosa retrieve, in their return to an ideogrammic method, is an 'irreducibly graphic poetics', and that one could never think of an original or primary poetics as purified of writing, the graphic, that poetic language cannot be idealized as natural and immediate—all such suggestions must employ, even as they deny and undermine, an historicist rhetoric, which Derrida identifies with the 'dominant category of the *épistémè*: being'. It is this *épistémè* of being as 'transcendental authority', Derrida argues, which modernist poetry, along with philosophy and even before it, 'at first destroyed and caused to vacillate'.[18] To 'destroy' takes on a radically different, Nietzschean, implication from annihilate, so that in contemplating an 'irreducibly graphic poetics' one has to think the oxymoron of a *structure of destructions* or *field* (open) *of force*. Such structures are inseparable from language, or more precisely, from writing understood in the double sense of metaphor and rhetoric.

Still, Pound's own assaults upon nineteenth-century idealism and metaphysics notwithstanding, one must recognize in his somewhat belated rediscovery of the Chinese ideogram the familiar rhetoric of one hoping to recuperate an original or primordial poetic language. But it is just this irreducible double face of a 'graphic' poetics that intervenes and disrupts any nostalgia for origins and makes traditionalist poetics subject to a diacritical reading. Following de Man, as well as Derrida, it is therefore necessary to recognize that the 'neo-Nietzschean clatter' of modernism resides in a 'linguistic predicament' that is inextricable from the discourse of either philosophy or poetry, and which Nietzsche's most recent commentators—who also have uncovered a 'new' Nietzsche—have located in his deconstructed notion of 'Art'. Of art which is associated with, at the same time, a constructionist and a genetic notion, of the 'impulse' toward metaphor, sometimes called the 'will to power', which itself is allied with a certain, disorientated notion of 'repetition'.

Sarah Kofman, one of the best 'new' readers of the 'new' Nietzsche, has in a number of books explored the philosopher's so-called linguistic nihilism in terms contrary to the ethical and descriptive approach common to those who 'apply' philosophy rather than 'read' it.[19] And like de Man, she discovers already in his Nietzsche's first book, *The Birth of Tragedy*, the linguistic problematic most readers defer to later texts. As Kofman reads

204

him—and I am being overly schematic here—Nietzsche's privileging of music assumes from the outset the inadequacy or irreducible metaphoricity of language, and therefore ascribes to music the same condition of broken immediacy he ascribes to language. The privilege of music, then, cannot lie in its natural origin or transcendental authority. On the contrary, music is already a part of the realm of representation, or the symbolic language of feeling, of pleasure and pain. The privilege of the language of music to other, and not necessarily subsequent or more fallen, languages, Kofman goes on, is the result of a hierarchy which Nietzsche establishes to distinguish between the different levels of symbolic language.

Music can only be privileged over percept and/or concept, as one metaphor over another, because its intensity makes it the more general language or best representation of the 'primordial melody of pleasure and pain'; so that, for example, the lyric (with its images) stands as a metaphorical expression of music and is therefore a less privileged representation or metaphor, and so on down the scale of displacements to opera which makes sound the metaphor of the lyric image or text. Thus Nietzsche's hierarchy makes an uneasy distinction only between good metaphor (music) and bad metaphor, and not between ontological levels. And despite the insistence that music already belongs to metaphor and not presence, Nietzsche, according to Kofman, has to recognize that he has rebuilt the very metaphysical structure that he had begun by reversing. The problem led almost immediately, as Kofman reads it, to a questioning of the hierarchy. If Nietzsche's first manoeuvre had been to reverse the Aristotelian priority of thought to image or idea to representation, he had by his reversal reproduced a system in which metaphor was progressively devalued. Even good music or good metaphor is a devaluation, of which the image is a further figurative devaluation. Nietzsche's need to rehabilitate metaphor, in Kofman's readings, takes the form in subsequent texts, and most problematically in the fragmentary and incomplete *Book of Philosophy (Philosophenbuch)*, of a strategic reinscription. Metaphor re-turns but under another name, as the idea of *text* or *interpretation,* of the 'will to power' signified as the irruption of force, but an 'artistic' and not a natural force: 'The notion of metaphor now becomes entirely "improper" because it is no longer referred to a proper or natural term, but to an interpretation.'[20] If Nietzsche abandons the privileged name of metaphor at this point, however, he reprivileges it under the name of interpretation and ascribes to it a function of intervention rather than a function of representation or recuperation.

Though she does not in this context address directly that particular section, the only completed one, of the *Book of Philosophy* which has become the touchstone of recent criticism, she is without question referring to the significance of that philosophical fable we know as (in translation) 'Truth and Falsity in an Ultramoral Sense'.[21] Despite its recent currency as the basic text for deconstruction readings, with certain exceptions the essay continues to be employed rather than 'read'—as a categorical statement of the inadequacy of language to reality or to the presence of the 'Thing-in-Itself', and thus as an undoing of metaphysics of presence. Despite such warnings as de Man's concerning the problematic inscribed in any philosophical fable which must employ the very devices and concepts of metaphysics it is in the process of undoing, or despite Eugenio Donato's observations on the inevitable narrativity and hence belatedness of a form which can only tell the story of its own 'incapacity' to make its story adequate to the truth it espouses, there remains the tendency (at least for literary criticism) to read the 'fable' as a series of conceptual remarks.[22]

The first section of the 'fable', then, has generally been considered a philosophical truism denouncing or murdering 'truth', or relegating it to the vertigo of an endless recession of forgettings. But this reading in a sense elevates the aphoristic to an illusory if not sufficient substitute for 'truth'. We can recall the economy and aphoristic condensation of Nietzsche's definitions undoing definition: words are recognized as the expressions of a 'nerve stimulus in sounds', and everything after, percept or concept, consists of metaphors of metaphors deriving, though deriving no longer makes sense here, from that 'First metaphor'. There is no natural or 'proper' link, the fable asserts, between the 'First metaphor' which cannot be natural because it already belongs to the realm of sense (or the symbolic) and any presence or 'Thing-in-Itself' (TF, 506–7). Both nature and the 'Thing-in-Itself' are already and irreducibly metaphorical. This allows Nietzsche's famous and much-quoted conclusion: 'What therefore is truth? A mobile army of metaphors, metonymies, anthropomorphisms', and so on, including the figure of 'truth' as like effaced coins or 'illusions which one has forgotten that they *are* illusions' (TF, 508), a sentence which silently undermines the propriety of the copulative. (There is no nature in the copulative.) But the fable has not yet passed the mid-point of its first half, and continues to pile up metaphor upon metaphor as if to mock the very history of philosophy, building (as Nietzsche says) its own 'pyramidal order with castes and grades' (TF, 509) out of the very devalued figures it has forgotten to be illusions or metaphors. What the fable substitutes for the necessary 'laws' of causality and adequation is a concept or metaphor of '*aesthetical* relation', a 'suggestive metamorphosis' which is also a 'stammering translation into a quite distinct foreign language', a force which undoes the stabilizing concept of 'phenomena' as a necessary intermediary dialectically conjoining symbolic or figural levels. Not only has Nietzsche undone the ontological or natural origin of figure, he has disrupted the notion of rational and economical transfer between levels of metaphor. But even the 'aesthetical' is one of those laborious constructions at which language has worked, the very metaphor of a genetic myth which must also be undone. The aesthetical has always grounded philosophy, in language *habits* and not natural laws.

But when Nietzsche turns to the second part of his fable, he must tell, or repeat, a slightly different story; or perhaps one could say he must repeat a story of repetition. If, as he asserts, the history which the fable narrates can be condensed into two general phases—'it is *language* which worked originally at the construction of ideas; in later times it is *science*' (TF, 512)—this compressed history is at once vindicated and undone by the very narrative structure in which it has to be told. It is not at all improbable that Nietzsche's history of, first, language's and, then, science's (or philosophy's) construction allegorizes a general history of philosophy, developing from a logic which draws its metaphors from nature (and thus from a forgotten figurality) to a science or logic which builds paradigmatically (and categorically) like Kant's or syntagmatically (and dialectically) like Hegel's by attempting to efface and overcome the metaphoricity of its means. If the scientific phase imitates and repeats by forgetting the symbolic or linguistic epoch—in the way, to follow Nietzsche's metaphors, that the builders of the 'great columbrarium of ideas, the cemetery of perceptions' imitate the working of bees at building cells and then filling them with honey—the original builders and those who build their huts, like worshippers, beside the 'towering edifice of science', have only forgotten that they are condemned to repetition, and to metaphors of metaphors (TF, 512–13). It is Kant's columbrarium and Hegel's pyramidal tomb that already contains not the truth or honey but only embodied signs of it. The 'honey'—and one might evoke here for Wallace Stevens' paradoxical line, 'The honey of heaven may or may not come,/ But that of earth both comes and goes at once'—is not a natural presence but a product, even a by-product. The image or form is not derived from presence, but presence (as the sign or body) is produced in the image or form. Yet not in imitation of the form, nor derived from it. It is because form and content have no natural affinity (or no ontological definition) that a generative repetition seems to take place:

> That impulse toward the formation of metaphors, that funda-
> mental impulse of man, which we cannot reason away for one
> moment . . . is in truth not defeated nor even subdued by the
> fact that out of its evaporated products, the ideas, a regular and
> rigid new world has been built as a stronghold for it. This
> impulse seeks for itself a new realm of action and another river-
> bed, and finds it in *Mythos* and more generally in *Art*. This
> impulse constantly confuses the rubrics and cells of the ideas by
> putting up new figures of speech, metaphors, metonymies; it
> constantly shows its passionate longing for shaping the existing
> world of waking man as motley, irregular, inconsequently
> incoherent, attractive, and eternally new as the world of dreams
> is. For indeed, waking man per se is only clear about his being
> awake through the rigid and orderly woof of ideas, and it is for
> this very reason that he sometimes comes to believe that he
> was dreaming when that woof of ideas has for a moment been
> torn by Art. (TF, 513)

Art is one of the names of that 'impulse' or repetition earlier called 'aesthetical'; or better, it is the intervention or re-turn of this force upon itself. This impulse has always inhabited

208

language, and not simply as its negative or counterforce. Art does not simply reverse the construction impulse, but disrupts it from the inside, since Art and Mythos are already archaic forms ('another river-bed') to which the 'impulse' returns, structures once constructed by the 'impulse'. Art, then, is not primordial, but the scene of reinscription, and the artistic 'impulse' was never constructive or generative but primordially deconstructive, always already an opposition or divided within itself. Nietzsche has reversed the privilege of metaphor by first devaluing it, and then in the same gesture re-privileging the devalued. Metaphor becomes irresistible. This reinscription of Art—another name for interpretation's will to power—is a double inscription of the heterogeneous, best described in Derrida's phrase as the 'primordial structure of repetition', which, as Rodolphe Gasché has recently observed, borrows the name primordial while cancelling the metaphysical implications of its deriving from presence.[23] Art or interpretation, in Derrida's terms, obeys the 'strange structure of the supplement': that which is added on, or is reinscribed, both reverses and intervenes, tearing at the very structure which has been constructed out of it. Art is originary figure, a combat—a *war*—and in de Man's sense, a tropic dis-figuring.

Now, I have been arguing all along that something of this kind is already implicated in Pound's efforts to describe how poetry 'makes it new', which means something quite different from making poetry new or recuperating an original self-presence of language called poetry or poesy. What Pound calls the Image, or 'interpretative metaphor', may be said to follow the movement of double inscription or the 'strange structure of the supplement'. Indeed, Pound's very choice of names for this structure takes a devalued concept of the image (as imagery, or ornamental metaphor, or representation), and reprivileges it. His Image, with a capital 'I', or Imagisme, with its French suffix, is another figure for the poem, a figure of figurality or 'interpretative metaphor'. One cannot think of the Image, whether as the name for a single poem or as a generic concept, without thinking its irreducible double nature, or without thinking of it as a reinscription. And Pound's definition of the 'one image poem' as a 'form of super-positions', as 'one idea set on top of another', as 'cinematographical', almost literally details a reinscriptive logic: 'In a poem of this sort one is trying to record the precise instant when a thing outward and objective transforms itself, or darts into a thing inward and subjective' (G-B, 89). Therefore, he can speak of the Image as 'analytical', and call upon the analogy of analytical geometry in contrast to other mathematical models which are descriptive. The analytical Image is productive rather than representative, in the sense, as Pound argues, that it transcribes and erases the *re*, producing a presentational or re-petitional effect, a figure instead of some *res* itself. The Image proposes a reinscriptive logic, a 'phantastikon', which Pound once said was the right name for Imagination.

We have already seen how Fenollosa's remarkable essay has equated nature with poetry or metaphor, and how Pound understands this return to the verbal, or the reinscription of the visual into the verbal in ideogrammic writing, as a critical or interpretative figure. A close reading of that essay, which I have attempted elsewhere,[24] has to recognize, as Pound explicitly remarked, that Fenollosa chose to tell the story of language's origin, its historical dispersal or de-Orientation, and its recuperation of power through the reintroduction or reinscription of graphic writing into phonetic writing, in a 'narrative' mode. So that one should be as cautious of reading it is a descriptive history as in reading Nietzsche's 'fable' as a decisive ontological argument. That the story he tells both follows Hegel's and reverses it is self-evident, but also deceiving, since Fenollosa in his other writings interpreted the return to the Chinese character in terms of a curious historical reversal, or retreat, of poetry.

It was Fenollosa's contention that American thought, or Transcendentalism, was not only compatible with Oriental thought or Zen doctrine, but that it had been a virtual recuperation of the Oriental—the result of a very strange double movement. On the one hand, he argued, the Zen 'book of nature', which had already derived the 'categories of thought' from the 'basis of nature's organization', was an 'independent discovery of Hegelian categories that lie behind the two worlds of subject and object'.[25] On the other, American thought had been touched by Oriental thought in a manner more direct than the Hegelian or historical mediation of the West; that is, in a

way contrary to any thinking of the western movement
(grammatical) of thought. Fenollosa hypothesized a Pacific
'stage' for this interaction of American and Oriental thought, a
'Pacific School of Art', he called it, generated by 'actual dis-
persion and control throughout the vast basin of the Pacific'.
Pacific art accentuated the Eastern 'centre of dispersion' in
contrast to the Western centring—while Chinese art was the
only 'large form of world art that combine[d] both impulses'.
The Chinese ideograph therefore, is not Idealistic or synthetic:
'It thus becomes a great school of poetic interpretation', though
interpretation here for Fenollosa meant reading nature as a
'storehouse of spiritual laws'.

The freshness of Emersonian thought, or Transcendentalism,
he appeared to conclude, was the result of its more direct
apprehension of the originary interpretative thought of the
Chinese, though Transcendental thought necessarily inscribed
its intuitions in what Whitman had called 'Hegelian formulas'.
However bizarre the historical formulation, and despite the
incoherence or blindness that permits him to find the origins of
western humanism in the forgotten nature of oriental graphism,
and to forget that his own reading of the ideogram is a purely
western idealization, Fenollosa may be said to *radicalize* the
thinking of the Chinese grapheme in a way he could not have
understood. His view of the historical 'retreat' of Chinese
poetry, a retreat or withdrawal which in its way returns to meet
or intervene upon the advance and historical decline of western
thought, is indirectly recounted in 'The Chinese Written
Character . . .', as Pound noted, as a completed history of
language. Yet, this history will not end or close. Fenollosa's
narrative disrupts its own advance and defers any return. The
keynote of all Fenollosa's teaching of the meeting between East
and West lies, according to Van Wyck Brooks, in his notion of
'spacing'. Spacing and dispersal—and while we have come to
think of spacing in a sense quite different from Fenollosa's
definition that 'all art is harmonious spacing', his notion of
Oriental dispersion and decentring as preceding western
centring has critical implications which explode the idea of
cyclical history. Therefore the Chinese ideograph was the sign
that there could be no unitary style, or no pure cultural style,
but only a curious interweaving of the heterogeneous: 'just as

211

it is true that the alien influence lies at the very core of the national.' The return to the 'method' of Chinese writing, prophesied at the very conclusion of 'The Chinese Character', would not be the culmination or closure of a western poetics, nor a recuperation of some primordial method, but a sign of another poetic 'beginning', of return or inaugural repetition.

It is no accident, then, as I have suggested elsewhere, that the ideographs Fenollosa chooses to exemplify this return to a natural writing, which is to say, to metaphor, are ideographs of the sun-rising, or more accurately, ideographs retranscribing the English sentence, 'Sun rises (in the) East', back into a language which the western grammar had murdered, or stablized. The return of the sun is enabled by the intervention, or reinscription of the 'visible hieroglyphics' of Chinese radicals, so that the sign of the Orient is the sign of the 'sun entangled in the branches of a tree', a sun that rises by passing over and erasing the 'horizon' which it projects in its turning. Here is the curious figure of metaphor returning upon itself, of metaphor withdrawing into metaphor advancing, and re-drawing a *radical* horizon: 'the sun is above the horizon, but beyond that the single upright line is like the growing trunk of the tree sign' (CWC, p. 33). Recall Williams in *Paterson*, where the poem is 'the ignorant sun/ rising in the slot of/ hollow suns risen . . .'; 'When the sun rises, it rises in the poem/ and when it sets darkness comes down/ and the poem is dark.'[26]

And Fenollosa: 'Thus in all poetry a word is like a sun, with its corona and chromosphere; words crowd upon words, and enwrap each other in their luminous envelopes until sentences become clear, continuous light bands' (CWC, p. 32). This figure of the innate harmony and natural affinity of things discovered and 'enveloped' in a horizon ordered and centred upon the poetic word is, in its way, an euphoric affirmation of Hegel's 'symbol'. But if the 'poetic word' is 'like' a sun, Fenollosa can only recur to the tautology implicit in his circular definition. The sun never appears except in its sign, which can rise only in the text it presumably illuminates and envelopes. It rises only in its corona. The sun—which projects horizons and erases them at the same time, breaching the very boundaries it produces—is a figure for all the other figures which are its 'light bands'. This sun never properly arrives or re-orients itself.

R..ther, its turning is dis-orienting. Fenollosa ascribes to poetic words not only luminosity but excess, 'overtones', which are like nature's excess. The clarity of poetry, its luminosity, lies in the 'delicate balance of overtones' or the plurisignificance of radical relations which are repeatedly re-drawn. The sun does not close upon itself, or return, but re-turns, and in an orbit that marks a double track.

Fenollosa's essay (or is it Pound's rewriting, 'translation'?) does not conclude by rejoining West to East, by a re-Orientation which would fulfil the Emersonian dream he brought to Japan. Nor does it recuperate a primordial Chinese writing which, as we know, Fenollosa thought to be essentially uncontaminated by Western phonologism. Can one say, then, that he does indeed recuperate the Oriental 'nature' (a vital heterogeneity), but in the graphic rupture which marks every myth of origins and the circle of eternal return that is its figure? Does Fenollosa simply repeat the Hegelian sublation in an ideal graphism, thereby refining upon Hegel's devaluation of the 'hieroglyph'? Not quite. The Pound/Fenollosa text ends in a crux of translation that resists sublation, or marks its reinscriptive *character*. It ends not in a translation that writes Western dispersal back into Eastern unity, but on the contrary folds that dispersal back into a more originary (not original) dispersal. In his concluding example of an English sentence translated *back* into a more primordial Chinese writing, what at first appears to be the evidence (visible) of the ideograph's priority to a fallen or arbitrary western phonetic representation of 'nature' has to be itself presented as a question of priority, as if the ideograph almost manages, but in a way cannot, purify the language into which it has fallen. The ideogram (ideographs), which would make 'time' and therefore natural transformation visible, can only translate its dependence on that which has derived from it. In that Western sentence—'The sun rises in the east' or, as the words are placed *under* the ideographs, 'Sun Rises (in the) East'—the sun which resides in the position of the (Western) subject is 'set', as it were, in a movement that marks its eclipse (CWC, 33). For the sentence, Western or Eastern, moves inexactly from left to right, and not as in Chinese 'writing', from the top to the bottom of a column. It continues to move within the track of a Western grammar even as it receives its definition only with its arrival on the right, within the sign of the East. Within parentheses. Writing has had to pass through its own myth, of 'shining', of arising to a visibility, the issue of some luminous origin, the 'sun' as the name of that which goes out of itself. This Chinese graphic does not speak outside of the metaphysics (born of Western phonologism) which Fenollosa at one time seems to say is a mistake and contamination of the Oriental and at another claims is only the historical detour back to 'nature'. The origin and unity of nature must pass through nature, as Emerson tried to argue, and must be eclipsed; but on the other hand, since nature, or the organic, has neither beginning nor end, and hence *is* not unity or even the figure of origin, the name of the sun, or of the subject, arises only in figure, in heterogeneity. Writing is the 'origin' of the 'sun', which rises only by re-arising.

Strictly speaking, then, there is no 'nature' or natural language, no Orient. No primordial writing. No origin or East to pass into the West. No unity to be eclipsed in its image. But Fenollosa, we remember, ascribed to a most curious notion of the West—arguing at one time that western grammar or phonologism had denatured language, and at another that Hegel had perceived and reinscribed the Oriental (in this specific case, the Zen) in his metaphysics. In either case, phonologism has its origin in culture, and not nature, and thus in a writing, as Derrida tells us, which marks a culture which cannot be sublimated (or sublated) by logocentrism.[27] Fenollosa's admission of the 'dispersal' and the 'alien' element inscribed in Oriental languages and cultures locates origins in the horizons of the sun, in a writing that precedes all presence. Just as Derrida questions the story or narrative told by Western sinologists, of a natural speech *eclipsed* by writing which characterizes the historical foundering of Chinese culture and signifies its failure to advance into the enlightenment of the West, Fenollosa seems to tell a counter story; but at the same time he ascribes to the mysticism of a language/writing which is primitive (or primordial) to the very degree that its inscribed sign (or signifier) retains an ideal relation (as image or resemblance) to a unique reality or signified (nature) that grounds it. Thus Fenollosa's sense of nature as a text(ure) of analogies.

Pound's appropriation of Fenollosa cannot but reinscribe

this problematic of the image that at once breaks up referentiality (representation) and symbolization (the sign as synecdoche), or dis-orients this narrative of an eclipsed writing into radical Image, an Image that marks the breached horizon which would allow us to think the history and grammar of the sun. Pound's theory of the Image is in effect a theory of radical translation, of a double writing that does not eclipse the 'sun' but rather deflects its orbit or produces an ellipse. The Image reinscribes but cannot efface Western grammar, just as Fenollosa's example cannot recuperate some purity of a primordial writing nor leave the grammar of the Western (phonetic) sentence intact, that is, disentangled. The sun rises (again) only in the branches of a tree or text. Pound's noun/verb Image, one also wants to observe, cannot discount the categories of logocentric or philological description; it cannot be described without the subject/verb/object distribution. And if the Image is also his reification (if not reinscription) of the devalued, representational sign, it is also a trans-valuation of any metaphysical notion of image. For Pound's Image/Poem is not only a 'figure' of heterogeneous or originary force (which he likes to call verbal and 'natural'), it is *pre*sentational and not *re*presentational precisely in the sense that it violates grammatical propriety.

There is no example of the Image in Pound, not even a poem like 'In a Station of the Metro', that exemplary Imagist poem. The Image cannot be exemplified. And therefore, any prefiguration of it, any figure for it, like the 'rose in the steel dust' mentioned earlier, can only poeticize or metaphorize its enigma. The Image is Pound's name for the primordial, but the primordial is always already 'translation' of the translative effect itself. A gathering of dispersed and even alien fragments, an ideo-grammatizing of them, it at the same time disturbs that grammar or marks the *time* between the idea and the gramma, between idea and image or between the image and its graph, between what Fenollosa wanted to distinguish as the visible and abstract and Pound the noun and verb of a defective and deflected Western language. Between philosophy and literature? Thought and metaphor? Which is only to say that these metaphors of oppositions or difference no longer hold: that the image, for example, can no longer be conceived as the issue of

215

some *being* which precedes and gives rise to it.

Pound, of course, habitually wrote in the language of such privileged oppositions and hierarchies, as if to affirm some primordial being or luminosity which would not only be revealed but, in the terms of the essay mentioned previously, would be reinscribed as a force in some 'method' of 'luminous detail'. Luminous detail, then, would be not only a manifestation of the sun, but in a sense be older than the 'sun' itself, older than any being or truth. This is why I do not hesitate to translate Pound's language of the primordially privileged poetic language into the equivocations of a notion or non-concept like Derrida's *différance*. Like Derrida, Pound cannot find language or definition for that which exceeds all names and in effect produces them. The Image produces images, but it is also the becoming-unmotivated of the image or sign. And Pound would need other names for it: Vortex, Ideogram, even Paideuma (a word which inscribes the radical *play* or *paidia* of the mark or 'complex' as Pound would call the de*sign* of 'inrooted ideas' which characterized a culture, a concept recuperated from Plato's devaluation of language's false image). Thus, when in *Guide to Kulchur* Pound amplifies his recurrent argument for the difference between received or static ideas (as in a history of ideas) and 'ideas in action', the latter, like the 'moving Image' he privileges in the *ABC of Reading,* marks the irreducible temporality (hence, in grammatical terms, verbality) of the Image (see GK, 34).

The Image is (one of) Pound's names for the 'poetic', itself already a name in quotation marks, a name for that which is borne within, as the difference of, those recurrent works or classics of literature he envisions not as a progressive history of 'culture' but as re-agents to any history of design. The Image, like Nietzsche's figure of Art, is the name of the vital contradiction in Pound's 'method'. The Image is 'method', but a method that, as in Nietzsche, transvalues method; it methodically disorients or undoes method, as in Derrida's *Pas*. The Image is Pound's name for poetic language, or for language itself, that which disturbs and displaces the fiction of the mastering, human self and introduces the disturbing possibility of an It or Id that inhabits all taboos and grammars and in the disguise of artistic order subverts the fictions of power it perpetrates. Nietzsche, of course, had already written this fable of the totalitarian radical:

> Man himself . . . has an invincible tendency to let himself be deceived, and he is like one enchanted with happiness when the rhapsodist narrates to him epic romances in such a way that they appear real or when the actor on the stage makes the king appear more kingly than reality shows him. Intellect, that master of dissimulation, is free and dismissed from his service as slave, so long as It is able to deceive without *injuring*, and then It celebrates Its Saturnalia . . . Whatever It now does, compared with Its former doings, bears within itself dissimulation, just as its former doings bore the character of distortion. It copies human life, but takes it for a good thing and seems to rest quite satisfied with it. That enormous framework and hoarding of ideas, by clinging to which needy man saves himself through life, is to the freed intellect only a scaffolding and a toy for Its most daring feats, and when It smashes it to pieces, throws it into confusion, and then puts it together ironically, pairing the strangest, separating the nearest items, then It manifests that It has no use for those makeshifts of misery, and that It is now no longer led by ideas but by intuitions. From these intuitions no regular road leads into the land of the spectral schemata, the abstractions; for them the word is not made, when man sees them he is dumb, or speaks in forbidden metaphors and in unheard-of combinations of ideas, in order to correspond creatively with the impression of the powerful present intuition at least by destroying and jeering at the old barriers of ideas.[28] (TF, 514)

NOTES

1. 'The Case against Nietzsche', *The Complete Poems and Selected Letters and Prose of Hart Crane* (Garden City, N.Y.: Doubleday Anchor, 1966), pp. 197–98.
2. See *The Letters of Wallace Stevens*, selected and ed. by Holly Stevens (New York: Knopf, 1966), pp. 409, 431–32, 461–62, 486, 532.
3. *The Literary Essays of Ezra Pound*, ed. with introduction by T. S. Eliot (Norfolk, Conn.: New Directions, 1954), p. 32.
4. A. R. Orage, *Friedrick Nietzsche, the Dionysion Spirit of the Age* (London: Faulis, 1906). See also Orage, *Nietzsche in Outline and Aphorism* (Chicago: McClurg, 1910).
5. The question refers to the following lines, from 'Hugh Selwyn Mauberley', *Personae, Collected Shorter Poems* (New York: New Directions, 1971), p. 199:

Mildness, amid the neo-Nietzschean clatter,
His sense of graduations,
Quite out of place amid
Resistance to current exacerbations,

Invitation, mere invitation to perceptivity
Gradually led him to the isolation
Which these presents place
Under a more tolerant, perhaps, examination.

6. De Man, *Allegories of Reading* (New Haven, Conn.: Yale University Press, 1979), p. 79.
7. *Allegories of Reading*, p. 79.
8. *Allegories of Reading*, p. 119.
9. See Derrida, *Of Grammatology*, trans. by Gayatri Spivak (Baltimore, Md.: Johns Hopkins University Press, 1976), p. 92.
10. These tropes are taken respectively from the poems 'Saint John and the Back-Ache' and 'Not Ideas about the Thing but the Thing Itself', *The Palm at the End of the Mind, Selected Poems and a Play*, ed. by Holly Stevens (New York: Random House, Vintage, 1972), pp. 329 and 387–88.
11. I am referring to Derrida's essay, in part on Heidegger's notion of metaphor, entitled (in 'literal' English translation) 'The *Retrait* of Metaphor', *Enclitic*, II (Fall 1978), 4–33. The translation retains the untranslatable (non-) word *retrait* which 'bears' the various senses of retreat, re-drawing, withdrawal, recess, re-marking, retirement, as they touch upon notions of *trait* and trait, mark, line, etc.
12. 'Pas', *Gramma*, nos. 3/4 (1976), 111–215.
13. Subsequent quotations from Pound's writings (and including Fenollosa's essay) will be noted in the text, as follows:— G-B: *Gaudier-Brzeska, A Memoir* (New York: New Directions, 1970); GK: *Guide to Kulchur* (New York: New Directions, n.d.); L: *The Letters of Ezra Pound, 1907–1941*, ed. by D. D. Paige (New York: Harcourt, Brace, 1950); LE: *The Literary Essays of Ezra Pound* (see note 3); SP: *Ezra Pound, Selected Prose, 1909–1965* (New York: New Directions, 1973); SR: *The Spirit of Romance* (New York: New Directions, n.d.—first pub. in 1909); NPL: 'Postscript' to Pound's translation of Remy de Gourmont, *The Natural Philosophy of Love* (New York: Liveright, 1932—first pub. in 1922); CWC: Ernest Fenollosa, *The Chinese Written Character as a Medium for Poetry*, ed. by E. Pound (San Francisco: City Lights, 1969).
14. See Fenollosa, *CWC*: 'The wealth of European speech grew, following slowly the intricate maze of nature's suggestions and affinities. Metaphor piled upon metaphor in quasi-geological strata' (23). Nature, then, which 'furnishes her own clues', in 'homologies, sympathies, and identities' (22), can never appear outside of metaphor. It can never be other than its clues or signs. And if all one can know of nature is metaphor—that is, of the process passing from unseen to seen, from visible to invisible, the classical metaphysical definition of metaphor—all we can know is already 'figure': 'is it not enough to show that Chinese poetry gets back *near* to the

processes of nature by means of its vivid figure, its wealth of such figure?' (31—my italics). To say that poetry reveals nature as 'relations' can only mean that poetry reveals only metaphor, a tautology. Except that by revealing metaphor it reveals the undoing of grammar and logic and their accompanying systems of taxonomy: 'This was probably why the conception of evolution came so late in Europe. *It could not make way until it was prepared to destroy the inveterate logic of classification*' (27—F's italics? or P's).

15. See the last two chapters of *Blindness and Insight* (New York: Oxford University Press, 1971), pp. 142–86.

16. *The Will to Power*, ed. by Walter Kaufmann (New York: Vintage, 1968), p. 424.

17. See Jacques Derrida, *La dissémination* (Paris: Seuil, 1972). Like other Derridean terms, *dissémination* functions to defamiliarize conceptual notions of orderly (organic) dispersal, the concept of a broken but recuperable unity. Dissemination, he once remarked, in a non-definition, is that which does 'not return to the father'; it is an irreducibly doubled term, and, as he says, includes by semantic accident not only two incompatible and etymologically unconnected meanings, but meanings which are often, by linguistic habit, elided in an organic figure. It is not simply that *seme* and *semen* accidentally inhabit the same phonemic structure, but that, in a metaphor which has become a cliché, we have been accustomed to think of the naturalness of language in terms of the word as seed or vice versa. Derrida's coinage resists our either discarding the metaphor as false or forgetting its accidental, irrational, and non-ontological status.

18. *Of Grammatology*, p. 92.

19. Kofman, *Nietzsche et la metaphor* (Paris: Payot, 1972). A chapter of which appears in *The New Nietzsche, Contemporary Styles of Interpretation* (New York: Delta, 1977), pp. 210–14.

20. *The New Nietzsche*, p. 208.

21. For 'Truth and Falsity . . .', see *The Philosophy of Nietzsche*, ed. with an introduction by Geoffrey Clive (New York: Mentor, 1965), pp. 503–15. Clive's selections are taken from the Oscar Levy translation of Nietzsche's *Works*. Hereafter cited in text as TF.

22. See De Man, *Allegories of Reading*, pp. 111–13; and Donato, 'Divine Agonies: Of Representation and Narrative in Romantic Poetics', *Glyph 6* (Baltimore, Md.: Johns Hopkins University Press, 1979), pp. 98–100.

23. See 'Destruction as Criticism', *Glyph 6*, pp. 175–215, especially p. 193. Gasche's important essay elaborates the 'deconstructive' strategy of reversal and displacement (or intervention) in terms of the devaluation and then reinscription of the devalued term into the discourse, much in the way Nietzsche devalues and then reinscribes metaphor, and, one might add, the way Pound does the *idea* of image.

24. See 'Decentering the Image: The "Project" of "American" Poetics?' *Textual Strategies*, ed. with introduction by Josue V. Harari (Ithaca, N.Y.: Cornell University Press, 1979), pp. 322–58, especially pp. 332–40. Also published in *Boundary 2*, VIII (Fall 1979), 159–88.

25. The quotations from Fenollosa in the following paragraphs are from his

✓ *Epochs of Chinese and Japanese Art,* new and rev. ed. with copious notes by
   Professor Petrucci, 2 vols. (New York: Dover, 1963), an unabridged
   publication of a 1913 text. The remarks by Van Wyck Brooks are from his
   essay, 'Fenollosa and His Circle', *Fenollosa and His Circle* (New York:
   Dutton, 1962), pp. 1–68, especially p. 61.
26. William Carlos Williams, *Paterson* (New York: New Directions, 1963),
   pp. 4, 99.
27. See *Of Grammatology,* p. 91.
28. In *Allegories of Reading,* pp. 114–15, Paul de Man remarks on this passage,
   which culminates his reading of Nietzsche's philosophical 'fable', as an
   instance of the philosopher's double reading of the self. For de Man, this
   conclusion does not celebrate the triumph of the artistic 'self' but is a
   questioning of the valorization of an art which would presume to over-
   come or supplant a dead or sclerotic philosophy. Thus, the essay
   continues to exemplify de Man's ironic reading of the *play* between
   philosophy and literature.

Joseph N. Riddel's ' "Neo-Nietzschean Clatter"—Speculation and/on
Pound's Poetic Image' is a revised and shortened version of an essay which
originally appeared in *boundary 2*, IX, 3 (Spring 1981).

8

Icons, Etymologies, Origins and Monkey Puzzles in the Languages of Upward and Fenollosa

by RICHARD GODDEN

> The Question of the origin of language tends always to become a
> veritable monkey puzzle—Ernst Cassirer[1]

Language from the first to the last is social, and its meaning is
to be found between speakers. As a man talks so he identifies
his social position; as he listens so he receives the positions of
others. Dialogue, no matter how equable, involves modifica-
tions: the listener deals with an utterance by laying down a set
of answering words that are his own terms or at least versions
of those terms, 'therefore there is no reason for saying that
meaning belongs to a word as such. In essence meaning
belongs to its position between speakers.'[2] Perhaps the birth-
cry or the death-rattle, if they may be taken as signs, escape
sociability; they are unique in that they cannot stay to appreci-
ate their own effect—few signs are so singular. The hunger-
pang, the sexual-sigh, maybe even the sound of one's own
heart suddenly overheard, are events in a context that may
happen again; as such they take on the form of that context.
Only the rarest among signs escapes society, even

> . . . those vague, undeveloped experiences, thoughts, and idle
> accidental words that flash across our minds . . . are all of them
> cases of miscarriages of social orientations, novels without
> heroes, performances without audiences.[3]

Where signs are socially ubiquitous, neither their origins nor
the objects to which they refer lie beyond that ubiquity. The
troubling 'environment of what might have been meant'[4] is
the space in which the linguistic substance of both signifier
and signified originate.

Between 1910 and 1916, Pound was preoccupied with the
problem of reference. However, what emerges from the essays
of the period is not a concern for man's relation to other men,
but for man's relation to objects. Moreover, the socially vacant
but 'luminous' details of externality require diagrams not
script. 'Phantastikon', 'image', 'ideogram', and 'vortex' are
Poundian synonyms for energy which are easier to draw than
to describe verbally. Their line of development marks an
increasingly elaborate figure for that force which Pound
believed to exist between the word and the object. Effectively,
they stand as avatars for reference, and more particularly for
aesthetic forms of reference that would exclude or modify
language. If I may extend the conceit—and argue for it later—
they are shibboleths, not avatars, since, as the diagram grows
more complex, so spoken or speakable language gives way to
silent shapes.

'Phantastikon' makes its first significant appearance in
'Psychology and Troubadours' (1912); taken from the Greek
psychologists it refers to that state in which 'minds are . . .
circumvolved about them[selves] like soap-bubbles.'[5] 'Caval-
canti', written between 1910 and 1931, glosses this 'interactive
force' as a collapse of discreetness between subject and object:

> The senses at first seem to project a few yards beyond the body.
> Effect of a decent climate where a man leaves his nerve-set
> open, or allows it to tune in to its ambiance.[6]

Though Pound is unspecific as to his Greek sources, 'phan-
tastikon' has been traced to the Sophists; it describes 'the
realm of image-making . . . where "truth" is not only imitated
but offered through imitation as a plausible reality.'[7] The
troubadour cannot help himself, he is an iconicist. He appre-

hends and uses only icons and indices, that is to say, signs which 'stand for something because they resemble it' (icons), or signs which have 'a real connection with the object' (indices). Where the interface between the senses and the world is absolute, the mind cannot think in 'symbols' that depend upon 'mental association (or habit)',[8] since a conventional sign would interrupt that flow between the thinking body and the thought world:

> Any ordinary word as 'give', 'bird', 'marriage' is an example of a symbol. It is applicable to whatever may be found to realize the idea connected with the word: it does not, in itself, identify those things. It does not show us a bird, nor enact before our eyes a giving in marriage, but supposes that we are able to imagine those things and have associated the word with them.[9]

The iconicity of the troubadours' ideal language is removed from the twelfth century and converted into a general directive by 'A Few Dont's' (1913). Pound warns against expressions like 'dim lands *of peace*' which 'dull the image' and stem from writers' 'not realizing that the natural object is always the *adequate* symbol' (*LE*, p. 5). The gift of Fenollosa's notebooks, in the same year, intensifies Pound's interest in iconographic script. Fenollosa was predominantly concerned with those Chinese characters whose very shape records things, rather than the sounds given to things: furthermore, the lines drawn by Chinese calligraphers do not merely 'resemble' their referents but possess a 'real connection'—the icon becomes indexical as soon as it is recognized that the pen is informed by the eye's energy. Hugh Kenner catches this inclination, precisely:

> The ideogram, Fenollosa does not tire of repeating, sketches a process, seizes some continuous happening—the movement of attention through an eye . . . let[ting] no man with an eye forget what energy it is that fills words: the energy of process in nature.[10]

Equivalents are difficult to find in a phonetic language, but demonstrative-pronouns focus attention strongly upon their objects: 'this' or 'that' make the listener observe in order to establish an active connection, whether it be with a prior clause or some spatial location over 'there', on the right. As smoke is to fire, so the 'ideogram' is to its referent—both are cause and effect relations which Charles Sanders Peirce would describe as, 'essentially affairs of here and now, [their] office being to bring the thought to a particular experience or series of experience connected by dynamical relation.'[11]

The 'vortex' is dynamical and ultimately indexical, consequently it poses problems for language. Indices are rarely words: 'this' and 'that' turn the head or the mind's-eye becoming verbal pointers. More commonly, the index establishes connections through gesture, interjection and exclamation, its energy reduces linguistic mediation. Likewise, the 'vortex' strains Pound's capacity for analogy:

> The image is not an idea. It is a radiant node or cluster; it is what I can, and must perforce, call a VORTEX, from which, and through which, and into which, ideas are constantly rushing.[12]

Capitals turn the noun into an expulsive interjection, but the gesture is formal. The pattern in the energy is more nearly realized spatially when Pound charts the 'VORTEX' in terms of analytical geometry. The arithmetical, algebraic and geometrical are related in a graph of rising intensity. Arithmetic states facts; algebra provides laws of relation between those facts but 'IT MAKES NO PICTURE';[13] geometry gives an outline to algebraic signs, so that $a^2 + b^2 = c^2$, in Euclid, applies to the right-angled triangle. But the diagram of a right-angled triangle does not '*create* form'.[14] The graph describes a precise narrative: fact gives way to algebraic symbol, which achieves iconic stature in a diagram, only to be superseded by the indexical 'form'—an intuitive line expressive of motion. Reiteration turns the noun into a verb: like 'BLAST' and 'VORTEX', 'form' is an instruction, difficult to follow in that the line to be drawn is unspecified:

> But in analytics we come upon a new way of dealing with form. It is in this way that art handles life. . . . This statement does not interfere in the least with 'spontaneity' and 'intuition', or with their function in art. I passed my last *exam.* in mathematics on sheer intuition. I saw where the line *had* to go as clearly as I ever saw an image.[15]

Although no figure is available, Pound's desire to make a picture is plain; the impossibility merely intensifies his need. What would a 'radiant node' look like?

In 1914 Pound reviewed Upward's *The New Word*. Having met Upward at Yeats' soirées during 1911, it is probable that even as he was constructing his 'vortex' he had in mind Upward's figure for energy.[16] *The New Word* (1910) posits a fluid universe in which matter, although fixed, is actually an interlock of energies. A notion that precipitates Upward into Pound's representational difficulties. A sequence of verbal diagrams is offered:

> The Cross is a rude picture of a knot. As such it is a sign of Matter . . . (and) . . . reminds us of the nature of Matter. Not only is it the rude picture of a knot, that is to say, of a joint in the network, but it shows us how the knot is made. It is by two lines of string meeting crosswise. Thus it reminds us that two ways of Strength must meet crosswise to become entangled.[17]

The iconicity of resemblance passes into the indexicality of a 'real connection': a diagram is iconic, but if it is part of a set of rules for the construction of the object which it resembles, that diagram is indexical. (Clocks, sundials and Upward's bits of string are indices.) Nonetheless, a cross is static; it catches the hiatus of energy into matter, but cannot describe change:

> What is the sign of Change? . . . The least false sign that I can draw is a line turning from a round into an end, and back again into a round. The line going inward is the whirl, and the line coming outward is the swirl. It goes in black and comes out white . . . I find that I have drawn a Spring. (*NW*, pp. 192–93)

The figure of the spring (which Upward inserts pictorially in the text itself) would fit any number of trains, carts, bicycles, and cars in a child's book of optical tricks: it does indeed seem to whirl and swirl. But even the conversion of wheel into spring, though it grants the line a vertical axis, does not make the figure three-dimensional. Upward struggles to transcend the flatness of the page and the linearity of the phonetic alphabet so that 'the sign [may] . . . grow to a shape' (*NW*, p. 193). The spring is envisioned as a waterspout, whose crest 'unfold[s] like a fan, only it unfolds all round like a flower-cup' (*NW*, p. 194), while the same shape is repeated in the water from which the fountain rises. In linear terms Upward has drawn the infinity sign and added arrows. For three-dimensional emphasis he likens the

'flower-cup' to a chrysanthemum, and, by setting two chrys-
anthemums back to back, achieves a positive perpetuum-
mobile of Infinity. The sign is iconic in that it resembles, and
indexical in that it directs us to locate the current:

> It is the pure Shape, reached by the same road by which the
> mathematician reaches his flats and lines. It is the grin without
> the cat. It is the ideal whirl-swirl.
>   It is strength turning inside out.
> Such is the true beat of strength, the first beat, the one from
> which all others part, the beat which we feel in all things that
> come within our measure, in ourselves, and in our starry world,
> the beat that is called Action and Reaction. (*NW*, pp. 194–95)

This passage is a blue-print for an ur-icon, in which are
found characteristics so generic as to be considered iconic for
all phenomena. The figure for Strength lays the basis for many
maps—physiological, linguistic, celestial and neurological.

> Mind is Matter. It is the meeting place of these two strengths
> [inner and outer]. The seat of Mind is, verily speaking, in the
> skin; the brain itself is a fold of skin stuff caught between the
> bone-stuff, by the turning inside out of the life-seed while it is
> yet in the womb. (*NW*, p. 229)

Likewise, the skin, as matter that describes an outline, is a
struggle between exterior and interior power: 'To be real, the
outline must be gained in battle' (*NW*, p. 195). Not sur-
prisingly, language exhibits a similar opposition; pronuncia-
tion proffers 'two sounds beneath all spoken words', inhalation
and exhalation, 'That is the whirl-swirl in language' (*NW*,
p. 267). Not even God is exempt from schematic division:

> . . . the Man Outside could not know himself except by turning
> one half of his strength against the other half; that what I name
> Life and they name the Universe is One Strength turning into
> two, by turning inside out, and so, . . . the Twin Wrestlers of
> the whirl-swirl are both God. (*NW*, p. 217)

To present Upward's arguments as a diagrammatic sequence
inclining to a universal figure is to imply that *The New Word* is
little more than an erudite model-kit in a pop-out book. And
yet it is a reduction that Upward might have enjoyed, since
the impulse behind *The New Word* is the recovery of the old

word, or rather, 'the oldest and most catholic speech, the language of signs' (*NW*, p. 29). Such signs, though realized in phonetic script, are both indexical and iconic: 'Letters themselves are half-breeds, degenerate pictures merging into signs' (*NW*, p. 190). The phoneme, as Fenollosa recognized, resists iconic blandishment,[18] whereas the Chinese ideogram wears its etymology in its face. However, traced to its origin in 'the wild man's cry' (*NW*, p. 35), the primitive energy of language may still be heard within phonetic transcription. Many of Upward's etymologies, starting from 'the living mouth' rather than 'the dead manuscript', find an indexical residue in the most unpromising materials. Take the abstract noun 'truth'.[19] Apparently, 'no imaginary Aryan root' has been found, though Skeat offers a source for the term 'verihood' in 'war', meaning 'to choose' or 'to believe'. Upward has little time for philology and prefers 'the sensible' to the linguistic root, insisting that, 'there is in every word a native element of feeling or a mark set on it by the world of sense', and that as a consequence 'morphology . . . is . . . drudgery' unless it leads to physiology (*NW*, p. 54). 'Truth' is physically founded on 'try' and 'utter', even as 'verihood' rests in 'ware':

> For its sensible root we have only to go out into the playground. *Ware!* is a cry that can still be heard on the lips of the English schoolboy. It is found in written English in such words as *aware* and *wary*. The word *wary* calls up a picture of the wild man of the woods, crouched with one ear to the ground, his fingers tightening on his knife, and his whole soul astrain to catch the first faint rustle that shall bewray [*sic*] the hidden foe. Such a cry as *Ware!* is worth a library of manuscripts. We need no imaginary Aryan root to help us to its meaning. It means 'Hear with all your might!' It is the strength of the ear at its highest pitch. If there be any root in word-lore this cry must be it. It is perhaps the one word in English that has come straight down without a change from the real Aryans;—and it is not to be found in the Etymological Dictionary!

'*Ware!*' as an exclamation available in a playground and (fossilized) in the unvoiced dental 't' of 'truth', 'utter' and 'try', is an indexical sign as directional as an arrow. With hearing 'strained to highest pitch' it is just possible to witness the metamorphosis of the phoneme 't' into a primitive exhalation that will, in its turn, solidify into a word of warning. As an etymology this may be fanciful, but it indicates Upward's resourceful discovery of primitive forces in language. Abstract terms ('truth', 'idealist', 'self', 'soul'), and even those apparently non-semantic units—phonemes—are set in such proximity to the physicality of event or feeling that their status as conventional signs ('symbols') collapses. The arbitrary aspect of language fades once it is recognized that for Upward the etymology of any and every term is a path to a gesture or cry close to that term's inception. Nature and language recover one another. Origin itself, however, resists all representation, since 'feeling comes before thought and emotion before explanation' (*NW*, p. 231). But even end-stopped here the desire to re-originate is not entirely still. Upward notes enigmatically that, 'for the ontologist there are no coincidences, but only Rhymes' (*NW*, p. 43). The ontologist or 'learner of what words mean' (*NW*, p. 263) discovers an essence in language through the principle of rhyme. Despite his assurance that there are 'more Rhymes in heaven and earth than are dreamt of by etymology' (*NW*, p. 273), Upward's examples are often so partial as to be silent, and frequently fall on the first or central syllables, and are, therefore, hard to see: as rhymes they are problematic in that they wilfully strain the senses. Moreover, praise for 'the speech of the English fo'k' as 'a higher authority than any book' (*NW*, p. 61), appearances to the contrary, does not denote an interest in speech. The idioms of low Dutch or the dialects of the East coast concern Upward only in so far as they adjust conventional spelling, written with an eye to the Mediterranean languages. Nordic or Baltic pronunciation is used to divide words; phonemes are removed or installed and syllables are reshuffled in order to establish a rhyme between vocal sounds as they occur at different etymological levels and between different languages. Upward's etymologies are far from phonocentric; ontological grace falls not on voice but on the syllable or the phoneme, in so far as that unit demonstrates a propensity to be drawn into a line or rhyme. Take 'self'[20]: an anonymous intuition tells him that 'self' is shortened from 'Soul-elf', but 'Soul' yields nothing. Instead, he links 'S' to the Latin 'se', 'a sign for ownership', to produce 'own elf', written 'one's elf'. From here it is a small sidestep via a sight-rhyme from 'elf' to 'life' ('to me that elf looks very much like life'). Since 'elf' is 'aelef', or half, according to one philologist, and in Icelandic is 'lifa', 'a remnant' or 'what is left'—Upward is able to build the two halves of his whirl-swirl or All-thing into the etymological structure of 'Self'. Not since Thoreau bent the twenty-six letters of the alphabet into an 'O' on the strength of the words 'leaf' and 'leaves'[21] has so much been done with so little. In this instance, a rhyme strains eye and ear beyond linguistic constraint, to reinvent 'self' as a verbal icon—kin to Fenollosa's ideograms, and of a shape similar to the energetic figure at the centre of Upward's imagination:

> Such are those old, prophetic words. Such are the jewels, glowing with all the colours of the rainbow . . . To me these words seem flowers, which have been snatched from children's hands, and trodden underfoot, but which have seeded in the dust, and are ready to spring up again, and gladden our jaded senses with somewhat of the freshness of the foreworld. (*NW*, p. 209)

The translation of language to iconic and indexical forms is mythic in intention. Iconic logic leads to the 'freshness' of pre-history, in that it removes language from exchange and restores it, via proximity and resemblance, to Nature. It is possible to do many things with Upward's naturalized 'self', but one cannot use it in conversation. The justification for such translations might be schematized as:

iconic = analogic = motivated = Natural

Nature is both source and destination to mythic models of language, in which the sign arises from an intensification of the subject's encounter with the external world. Adorno likens mythic thought to that 'gasp of surprise which accompanies the experience of the unusual [and] becomes its name'.[22] Ernst Cassirer specifies the form of the gasp:

> If we would have a verbal analogue to the mythic conception— we must, apparently, go back to the most primitive level of interjections. The manitu of the Algonquins, the mulungu of the Bantus is used in this way—as an exclamation which indicates not so much a thing as a certain impression, and which is used to greet anything unusual, wonderful, marvelous or terrifying.[23]

In *The Divine Mystery* (1913), Upward's study of religious forms to the time of Christ, the interjection is made the special property of the Wizard; as spells and incantations its dynamic surge is contained within objective verbal structures that are considered magical:

> Before the imagination of man had peopled outside nature with unseen forms, gifted with human intelligence, the wizard had long been in communication with the clouds and winds. . . . The oldest methods of communication are still the most widely understood; the sign, [and] the emotional cry . . . reach the intelligence of children and foreigners, on whom grammatical speech would be wasted. In the same way they lingered in the usage of the wizard as the appropriate language in which to address his commands to the storm and flood.[24]

In his earliest guise the wizard is a weather prophet: his headache allows him to anticipate the storm and 'to be its Word' (*DM*, p. 2). The wizard's prophetic interjection, born of a gasp and becoming a magic term, is a 'figuring of the Creative strength [of Nature] as human strength', and is, Upward assures us, 'a necessity of the human mind' (*DM*, p. 40). If so, it is possible to argue that 'mythology is not the disease of language but its law' (*DM*, p. 40). Whether or not this is true or adequate, it is clear that a mythic scenario will stress particular linguistic features.

Whereas theoretical thinking is discursive and seeks to deliver the contents of sensory or intuitive perception from their isolation, by placing them in categories as part of a unified system of related elements—mythical thought rests solidly in immediate experience. The shape of a hill, a bird's breath in thawing air, or a movement on a body of water is so distinct to the perceiver that the object may be said to have a presence. The totality of the scene falls away and the encounter is resolved in the singular cry. Cassirer, following Usener and Spieth, sees that word as the creation of a 'momentary god' or Tro. Hopkins catches the uniqueness of this kind of linguistic event in his neologism, 'inscape'—an 'unspeakable stress of pitch, distinctiveness, selving'. 'Unspeakable' is well chosen: where individual phenomena are deified and their terms sacrilized, conversation will be scant. If mythic experience is intensive, compressive, immediate, perceptually overwhelming and incapable of generalization, it must resist language. Once the gasp has been specified as a word and the place designated holy, the quality of mythic ideation (inherently primary and singular) has passed over towards its antithesis in reasonable thought. Mythic experience is a frozen moment corrective of those moments that follow and would seek to represent it; as such, it is necessarily in retreat from its own designata.

Pound recognized the problem and perhaps read Upward as a kind of solution. Reviewing *The New Word* (1914),[25] he praised its etymological insights into myth. For both men mythic perception was current and available. Pound claimed kinship with one man who knew Artemis and another who understood Persephone and Demeter, while for Upward a bureaucratic posting in Nigeria led to an encounter with 'The Son of Thunder'. But as Pound notes, 'these myths are only intelligible in a vivid and glittering sense to those people to whom they occur': consequently the initial experience is followed by a number of lies or 'explications of mood'.[26] As the lies proliferate so a mythic or literary sequence emerges: each story, set in its sequence, being a stencil through which the original feeling state may be reapproached.[27] By implication language and art originate in a gasp of natural reverence, thereby raising interesting questions for linguistic and literary value. Is proximity to the gasp a guarantee of aesthetic or etymological truth? As a series extends does its power diminish? Certainly, an interest in icons and indices suggests that mythic ideation remains a prime component of value for Pound, as for Upward and Fenollosa. Nonetheless, the attraction of mythic seriality is that it offers the outward show of historical concern, while prompting the collapse of any and every historical instance into the moment of frozen intensity (the religious rictus in the throat) from which it is said to arise. *The New Word* and *The Divine Mystery* are exemplary exercises in mythic seriality. Each etymology registers a sequence of substitutions through which the shock of myth is translated and retained. The investigative structure of *The Divine Mystery* rests on the assumption that the wizard's headache passes through many manifestations into the agony of Christ crucified:

> The first scene in the life of the Divine Man, therefore, shows him as a half-naked savage, cowering in the cave before the coming

231

storm, and only half awake to the connection between the trouble inside his own head and the trouble outside in the sky. That trembling wretch is the first interpreter of Heaven, mediator and medium between man and his Creator. He is the father of all the human gods, of all the prophets and the priests, of the rude medicine man and of the College of Physicians, of the astrologer and the astronomer, of fetishism and philosophy; he is the teacher of the crafts and handycrafts, of art and science, of poetry and history, of the Law and the Gospel. So Heaven calls him visibly, calls him even as Paul of Tarsus was called, calls him in pain and anguish to take up his great ministry to mankind, and calls him its Son. (*DM*, p. 9)

The advantage of seriality is apparent—any level of the series may be compared to any other level. By dint of compression '*Ware!*' is found in 'Truth', and Christ and John Barleycorn share the crown worn by the Genius of Corn and woven from spiked wheat or barley (*DM*, pp. 104–8). Although for Upward, 'The greatest poetry . . . owes its magic to the echoes it awakes in the dark caverns of submerged memory' (*DM*, p. 105), such echoes offer a delusive density, in which every level merely repeats every other level in a weaker or stronger form. Sameness, not difference, governs the series, which is closed to those ideas that do not accord with the 'feeling' at its base. Moreover, the attention paid to that initial form implies, if not a golden-age, at least a golden-moment of mythology, in the luminescence of which later versions are corrupt. Mythic ideation, even in its serial form, can have no history. As with the icon and the index, a complicity with Nature guarantees the delights of primary intensity and singular experience and very little else.

Despite the limitations it seems that Pound had both Fenollosa and Upward in mind as he defined and redefined Imagism, between the summers of 1912 and 1913. Imagism is a mythic idea. Indeed, the celebrated Do's and Don't's are almost incomprehensible outside the constraints of that instantaneous and fleeting experience.

1 Direct treatment of the 'thing' whether subjective or objective.
2 To use absolutely no word that does not contribute to the presentation.

3 As regarding rhythm: to compose in the sequence of the musical phrase, not in the sequence of the metronome. (*LE*, p. 3)

The first directive is particularly odd and is made no clearer by Pound's subsequent assertion that, 'the natural object is always the *adequate* symbol'. Given that natural objects are generally converted into 'symbols' through social labour, Pound's claims seem misguided. But his reiterated insistence that 'the proper and perfect symbol is the natural object' (*LE*, p. 5) is accurate within the context of mythic ideation, where the 'subjective' and 'objective' fuse in a perception so intense that language is pared to interjection, and the senses focus on isolated phenomena. The rhythm of such apprehension is all that Pound might have desired: Cassirer notes, 'the formulation of language should be traced . . . to the dynamic process which produces the sound out of its own inner drive'[28]—he could be glossing Upward's 'rhymes' and Pound's rhythmical structures:

> I believe in an 'absolute rhythm', a rhythm, that is, in poetry which corresponds exactly to the emotion or shade of emotion to be expressed. A man's rhythm must be interpretative, it will be, therefore, in the end, his own, uncounterfeiting, uncounterfeitable. (*LE*, p. 9)

At the level of poetic practice myth is also a useful context, converting a brief flirtation (in which a methodology at a loss for an idea commits acts of verbal hygiene) into one phase of a more enduring involvement with the forms of mythic language.

IN A STATION OF THE METRO

> The apparition of these faces in the crowd;
> Petals on a wet, black bough.[29]

Gaudier-Brzeska offers a brief history of what has been called 'the model Imagist poem'.[30] On a visit to Paris in 1911, emerging from the Metro at La Concorde, Pound 'saw suddenly a beautiful face, and then another and another . . . I tried all day to find words for what this had meant to me, and I could not find any words that seemed to me worthy, or lovely as that sudden emotion.'[31] One and a half years later, and with two failures of thirty and fifteen lines destroyed, Pound produced the twenty-word success. Autobiographically the poem constitutes a small mythic series: a feeling state is attended by substitutions at different levels of proximity. Hugh Kenner adds the crowds seen underground by Odysseus, Orpheus and Koré, thereby extending the sequence. But in the poem, as in the mythic experience, 'the sensible present is so great that everything else dwindles before it.'[32] Direct articles and the demonstrative pronoun set a narrow perceptual focus. Sensitive, perhaps, to indexical insistence, the subject who perceives has no independent status but joins his object in 'apparitions'—a term which at an objective extreme means 'image', while a subjective inflection yields 'apprehension'. As passive as the notional primitive, the notional observer simply gasps. His vision does not construct an image but receives one. Consequently, the transition to the second line is neither a truncated simile nor a tensional metaphor[33]: if any word is silently read between the lines it is 'are' not 'like'. The linkage between 'faces' and 'petals' is stronger than similarity; they *are* the same—in that, as part of a single mythic series, each substitutes for the other in an approximation to that original 'sudden emotion'. Read in the context of myth, 'IN A STATION OF THE METRO' is intensive and without tension; its parts, far from releasing an open pattern of energy through dissonance,[34] are rigidly contractive.

I am reminded of Fenollosa's ideograms for 'Man Sees Horse' (*CWC*, p. 8). Each figure arises from a number of substitutions:

> If we all knew *what division* of this mental horse-picture each of these signs stood for, we could communicate continuous thought to one another as easily by drawing them as by speaking words. We habitually employ the visible language of gesture in much this same manner.
>
> But Chinese notation is something much more than arbitrary symbols. It is based upon a vivid shorthand picture of the operations of nature. In the algebraic figure and in the spoken word there is no natural connection between thing and sign: all depends upon sheer convention. But the Chinese method follows natural suggestion. First stands the man on his two legs. Second, his eye moves through space: a bold figure represented by running legs under an eye, a modified picture of an eye, a

modified picture of running legs, but unforgettable once you have seen it. Third stands the horse on his four legs.

The thought-picture is not only called up by these signs as well as by words, but far more vividly and concretely. Legs belong to all three characters: they are *alive*. The group holds something of the quality of a continuous moving picture. (*CWC*, pp. 8–9)

At every stage the movement from action to 'thought-picture' to gesture to sign is mimetic, motivated by a single desire to particularize. Depending upon the calligrapher's acuteness and the scene witnessed, the figure for man might contain an exact account of a degree of athleticism. However, an increase in potential for registering singularity is accompanied by a loss of power to propositionalize. Perhaps the non-predicative quality of Chinese script can best be caught by applying Frege's distinction between 'sense' and 'reference'. For Frege 'sense' is what the proposition states, and 'reference' is that about which the 'sense' is stated: he notes that in striving for truth we tend to advance from 'sense' to 'reference'. In the Chinese character, as in icons and indices, proposition has no place. We move from reference to 'reference', or at least from palpable signs to still greater palpability. It might be objected that Fenollosa's insistence that 'things are only the terminal points, or rather the meeting points, of actions' (*CWC*, p. 10), calls the referent into question and revises the whole notion of mimesis. This is exactly Hugh Kenner's reading:

> Ideographs, supposed to correspond with things, had sponsored the very habits Fenollosa was to refute by positing that ideographs corresponded with actions. His great and unassailable originality stemmed from his conviction that the unit of thought was less like a noun than like a verb, and that Chinese signs, therefore, denoted processes. . . . Metaphor so seen was a centrality not an embarrassment.[35]

But the shift from 'thing' to 'action' (from noun to verb) does not redefine 'reference' or open it to 'sense'. For example— Fenollosa's 'horse' stands firm on four legs and looks all the more *'alive'* for that—but whether it is perceived as a blur of action, or as one black line describing an outline, or as five phonemes is eventually irrelevant. Changes in representational conventions do not, in and of themselves, effect changes in thought. Only when the word for 'horse' (however written) is recognized as a position between speakers, having different accounts of horse-power, will narrowly mimetic accounts of 'reference' be overcome. Once sociability is readmitted to the sign, typographical distinctions *can* be treated as semantic issues. Indeed, I shall try later to explain Pound's iconic preoccupations in terms of a particular cultural need. However, the influence of Upward and Fenollosa encouraged no such historicizing of linguistic assumptions. Their models renovate mimesis through myth.

Just as Upward's etymological account of 'truth' contains 'a wild man of the woods, crouched with one ear to the ground', so Fenollosa's figure for 'horse' purports to such indexical energy that it scarcely warrants 'reading' at all—rather, it is a 'momentary god' registering a gasp. For both men language is phenomenologically intense because rooted in myth, and it is difficult to distinguish between their positions as Fenollosa insists that the earliest linguistic forms or 'original metaphors':

> . . . stand as a kind of luminous background, giving color and vitality, forcing them [the poet's words] closer to the concreteness of natural processes. . . . For these reasons poetry was the earliest of the world arts; poetry, language and the care of myth grew up together. (*CWC*, p. 24)

Their divergence is primarily one of sensory bias: Upward works with the ear while Fenollosa works with the eye. But in each case etymological ingenuity produces small objects with a large sensory pay-off. Upward's ear distinguishes the evocative value of particular vowels and consonants. Fenollosa's eye strains after graphic nuance. The reader's attention is focused on the sub-sections of signs which are not, in any conventional sense, units of meaning. Arguably, a phoneme or the thickening in a calligraphic line, freed from instrumentality, can play on the senses of the recipient, stimulating 'the exercise of perception and the perceptual recombining of sense data as an end in itself'.[36] Upward's reading of 'Self' is just such an exercise in auditory and visual sensitivity, undertaken on a semi-autonomous object—the phoneme 's'. Situated between 'one' and 'elf' (where 'elf'/'aelef' is 'half') the letter marks the division of a self-consistent unity (oneself) into those interdependent segments (one's elf: inner and outer) that lie at the centre of Upward's cosmology. Even as, apostrophized and possessive, it shuttles between one or other of its verbal sections, so the phoneme traces a whirl-swirl. Moving through its elements ('one' and 'elf'), much as the fountain's path moves through pool or air, 's' or 'se' (the Latin sign of ownership) stands as a man stands in Upward's world, at the focal point of a distinct pattern of energy. Cosmology and phonetics accord in a mythopoeic synesthesia of alarming condensation. Such 'rhymes' might find companion pieces among playground songs:

> Inty, ninty tibbety fig
> Deema dima doma nig
> Howchy powchy domi nowday
> Hom tom tout
> Olligo bolligo boo
> Out goes you.[37]

The child's count-out is gibberish in terms of rational lexis, grammatical function and semantic reference; luckily it is not interested in those terms. The children, unconsciously, and Upward, consciously, grant phonological structures a credence that subverts social semantics. Roman Jakobson, discussing the sound shape of language, argues that the non-signifying or differentiating features of language (phonemes and morphemes):

> . . . taken apart from [their] basic and conventional linguistic usage, carry a latent synesthesic association and thus an immediate semantic nuance. Their *immediacy* in signification of the distinctive features acquires an autonomous role in the more or less onomatopoeic strata of ordinary language. The habitual relation of *contiguity* between sound and meaning yields to a bond of *similarity*. This phenomenon goes beyond the limits of onomatopoeias proper and succeeds in creating submorphemic links between words of diverse origin. It is this similarity in sound and meaning which even assumes an active role in reviving or condemning lexical archaisms and in furthering viable neologisms.
>
> The significance of the play on words . . . in the life of language should not be underestimated. . . . And it is precisely 'play' and the mythopoeic transforms of language which help to dynamise the autonomous semantic potential of the distinctive features and of their complexes.[38]

If I understand this, Jakobson suggests that the sound of a sub-semantic unit may acquire 'by similarity' its own semantic content. He might be offering an account of Upward's etymological method. Take, once again, the 't' in 'truth'/'*Ware!*' which contains within its phonetic performance as an unvoiced dental, the panic of the hunted savage—if so, 'the turbulence . . . where the breath stream passes through narrow constrictions or across the teeth'[39] imbues a phoneme with oral, tactile and olefactory qualities which could be presented as its own semantic load.

I remain sceptical, though I am sure that Fenollosa would silently have applauded Upward's semantic predilections. C. S. Peirce, it seems, once copied out Poe's 'The Raven' in a hand that sought to convey the poetic ideas by means of the script itself; what resulted was a written analogue of onomatopoeic words, a kind of iconic handwriting that he called 'chirography'.[40] Fenollosa's essay is an anthology of chirographic examples, whose every line and segment of line protests an expressive relation to external process.

The problem with this kind of semantics is that it reduces the social content of meaning even as it renovates universalist claims for the physiology of language. My point is not to pursue the semantics of small linguistic units, but to stress the close kinship between icons and indices, mythical accounts of language and phenomenological attentiveness to linguistic production (be it phonetic or graphic). All by-pass social exchange in an attempt to grant language an inherent and empathetic immediacy. The tendency in each case is iconic in that it underplays the conventionality of the sign, and the historically specific dialogue that argues for meaning and achieves changes within meaning.

Pound found in Upward and Fenollosa what I am loosely describing as an iconically biased account of language. Its attractiveness may, quite wrong-headedly, have stemmed from its enormous weaknesses. Mythically intense, historically vapid, inflexible—not an inviting pedigree, unless it is placed within the larger context of social reification and its effects on the conventional levels of linguistic exchange. Fredric Jameson reads Conrad's impressionism and Wyndham Lewis's various modernisms as an expression of and compensation for what reification brings. Pound, too, sought compensation. Faced with a capitalist social organization—'the new social rhythms introduced by factory production, the market system, a generalized money economy, the commodification of labour power, and the omnipresence of the commodity form as such'[41]— Pound tended to retreat, in economic terms, to the notionally fixed systems of Confucius, Mencius and the medieval Catholic church. Linguistically, he found the stable solace of the icon, in which the sign's resemblance to what is signified removes man from signification and installs Nature there, in a comforting act of linguistic and social amnesia. Upward and Fenollosa offer double solace: not only do their mythic and etymological series posit continuity between primitive and modern, but the manner of their iconicity—concentrating on those linguistic units for which rationality has little time—beckons the senses towards an authenticity beyond the repressive needs of calculation, measurement and profit.

The consolations are illusory. Even when appealing to a nature ripe with the experiential fruits of mythic ideation, the index and the icon are contrived.[42] Their status as natural signs is a gestural and optical illusion. As with any other act of reference, be it effected by a pointer, a drawing or a word, the indexical and the iconic depend upon social conventions. If, for example, during a lecture, the speaker comments, 'This is no time to arrive', many of his listeners will glance at the door. No one is there. The audience response involved a shared expectation of proximity; it did not prove that the demonstrative pronoun and indexical sign, 'this', possessed a causal or 'real' connection with its object. Quite the opposite—there was no object. Likewise, Durer's account of the rhinoceros, covered with scales and imbricated plates, established an image that remained constant for two centuries and reappeared in the books of explorers and zoologists who had actually seen the animal, but could not portray its hide except by means of the conventionalized graphic signs for 'rhinoceros'—Durer's imbricated plates. Ernst Gombrich, who gathers the rhinoceroses,[43] does so to point out the cultural convention at the heart of iconic similarity. In this instance the convention is so strong that its rules seem more authentic than natural outlines; as Umberto Eco puts it:

At a certain point the iconic representation, however stylised it may be, appears to be more true than the real experience, and people begin to look at things through the glasses of iconic convention . . . [in a] sort of perceptual cramp caused by overwhelming cultural habits.[44]

Gombrich might correct Pound's enthusiasm for Gaudier-Brzeska's scarcely tutored ability to understand ideograms. Brzeska, though no sinologue, was 'accustomed to observe the dominant lines in objects',[45] and it is his training in linear convention, not a natural eye for similitude, that informs his guesses and makes him a better translator of the Chinese written character than most. It would seem that resemblance, too, is learned. Brzeska can only insist 'that *that* was a horse . . . what the . . . else could it be!'[46] because it has been agreed by a previous graphic convention that black pen strokes may refer to and perhaps even resemble a horse.

One problem remains: if the nature in natural language is put there socially, why is it that Upward, Fenollosa and at times Pound remain content in a primitive contrivance—their languages and their perceptions cramped in a desire to venerate an unnatural shibboleth, the natural sign? Unable to answer, I offer as a suggestion Marcuse's comments on the totalitarian tactic of displacing social dissent by turning Nature into 'the great antagonist of history':

The mythical glorification of the renewal of agriculture has its counterpart in the fight against the metropolis and its 'unnatural' spirit. This fight expands into an attack on the rule of reason in general and sets loose all irrational powers—a movement that ends with the total functionalization of the mind. 'Nature' is the first in the series of restricting conditions to which reason is subordinated. The unconditioned authority of the state seems to be the last. 'Nature' as celebrated by organicism, however, does not appear as a factor of production in the context of actual relations of production, nor as a condition of production, nor as the basis, itself historical, of human history. Instead it becomes a *myth*, and as a myth it hides the organicist deprivation and forcible displacement of historical and social processes. Nature becomes the great antagonist of history.[47]

If I may adapt—for Upward, Fenollosa and Pound language

is mythic, and becomes, under the incentive of iconicity, antagonistic towards history.

NOTES

1. E. Cassirer, *Language and Myth* (New York, 1953), p. 31. Subsequent pagination refers to this edition.
2. V. N. Volosinov, *Marxism and the Philosophy of Language* (New York, 1973), p. 102. Subsequent pagination refers to this edition.
3. Ibid., p. 92.
4. M. A. K. Halliday, *Language as Social Semiotic* (London, 1978), p. 137.
5. E. Pound, *The Spirit of Romance* (London, 1970), p. 92. Subsequent pagination refers to this edition.
6. E. Pound, *The Literary Essays of Ezra Pound*, ed. T. S. Eliot (London, 1960), p. 152. Subsequently, when referring to this collection, I shall adopt the abbreviation *LE* and include the reference in the body of the text.
7. I. F. A. Bell, 'The Phantasmagoria of Hugh Selwyn Mauberley', *Paideuma*, Vol. 5, No. 3 (Winter 1976), 384.
8. In defining icon, index and symbol, I have adopted the triadic account of signs offered by Charles Sanders Peirce. My quotations are drawn from *The Collected Papers of Charles Sanders Peirce*, ed. C. Hartshorne, P. Weiss and A. Burks, 8 Vols. (Cambridge, 1931–35, 1958). The general definitions refer to Vol. 3, p. 365. Peirce developed his language theories throughout his career and references are scattered. I found two commentaries particularly helpful: J. F. Fitzgerald, *Peirce's Theory of Signs as a Foundation for Pragmatism* (The Hague, 1966) and D. Greenlee, *Peirce's Concept of Sign* (The Hague, 1973).
9. *The Collected Papers of Charles Sanders Peirce*, Vol. 2, p. 298.
10. H. Kenner, *The Pound Era* (London, 1972), p. 196. Subsequent pagination refers to this edition.
11. *The Collected Papers of Charles Sanders Peirce*, Vol. 4, p. 56.
12. E. Pound, *Gaudier-Brzeska: A Memoir* (New York, 1970), p. 93. Subsequent pagination refers to this edition.
13. Ibid., p. 91.
14. *Idem.*
15. *Idem.*
16. For useful accounts of Pound's response to Upward see R. Bush, *The Genesis of Ezra Pound's Cantos* (Princeton, 1976), pp. 91–102, and D. Davie, *Pound* (London, 1975), pp. 62–74.
17. A. Upward, *The New Word* (London, 1908), p. 192. Subsequently, when referring to this work, I shall adopt the abbreviation *NW* and include the reference in the body of the text.
18. E. Fenollosa, *The Chinese Written Character as a Medium for Poetry*, ed. E. Pound (San Francisco, n.d.), pp. 24–5. Subsequently, when referring to

241

this work, I shall adopt the abbreviation *CWC* and include the reference in the body of the text.

19. See *The New Word*, pp. 41–3.
20. Ibid., pp. 205–9.
21. H. Thoreau, *Walden* (New York, 1893), pp. 469–77.
22. T. Adorno, *Dialectic of Enlightenment* (London, 1979), p. 15.
23. E. Cassirer, *Language and Myth*, p. 71.
24. A. Upward, *The Divine Mystery* (Santa Barbara, 1976), p. 27. Subsequently, when referring to this work, I shall adopt the abbreviation *DM* and include the reference in the body of the text.
25. E. Pound, 'Alan Upward Serious', *The New Age*, XIV, 25 (23 April 1914), 779–80.
26. E. Pound, 'Psychology and Troubadours', in *The Spirit of Romance*, p. 92.
27. I have taken this account of mythic seriality from Peter Munz, *When the Golden Bough Breaks: Structuralism or Typology* (London, 1973). 'Feeling state', 'sequence', 'stencil', and 'typological series' are his terms; their relevance to Pound is plain from 'Arnold Dolmetsch' (1915): 'The first myths arose when a man walked sheer into "nonsense", that is to say, when some very vivid and undeniable adventure befell him, and he told someone else who called him a liar. Thereupon, after bitter experience, perceiving that no one could understand what he meant when he said that he "turned into a tree" he made a myth—a work of art that is—an impersonal or objective story woven out of his own emotion, as the nearest equation that he was capable of putting into words. That story, perhaps, then gave rise to a weaker copy of his emotion in others, until there arose a cult, a company of people who could understand each other's nonsense about the gods' (*LE*, p. 431).
28. E. Cassirer, *Language and Myth*, p. 34.
29. E. Pound, *Collected Shorter Poems* (London, 1968), p. 119.
30. J. N. Riddel, 'Pound and the Decentered Image', *The Georgia Review*, XXIX, 3 (Fall 1975), 576.
31. E. Pound, *Gaudier-Brzeska: A Memoir*, pp. 86–7.
32. E. Cassirer, *Language and Myth*, p. 32.
33. Aristotle spoke of the 'epiphora', or the transfer of meaning within metaphor. Paul Ricoeur expands the idea to encompass a shift in logical distance from far to near. The mind's eye responds to likeness while recognizing a continuing difference. Coming to terms with congruent incongruence involves tensions that are avoided by the substitutional accounts of metaphor: 'All new rapprochement runs against a previous categorization which resists, or rather which yields while resisting . . . This is what the idea of semantic impertinence or incongruence preserves. In order that a metaphor obtains, one must continue to identify the previous incompatibility *through* the new compatibility. The predicative assimilation involves, in that way, a specific kind of tension which is not so much between a subject and a predicate as between semantic incongruence and congruence. The insight into likeness is the perception of the conflict between the previous incompatibility and the

new compatibility. "Remoteness" is preserved within "proximity". To see the *like* is to see the same in spite of, and through the different. This tension between sameness and difference characterizes the logical structure of likeness' (Paul Ricoeur, 'The Metaphoric Process as Cognition, Imagination and Feeling', collected in *On Metaphor*, ed. S. Sacks (London, 1979), pp. 146–47). Within the mythic scheme of things metaphors are scarcely metaphoric since any active exchange between distinct parts would challenge the principle of 'pars pro toto', dear to mythic and organicist thought: 'Here we find in operation a law which might actually be called the law of levelling and extinction of specific differences . . . every specimen is equivalent to the entire species. The part does not merely represent the whole, or the specimen its class; they are identical to the totality to which they belong; not merely as mediating aids to reflective thought, but as genuine presences which actually contain the power, significance and efficacy of the whole' (E. Cassirer, *Language and Myth*, p. 92).

34. I find closure where others find openness. Hugh Kenner reads the contrast between vegetal and mechanical as one element in an allusive 'complex' that 'concentrates far more than it need ever specify' (*The Pound Era*, p. 185). Herbert Schneidau puts 'process' into 'complex', arguing that the Imagism Pound derives from Fenollosa 'yields a world not of static objects with meanings imposed on them, but a drama of meanings unfolding from actions and processes' (*Ezra Pound: The Image and the Real*, Baton Rouge, 1969, p. 68). More open than any, Riddel employs Derridean deferal to establish that 'There never was any "perception"' and that therefore the poem is best read as 'a transaction without origin or end' ('Pound and the Decentered Image', pp. 577 and 585). I could not agree less.

35. H. Kenner, *The Pound Era*, p. 225.

36. F. Jameson, *The Political Unconscious* (Ithaca, 1980), p. 230. I am heavily indebted to Jameson's account of Conrad's impressionism for my own reading of Upward's 'rhymes' as perceptual experiences 'heightened to the point at which [they] touch [their] own outer limits and cause [their] own outer edge in the non-perceivable to rise before us' (Jameson, pp. 240–41). However, I have my doubts as to whether sensory recovery necessarily hinders the translation of materiality into the repetitive diversions of the dominant social system.

37. Quoted, R. Jakobson and M. Taylor, *The Sound Shape of Language* (London, 1979), p. 218.

38. Ibid., pp. 235–36.

39. See, *Manual of Phonetics*, ed. L. Kaiser (Amsterdam, 1957), p. 202, for a fuller definition of 'unvoiced' speech.

40. See, A. W. Burks, 'Icon, Index and Symbol', *Philosophy and Phenomenological Research*, Vol. 9, No. 4 (June 1949), 674.

41. F. Jameson, *Fables of Aggression* (London, 1979), p. 133.

42. In my initial description of Peirce's subdivisions I simplified in order to make clear what remain for Peirce three distinct orders of signification. I

was interested in general types rather than in the exceptions and contradictions that Peirce acknowledges. Umberto Eco's critique (*A Theory of Semiotics* (London, 1977), particularly pp. 190–224) extends many of Peirce's own criticisms in a comprehensive attack on the 'naturalness' of iconicity. For Peirce, too, no icon could be entirely free of a conventional element, for example, 'a diagram . . . is predominantly an icon of relations and is aided to be so by convention' (*The Collected Papers of C. S. Peirce*, Vol. 4, p. 448). Indexicality is also a matter of degree. Peirce notes that all language is indexical in that it focuses our attention on its objects, but marks the weakness of this kind of directive by describing the sentence as a 'subindex', observing that since language is a 'symbolic' proposition it cannot be truly indexical.

I believe that my initial simplification remains true to Peirce's concern to distinguish three general inclinations within signification.

43. E. Gombrich, *Art and Illusion* (London, 1972), pp. 70–1.
44. U. Eco, *A Theory of Semiotics* (London, 1977), p. 205.
45. E. Pound, *Gaudier-Brzeska: A Memoir*, p. 46.
46. *Idem.*
47. H. Marcuse, *Negations* (Harmondsworth, 1972), p. 23. I. F. A. Bell has traced connections between Fenollosa's organicism and the Transcendentalists, linking both to theories of popular science and to Pound. See, *Critic as Scientist: The Modernist Poetics of Ezra Pound* (London, 1981), particularly Chapters 3 and 6. From a historical account of influence he elaborates a criticism of Pound's poetics as a poetics of closure. The argument can be used to underline Marcuse's points about 'organist deprivation . . . and displacement' of social processes.

Index

245

246

247